PLANNING AND EVALUATING SPECIAL EDUCATION SERVICES

CHARLES A. MAHER
Rutgers University

RANDY ELLIOT BENNETT
Educational Testing Service

PRENTICE-HALL, INC., Englewood Cliffs, New Jersey 07632

Library of Congress Cataloging in Publication Data

MAHER, CHARLES A.
  Planning and evaluating special education services.

  Bibliography.
  Includes index.
  1. Exceptional children—Education—United States—
Planning. 2. Exceptional children—Education—United
States—Evaluation. I. Bennett, Randy Elliot. II. Title.
LC3981.M23 1984   371.9'0973   83-17627
ISBN 0-13-679481-5

Editorial/production supervision: Colleen Brosnan
Cover design: Celine Brandes/Photo Plus Art
Manufacturing buyer: Ron Chapman

Printed in the United States of America

10 9 8 7 6 5 4 3 2 1

ISBN 0-13-679481-5

Prentice-Hall International, Inc., *London*
Prentice-Hall of Australia Pty. Limited, *Sydney*
Editora Prentice-Hall do Brasil, Ltda., *Rio de Janeiro*
Prentice-Hall Canada Inc., *Toronto*
Prentice-Hall of India Private Limited, *New Delhi*
Prentice-Hall of Japan, Inc., *Tokyo*
Prentice-Hall of Southeast Asia Pte. Ltd., *Singapore*
Whitehall Books Limited, *Wellington, New Zealand*

CONTENTS

PLANNING AND EVALUATING
PERSONNEL DEVELOPMENT SERVICES   147

PLANNING AND EVALUATING
ADMINISTRATIVE SERVICES   175

REFERENCES   199

FOREWORD

Service delivery in special and remedial education involves a complex interaction of many factors. Students must be assessed, and somehow we must decide specifically who, among the many students experiencing academic and behavior problems, is eligible for special education services. Then, we must decide specifically how, where, and what to teach those students. Some require related services—such as physical therapy or speech and language intervention. But who? And how does one articulate related services with "typical" instructional services? How does one select personnel to work in special education or provide in-service training to those now doing so? How does one supervise, administer, or coordinate the services delivered?

There are no easy answers to these questions. That there are no easy answers creates a very complex dilemma for administrators, coordinators, supervisors, school psychologists, and others: Decisions must be made *now* so that services can be provided. Yet, defensible methods for decision making are hard to find. This book describes how planning and evaluation can be employed to arrive at and defend a wide range of special education decisions. The planning and evaluation process described encourages a systematic, explicit, data-based approach to decision making.

Planning and Evaluating Special Education Services shows how evaluation can be used to facilitate judgments about the need for, design, implementation, and outcome of a range of special education services and programs. The book illustrates how planning and evaluation are interdependent, by describing ways in which evaluation information may be used for program development and improvement.

The point of view expressed in this text is refreshing. The authors have not specified a particular model for delivering special education services. Rather, they have presented an approach to planning and evaluation that enables school personnel to develop programs targeted to the needs of their school district. The authors' approach suggests that planning and evaluation are ongoing activities and that changes in the service delivery system should be based on the data derived from these activities.

The authors, who have extensive experience in planning and evaluating special education services, have drawn on their own experiences to provide a range of practical approaches to planning and evaluating special education services. The methods and procedures they describe are integrated into an overall framework that allows the practitioner to apply planning and evaluation activities to developing and improving assessment, teaching, the delivery of related services, personnel development, and administration.

JAMES E. YSSELDYKE
University of Minnesota

PREFACE

The delivery of educational services to children and youth with special needs is a complex endeavor requiring the careful coordination of people, materials, and activities in various parts of a school system and community. Most school districts, for example, mainstream special needs children into regular education classes for some portion of the school day in order to facilitate their academic and social development. The success of such efforts is in no small way dependent on close collaboration and thoughtful planning. Regular and special education supervisors, teachers, and parents must come to a mutual understanding about such things as the purpose and goals of mainstreaming, the general methods and materials to be used, and the responsibilities of those involved. In addition, mechanisms for monitoring the implementation of the mainstreaming effort and for addressing the difficulties that will inevitably arise need to be established. Finally, after a reasonable period of time, the success of the effort must be reviewed so that needed improvements can be identified and effective practices put to more widespread use.

Whether the task is planning a mainstreaming program, developing an inservice training effort for paraprofessionals, or establishing a legally defensible preplacement pupil evaluation process, a generic set of planning and evaluation activities can be used to facilitate program development and improvement. These activities include (1) clarifying the need that the program will be designed to address, (2) designing the program to address the identified need, (3) carrying out the program and monitoring its implementation, and (4) evaluating the effectiveness of the effort so that improvements can be made and best practices disseminated.

Planning and Evaluating Special Education Services is a resource book of methods and procedures that describes this generic process and its application to the particular problems of special education service delivery. As such, the book has two primary goals:

1. To provide information about methods and procedures for planning and evaluating the range of special education programs and services that comprise a special education services delivery system.
2. To provide information about how to apply planning and evaluation methods and procedures to common special education services delivery problems.

This text is primarily meant for those administrators, supervisors, and program coordinators responsible for developing and improving the wide variety of special education programs in schools, school districts, and related agencies. Such programs mainly include those designed for handicapped and gifted students and, to a lesser extent, those meant to serve remedial, compensatory education, and Title I (now Chapter I) populations. Professionals with leadership roles in these programs will find the book to be a valuable compendium of suggestions and procedures for program planning and improvement as well as a useful reference for more fully understanding the work of educational evaluators.

Professional evaluators constitute a second appropriate audience for this book. Because the routine evaluation of special education programs is a relatively recent phenomenon, many educational evaluators are new to the task of evaluation in this context. These professionals will find *Planning and Evaluating Special Education Services* useful for gaining a clearer understanding of the special education context and the peculiar evaluation problems it poses.

Others who will find this book useful are program providers, university trainers, and educational consultants. School psychologists, special education teachers, and others involved in the direct delivery of services will discover a good deal of specific guidance on how to more effectively plan, monitor, and improve their own intervention efforts. University faculty will likewise discover the book useful in the training of leadership personnel and consultants will find the content offered a valuable aid in providing technical assistance to school districts and other educational agencies.

Planning and Evaluating Special Education Services is organized into seven chapters, each of which presents material about one or more important aspects of special education program planning and evaluation. Chapter 1 presents an overview and framework for program planning and evaluation in special education. Chapters 2 through 7 describe methods for planning and evaluation in each of five domains of special education. One chapter each is devoted to assessment, related services, staff development, and administration. Two chapters are devoted to the planning and evaluation of instruction as this is the special service to which the most professional time and effort is directed; one chapter focuses on those problems peculiar to individualized programs and the second centers on group instructional problems.

The material presented in this book is based largely upon the practical experience and research of the authors. The large majority of methods and procedures discussed have been successfully applied in actual school settings. The examples used to illustrate these methods and procedures are frequently actual occurrences drawn from our experiences.

The planning and evaluation methods discussed are also generally applicable to more than one kind of service. In most cases, however, each method is thoroughly discussed in only a particular chapter with the applicability of the method to other service areas specifically noted where appropriate. Through this approach, a wider variety and greater number of planning and evaluation methods are covered.

The careful planning and evaluation of special education services should be the concern of all those interested in improving the service delivery process. It is our hope that this book will encourage attention to the positive role that planning and evaluation can play in designing and improving programs to address the needs of children, staff, parents, and schools.

We would like to express our appreciation to Gary Echternacht, Educational Testing Service; Natalie Elman; Garry White, Winthrop College; Paul Wehman, Virginia Commonwealth University; Thomas Lovitt, University of Washington; Richard Shick, Mansfield University; James Ysseldyke, University of Minnesota; Sandy Cohen, University of Virginia; Daniel D. Sage, Syracuse University; and Nora Martin, Eastern Michigan University, for reviewing earlier drafts of this manuscript.

Finally, we should note that writing this book was a cooperative endeavor to which both authors contributed equally.

C.A.M.
R.E.B.

1

PLANNING AND EVALUATING SPECIAL EDUCATION SERVICES
An Overview

In most school districts, a service delivery system exists to support the education of exceptional children and youth. Such systems generally subsume a wide range of services, including assessment, instruction, related services, personnel development, and administration. Each type of service is usually delivered through various kinds of targeted programs. The effective delivery of these programs is very much dependent on the extent to which they are carefully planned, carried out, and modified to respond to changing conditions and needs.

This chapter introduces program planning and evaluation as a set of activities designed to assist the development and improvement of special education services. In the chapter, the need for planning and evaluating special education services delivery is described, perspectives on both special education services delivery and planning and evaluation are offered, and a framework for planning and evaluating special education services is introduced.

NEED FOR PLANNING AND EVALUATING
SPECIAL EDUCATION SERVICES

The importance of planning and evaluation is readily evident to most of those involved in special education. Public pressures and events, as well as professional concerns and interests, have created a need for practical approaches to planning

1

and evaluating special education services in public and private schools and human-service agencies.

Public Events and Pressures

The enactment of the Education for All Handicapped Children Act of 1975 (PL 94-142), more than any other public event, directed national attention to the need to educate all handicapped children and youth. This landmark legislation, its rules and regulations (U.S. Office of Education, 1977a, 1977b) and derivative laws designed to enforce its intent in the states, mandated delivery of a broad range of services, including assessment, instruction, related services, personnel development, and administration. Within each of these service delivery areas, regular planning and evaluation activities were specified or implied. Such activities included the annual development and review of individualized education programs (instruction), the periodic evaluation of staff-training needs (personnel development), and the routine construction of district service delivery plans (administration).

A second environmental condition with direct implications for special education program planning and evaluation has been the trend toward reduced spending for public education. The effect of this trend on the schools is clear: boards of education and school administrators must attempt to satisfy the same educational needs with fewer human and financial resources. For those involved in educating exceptional children, this will often mean using planning and evaluation activities for identifying and shutting down ineffective programs, improving program efficiency to generate more "bang for the buck," and gathering the evidence needed to argue against further spending cuts.

A third important trend is that of parental concern about, and involvement in, special education. As a result of PL 94-142, parents of special students have won the right to participate in the educational decision-making process. In addition, parents have continued to affect the nature and shape of special education through frequent litigation (e.g., *Armstrong* v. *Kline*, 1980; *Larry P.* v. *Riles*, 1979) and through the lobbying efforts of advocacy organizations (e.g., the Association for Children and Adults with Learning Disabilities). This trend has created a need to carefully integrate parents into the educational decision-making process, to improve existing services (e.g., preplacement evaluation practices), and to develop new ones (e.g., summer programs for the profoundly handicapped).

Professional Concerns and Interests

No doubt largely as a result of public events and pressures, school professionals have become more concerned about assuring and improving the quality of their work. The results of this concern are evident in the standards developed by professional associations to guide their constituents' practice. Both the American Psychological Association and the National Association of School Psychologists have issued codes for the delivery of school psychological services (Pennington,

1977; Specialty Guidelines, 1981). Similar codes have been promulgated for learning-disability specialists and for regular education teachers (*Code of Ethics and Competencies,* 1978; NEA Representative Assembly, 1981). These codes, in addition to setting performance standards, encourage evaluation by requiring professionals to routinely monitor and review the appropriateness of the services they provide.

The concerns of teachers, related specialists, and administrators for providing more appropriate services have also focused attention on planning and evaluation as a means for developing and monitoring the quality of educational programs. This emphasis is evident in the increased numbers of pre- and in-service offerings devoted to program planning and evaluation (Maher & Kratochwill, 1980) and in the many articles on planning and evaluation that have appeared recently in the general- and special-education literatures.

PERSPECTIVES ON THE DELIVERY
OF SPECIAL EDUCATION SERVICES

Special education is not a unitary concept or entity; it means different things to different people. To a regular classroom teacher, the term may bring to mind only those activities provided to handicapped children in self-contained classrooms; a school nurse, on the other hand, may consider a vision-screening program for elementary-school children a special education service, while the supervisor of compensatory education may view remedial programs as falling within this domain; parents of handicapped children may consider special education to encompass the wide range of services their children receive.

A Systems Perspective
on Special Education Services Delivery

For planning and evaluation to benefit fully the delivery of special education, the nature and scope of the special services delivery process must be defined. Without such a definition, the focus of planning and evaluation efforts will be unclear.

Figure 1-1 presents a conceptual scheme for organizing the special services delivery system. The scheme both helps to define the special services delivery system and divide it into manageable parts that can be dealt with more easily than the system as a whole. The five parts composing our conceptual scheme are: assessment, instruction, related services, personnel development, and administration. Each of these parts represents a service area. Assessment, instruction, and related services are delivered directly to children; personnel development and administration constitute support services. In toto, these services are designed to achieve a single overall goal: the provision of an appropriate education to exceptional children and youth.

Each special education service area depicted in Figure 1-1 is composed of

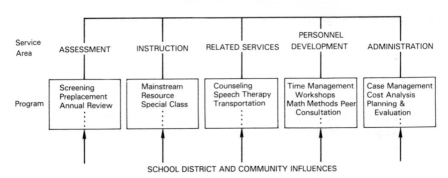

FIGURE 1-1 *A SPECIAL EDUCATION SERVICES DELIVERY SYSTEM*

a series of specifically targeted programs. *Programs* are organized configurations of resources—people, materials, and facilities—designed to assist an individual, group, or organization meet a specific need. The instructional service area, for example, may include, among other things, resource programs to meet the academic-support needs of mildly handicapped pupils, itinerant arrangements to address the problems of pupils unable to leave their homes, and special class programs for the functional-living needs of students with severe mental retardation.

The special services delivery system, in whole and in part, both influences and is affected by other systems in the school district (e.g., regular education) and in the general community. The special education services director, for instance, is typically responsible to the district school superintendent and, through that individual, to those members of the community represented on the local school board. Particular special programs may likewise be party to such interaction, as when efforts are undertaken to locate unserved handicapped children in the community through media advertisement, or to mainstream children into regular education classes.

In addition to interacting with the school system and community, the components of the special services system continuously interact among themselves. At the service level, for example, a clear set of interrelationships exists: assessment is primarily meant to provide information for making decisions about instructional programming and placement, the role of related services is to help students profit from direct instruction, personnel development is aimed at insuring that staff members possess the competencies needed to deliver services in all areas, and administration serves the function of overall service coordination.

Attempting to understand and work within the various internal and external relationships that influence the special education services delivery system is the heart of the systems perspective on planning and evaluation that we offer in this book. Recognition of these various interrelationships and their effects on service delivery will be repeatedly emphasized as we proceed in our discussion of the planning and evaluation process and its application to special education.

PERSPECTIVES ON PROGRAM PLANNING
AND EVALUATION

The successful application of planning and evaluation to special education requires, among other things, some understanding of what planning and evaluation are, the characteristics that provide quality in them, and how they have traditionally been applied in the schools.

Defining Planning and Evaluation

Planning is the process employed in developing a new program or improving an existing one. The planning process includes determining (1) the need for a program, (2) its goals, (3) the staff, materials, activities, schedule, and other elements that should compose it, (4) the methods for its evaluation, and (5) how it should be changed for the better (including its possible termination). Planning is based on the results of evaluation and occurs prior to, during, and following the implementation of a program; it is a continuous process.

Evaluation is also a process employed in designing or modifying a program. Evaluation involves gathering information about the various aspects of a program so that judgments about the program can be made. Evaluation provides information for judgments about the need for the program, the appropriateness of program goals, the strengths and weaknesses of different development options, the manner in which the program is carried out, and the ultimate success of the effort. This information becomes the basis for program improvement. Evaluation supplies the information on which planning decisions should be made.

A brief example may help to illustrate the relationship between planning and evaluation. The New Jersey Department of Education recently notified school districts of their responsibility to investigate and justify ethnic disproportions in programs for the educable mentally retarded (EMR). In a district where we helped deal with this problem, the special services director first initiated a review of the manner in which students placed in the EMR program had been assessed. The results of the director's evaluation indicated deficiencies in assessment procedure; in particular, failure to gather information on pupils' adaptive behavior, a central consideration in the diagnosis of mental retardation (Grossman, 1973). The director was led by this result to gather further information about assessment-team members' awareness of the underlying rationale, professional roles, and methods for assessing adaptive behavior. The evaluation data gathered by the director suggested that team members did not perceive the reasons for assessing adaptive behavior, the responsibilities of each team member in conducting such an assessment and, finally, the measurement tools available. These evaluation data were then used to plan an in-service program for pupil-assessment team members as well as to establish a means for regularly monitoring the assessment process.

Characteristics of Good Planning and Evaluation

Good planning and evaluation can be characterized by four major factors. These factors are based upon the *Standards for Evaluations of Educational Programs, Projects, and Materials* (Joint Committee, 1981), though they are modified somewhat to apply to planning as well as evaluation practice.

The first of these characteristics, *utility,* relates to the extent to which planning and evaluation efforts serve the program-development and -improvement needs of users. Utility means focusing planning and evaluation efforts on important program improvement concerns, conducting planning and evaluation in a timely manner, clearly documenting and communicating program plans and evaluation results, and working closely with program staff and decision makers to insure the positive use of planning and evaluation information.

Feasibility constitutes the second major characteristic of good planning and evaluation. This factor is intended to reflect the need for program-planning and -evaluation efforts to be realistic, diplomatic, and frugal. Activities should require reasonable amounts of staff time and disrupt operating programs to the minimal degree possible. Planning and evaluation efforts should also be carried out in a manner that is sensitive to the concerns of various interest groups (e.g., teachers, parents, administrators) so that the assistance of these groups is secured. Finally, activities should be of sufficient value to the program-development and -improvement process to justify the cost of carrying out those activities; if the evaluation costs more than the program, something has gone seriously awry!

Propriety represents yet a third characteristic of good planning and evaluation practice. Propriety refers to the degree to which efforts are carried out in legally and ethically responsible ways. Care should be taken to see that the rights of evaluation subjects are protected; their informed consent should be obtained and their right to needed programs preserved even if participation in such programs runs counter to the dictates of rigorous evaluation design (e.g., true experimental designs call for the random assignment of pupils to treatments, a situation that may not be tolerable in most special programs). Finally, propriety concerns the ready availability of planning and evaluation results. Such availability allows all interested parties the opportunity for critical examination and review.

The final factor that should be mentioned is *accuracy.* Planning and evaluation activities should be conducted in technically defensible ways. The context in which activities will be carried out should be examined, so that its likely effect on planning and evaluation can be anticipated. Input for program planning and evaluation should be gathered from a variety of sources (e.g., students, teachers, parents, administrators) and data-gathering procedures should be constructed and used to assure sufficient validity and reliability for program development and improvement purposes. Last, evaluation conclusions and planning decisions should be explicitly justified, so that their soundness can be assessed.

Planning and Evaluation in the Schools

Planning and evaluation have been practiced in the schools in one form or another for a long time. Traditionally, efforts have been informal. Administrators, for instance, have long based judgments about the need for new programs on their own subjective impressions and observations as well as on the input of others (e.g., parents, school-board members). Teachers, too, have constantly come to judgments about the success of their own classroom efforts (e.g., through classroom testing, homework, classwork) and changed program content and methods accordingly.

While informal planning and evaluation is frequently appropriate, it has serious limitations. First, planning and evaluation efforts of this kind are usually subject to criticisms of utility and propriety, because of their typical lack of documentation. Lack of documentation reduces utility, in that program staff members have no explicit plan to guide their service delivery efforts. It raises questions of propriety because the bases on which program modifications are made cannot be traced nor the procedures of evaluation inspected and critiqued by others.

Informal approaches also call into question the accuracy of planning and evaluation efforts. Such approaches are frequently unsystematic, characterized by minimal forethought and poor organization, resulting in program designs and evaluations that are often of low technical quality. Finally, informal approaches imply reliance on technically inadequate data-gathering procedures (e.g., unstructured observations) that may allow the results of evaluation to be contaminated by irrelevant influences (e.g., subjective biases) and the existence and effects of those influences to remain undetected (Bennett, 1982a).

While the large majority of planning and evaluation efforts traditionally undertaken in the schools have been informal, some districts have put more thoughtful approaches toward evaluation into practice. Districts receiving support through Title I (now Chapter I) of the Elementary and Secondary Education Act have for a number of years periodically evaluated these programs, using a formal set of federally prescribed procedures. Local education agencies in California are guided in their evaluation efforts by a state-supported technical-assistance network and tutorial materials developed by the Evaluation Improvement Project (California State, 1979). Finally, most big-city school districts have long-established evaluation units that take substantial care in conducting evaluation efforts.

Despite these praiseworthy efforts, many of the formal evaluations conducted in schools have been criticized by educators as being of limited use for program development and improvement. Such evaluations, in particular those of Title I, have had to operate within the constraints of a relatively rigid set of procedural guidelines. These guidelines have tended to divorce planning from evaluation by focusing on accountability issues, such as documenting the success or failure of programs, rather than on questions of how programs might be enhanced.

In this book, we encourage an approach to program planning and evaluation that is less rigid and more formative than the accountability-oriented schemes mandated for such programs as Title I but more formal, explicit, and systematic than that traditionally practiced in the schools. The approach we suggest helps to make planning and evaluation efforts open, routine activities that become an integral part of program functioning. In addition, it encourages the documentation of planning and evaluation efforts, so that recommendations for improving program delivery can be easily communicated and the methods used to reach those recommendations critically reviewed. Finally, and perhaps most important, the approach focuses planning and evaluation efforts on the critical educational concern of program improvement. For these reasons, the approach we recommend has generally proven useful, feasible, proper, and accurate in addressing problems common to educating exceptional children and youth.

A FRAMEWORK FOR SPECIAL EDUCATION
PLANNING AND EVALUATION

Many useful approaches to planning and evaluation exist. Some of the more popular of these approaches, or "models," as they are frequently called, are described in Table 1-1. Any one of these models can be successfully applied to the solution of particular special education planning and evaluation problems. However, it is our belief that no single model is best suited to the entire range of services that compose special education. Rather, some models are more appropriately applied to particular areas of special education than others.

The conceptual scheme we use for organizing planning and evaluation in special education draws heavily upon the many good ideas offered by existing approaches to planning and evaluation. Undoubtedly, you have already noted our endorsement of the basic premise underlying systems-analysis models: programs both act as and exist within systems of interrelated components; understanding these interrelationships is necessary for effective planning and evaluation. As the framework we suggest is introduced, key elements borrowed from these various planning and evaluation models will become recognizable and the debt we owe to those who have pioneered this field evident.

Our approach to special education planning and evaluation is represented by the framework presented in Figure 1-2. The framework is an integration of two concepts introduced earlier in this chapter. The first of these is the special education services delivery system, the major elements of which are located along the vertical dimension of the figure. The second important concept is that of planning and evaluation as a process. The components of this process are depicted as the horizontal dimension of the figure. Planning and evaluation in special education occurs when this process intersects with the special services delivery system.

Figure 1-2 implies a number of fundamental characteristics about the nature of special education planning and evaluation. First, planning and evaluation is

TABLE 1-1   Some Popular Planning and Evaluation Models

MODEL	DESCRIPTION	PROPONENT
Goal-Based	Goals and objectives, and activities needed to achieve them, established. Success determined by extent to which goals and objectives achieved.	Bloom, Hastings, & Madaus (1971)
Systems Analysis	Program inputs (e.g., staff, materials), processes (e.g., activities), and outputs (e.g., achievement) specified. Efficiency and effectiveness assessed by measuring these elements and their interrelationships within and across programs.	Kaufman (1972)
Decision Making	Delineation of key program questions and collection of relevant information to facilitate program decision making.	Stufflebeam, Foley, Gephart, Merriman, & Provus (1971)
Accreditation	Development according to conventional standards and criteria. Assessment of program quality through compliance audit often conducted by an external agency.	National Study of School Evaluation (1978)
Goal-Free	Complement to goal-based evaluation, involving detection of positive and negative effects of a program not reflected in program-goal statements.	Scriven (1974)
Adversarial	Opposing evaluation teams present evidence of program worth to a "judge" and "jury" using quasi-legal procedures.	Worthen & Owens (1978)
Art Criticism	Impressionistic critique of a program by an outside content expert, often without explicit standards, to obtain a judgment of program worth.	Stake (1975)
Transactional	Qualitative assessment of a program, often through case studies, to develop an understanding of how staff and consumers interact in and experience the program.	Parlett & Hamilton (1978)

applicable to the *range* of elements that compose the special education services delivery system. The common perception that only instructional programs need be carefully planned and evaluated is both inaccurate and unfortunate. Second, the planning and evaluation process is generic; its general form can be applied, without modification, to any area of service delivery.

Third, planning and evaluation in special education is a team effort requiring the input of professionals involved in planning and evaluation (the horizontal dimension of Figure 1-2) and special education services delivery (the vertical dimension of Figure 1-2). This collaboration brings both methodological and programmatic expertise to the planning and evaluation effort. In addition, involving special educators—especially those staffing a program—encourages a sense of ownership in the program as well as a greater willingness to accept and use evaluation results.

	PLANNING AND EVALUATION PROCESS			
SERVICE AREA	Problem Clarification	Program Design	Program Implementation	Outcome Assessment
Assessment				
Instruction	*PLANNING*			
Related Services		*AND*		
Personnel Development			*EVALUATION*	
Administration				*CONTENT*

FIGURE 1-2 *A FRAMEWORK FOR PLANNING AND EVALUATING SPECIAL EDUCATION SERVICES*

Finally, while the general process of planning and evaluating special education is the same regardless of service area, the specific models and methods used to apply any given segment of the process to any one service may differ from that used in another part of the process or for another service. The content of planning and evaluation—the models, methods, staff, and activities—will, therefore, frequently differ as the focus or stage of the planning and evaluation process changes.

Special Education Services

The focus of the planning and evaluation process is the special services delivery system. Earlier in this chapter, this system was conceptualized to include five areas: assessment, instruction, related services, personnel development, and administration. Each area was in turn seen as being composed of targeted programs directed at addressing the needs of an individual, group, or organization.

The assessment service area is intended to provide information for use in making educational decisions about individual children. The decisions typically made on the basis of assessment data are primarily of two types: those related to service eligibility and those tied to educational programming. Examples of programs within the assessment service area are school- and community-based child-find, preplacement evaluation, formative instructional assessment, and individualized program review. These programs typically interact with programs in other service delivery areas. Assessment information is, for example, used to suggest instructional and related service needs for individuals; likewise, personnel development efforts are often directed at improving assessment practice.

Programs for both individuals and groups compose the instructional service area. Such programs are generally aimed at directly facilitating the academic skill development and functional-living-skill development of exceptional students and, as such, comprise the core of special education. The most widely known instructional program for individuals is PL 94-142's individualized education program (IEP). Examples of group programs include resource rooms and special classes for the severely handicapped. The successful operation of instructional programs depends heavily upon programs housed in other service delivery areas, from assessment for information on which to base instructional goals, to administration for management and coordination.

Related services include such programs as speech, occupational, and physical therapy; counseling; transportation; and medical diagnosis. These programs are meant to provide children with the support needed to benefit from specialized instruction. Related service programs are delivered to both individuals and groups.

The goal of personnel development, the fourth component of the special services delivery system, is to insure that those involved with the education of exceptional children possess the competencies necessary to perform their jobs adequately. In-service workshops, graduate courses, organized consultation, and professional conferences all constitute examples of personnel development efforts.

The fifth special education service is administration, the management function that coordinates the delivery of all services in the system. Administration includes staff supervision, student case management, cost analysis, program compliance monitoring and reporting, and planning and evaluation. Administrative services set the organizational conditions needed for all other special services to function.

The Planning and Evaluation Process

The second dimension of our framework for special education planning and evaluation is the planning and evaluation process. As shown in Figure 1-2, this process is composed of four phases: problem clarification, program design, program implementation, and outcome assessment. Like the elements that compose the special services system, the phases of planning and evaluation can only be seen as distinct for discussion purposes. In reality, planning and evaluation phases, like special services, build upon and interact with each other. Program design is based upon problem clarification; implementation is guided by and often suggests changes in program design; outcome assessment indicates the existence of heretofore unknown service delivery problems that may necessitate design of new programs.

The major elements of the planning and evaluation process are listed in Box 1-1.

BOX 1-1 *ELEMENTS OF THE PLANNING AND EVALUATION PROCESS*

I. Problem Clarification

    A. Assessing service delivery needs
    B. Assessing service delivery context
    C. Describing the problem

II. Program Design

    A. Describing program purpose, goals, and objectives
    B. Evaluating program alternatives
    C. Developing the program design
    D. Evaluating the program design

III. Program Implementation

    A. Facilitating program implementation
    B. Evaluating program implementation

IV. Outcome Assessment

    A. Evaluating goal attainment
    B. Evaluating related effects
    C. Evaluating consumer reaction
    D. Evaluating cause-effect relations
    E. Evaluating cost-effectiveness
    F. Deciding about program change
    G. Communicating evaluation results

Problem clarification.   A service delivery problem can be thought of as an unsatisfactory state of affairs existing with respect to one or more special education services. The purpose of problem clarification is to define the nature and scope of this unsatisfactory state so that a special education program can be designed to improve it.

Needs assessment is the first activity of the problem-clarification phase. A service delivery need is a discrepancy between an actual condition and a desired state of affairs. Needs assessment is the process of gathering information about actual conditions and comparing that to the desired state.

The context in which particular service delivery needs are embedded is a second important factor in problem clarification. Such things as the ability of the school district to commit financial and staff resources to solve the problem, the interest district officials express in addressing it, and the likely resistance of staff to different solutions should be incorporated into the description of the service delivery problem.

Problem clarification concludes with a full description of the problem that is to be addressed. The description specifies the individual or group experiencing the problem, the service delivery needs of this target, and the organizational context in which the problem exists. This description forms the basis for program design, the second phase in the planning and evaluation process.

Program design. Program design is the process of constructing a program to address the service delivery needs defined as a result of problem clarification. The first concern in designing a program is specifying the purpose, goals, and objectives of the service delivery effort. These elements detail the rationale for the program's existence, whom it is meant to serve, and what it is meant to accomplish.

Evaluating program options is the second element of the program-design phase of the planning and evaluation process. Alternatives are identified on the basis of their match with program purpose, goals, and objectives. Once identified, options are compared in terms of such contextual factors as resources needed for implementation and staff reaction to the alternative, as well as the likelihood of goal attainment.

The process of developing the selected alternative into an operational program primarily involves the task of constructing a written program design. The program design reiterates the purpose of the effort, how it is to be carried out, and what it is expected to achieve. As such, the design guides both the implementation and evaluation of the program. An organizational structure for the program design is presented as Box 1-2.

BOX 1-2 *COMPONENTS OF A PROGRAM DESIGN*

I. Purpose

    A. Program rationale
    B. Scope
        1. Activities
        2. Client population
        3. Staff
    C. Major outcomes

II. Implementation

    A. Preconditions for operation
        1. Human resources
            a. Number, type, and qualifications of required staff
        2. Informational resources
            a. Policies and procedures
                (1) Criteria for selecting program clients
                (2) Evaluation plan
        3. Technological resources
            a. Materials
            b. Equipment
        4. Financial resources
            a. Budgets
                (1) Developmental
                (2) Operational
        5. Physical resources
            a. Facilities
                (1) Rooms
                (2) Buildings
                (3) Sites
    B. Nature of methods and activities
    C. Roles, responsibilities, and relationships of staff members

```
    D.  Sequence and timing of activities
    E.  Amount of permissible variation across sites

III. Outcomes

    A.  Program goals
        1.  Objectives cross-referenced to activities
```

The final consideration in program design is the quality of the proposed program. Program quality can be evaluated in terms of five criteria suggested by Provus (1972). The first criterion, clarity, refers to the extent to which the design is understandable and its components objectively measurable. Second, the design is inspected to insure that it is comprehensive, that it fully describes the purpose, implementation, and expected outcomes of the effort. Third, the components of the design are assessed to make certain that they are logically interrelated, or internally consistent. Compatibility with the need the program was established to address, with existing support conditions, and with other related programs is reviewed next. Finally, theoretical soundness is considered in terms of the degree to which the design describes a program that is consistent with current professional knowledge and principles of good practice.

Program implementation. The program-implementation phase of the planning and evaluation process centers upon facilitating the conduct of a program and upon evaluating and improving its operation. As we stated, the basis for implementation is the program design. The design describes the human, informational, technological, financial, and physical resources needed for the program to function properly. In addition, it details activities, staff responsibilities, schedule, and permissible variation in functioning across program locations. Making staff members aware of this information and working with them to see that it is used is essential if a program is to function successfully.

Implementation evaluation, or monitoring, serves to document how a program is being provided. This evaluation focuses on describing the context, or conditions, under which the program is actually operating, and the activities occurring and their timing, as well as other factors. Monitoring can reveal discrepancies between program plans and operations that may suggest the need to rethink aspects of design, improve program functioning, or both. In addition, information documenting what was delivered can help suggest the causes of positive and negative effects discovered through outcome assessment.

Outcome assessment. The fourth, and final, phase of the planning and evaluation process is outcome assessment. Outcome assessment is meant to describe the impact or effects that a program has had. This information may imply the need to revise the program to better achieve desired effects, expand the program so that its benefits can be brought to others, or terminate it to prevent further unjustified expenditures or harmful results.

Outcome assessment helps to clarify a broad range of decision-making concerns (see Table 1-2). However, because of the demands that such assessment places on school resources, it is rare for the outcome assessment of any given program to intensively address more than two or three of these concerns. The first decision-making concern is determining if a program was responsive to the service delivery problem it was meant to address. This determination is typically made by assessing the extent to which the program achieved the goals set by its designers.

A second common concern of outcome evaluation is for related program effects. Most educational programs have effects on students, staff, or community in addition to the ones they were primarily intended to produce. These effects may be positive, as when the introduction of microcomputers to assist instruction increases school attendance; they may also be negative, as in the case of a mainstreaming program that creates feelings of resentment toward handicapped students because of the extra work it creates for regular class teachers. Program side effects have obvious implications for program improvement—especially when negative— and hence constitute an important focus for outcome assessment.

Consumer reaction is a third decision-making concern that falls within the purview of outcome assessment. The reactions of program consumers—for example, parents and even the students themselves—can aid in determining the social value of a program as well as point to ways in which it can be improved.

A fourth possible focus for outcome assessment is determining the relationship between a program and its observed effects. Because the effects observed at the conclusion of a program can be due to particular elements of the program (e.g., a singular teacher, method, or set of materials) or to elements totally outside the effort (e.g., another program, poor evaluation design, pupil maturation), the object of outcome assessment is sometimes the exploration of cause-effect relationships. Strong statements of cause-effect relationship, however, require elements of experimental design often inappropriate in school settings (e.g., random assignment of

TABLE 1-2   Decision-Making Concerns Addressed by Outcome Evaluation

DECISION-MAKING CONCERN	EVALUATION FOCUS
To what extent have program goals been achieved?	Goal Attainment
Have any positive or negative results not reflected in program goals been produced?	Related Program Effects
What do consumers think of the program?	Consumer Reaction
Did the program cause the observed effects? What particular program elements were responsible for given effects?	Cause-Effect Relations
Was the program worth the resources invested in it?	Cost-Effectiveness
How should the program be changed?	All of the above

students to programs). For this reason, the practical examination of cause-effect relations is frequently focused upon gathering evidence to *rule out* likely competing causes (e.g., novelty) of program outcomes. The results of such exploration may support the success of a program so that it can be more widely disseminated or suggest particular elements (e.g., methods and materials) responsible for given effects.

The cost-effectiveness of school programs represents yet another legitimate concern that can be addressed by outcome assessment. This type of outcome evaluation has rarely been utilized in the schools because of the complex economic, educational, and methodological issues it entails (e.g., see Levine, 1981). Interest in cost-effectiveness evaluation, however, is increasing as resources for education become more limited and allocating funds to programs that produce the biggest impact becomes more critical.

A sixth concern of outcome assessment is deciding how a program should be changed to more effectively achieve program, system, district, or community goals. The notion of change includes modifications in program design and implementation, expansion of the program to other sites or target populations, and, where appropriate, termination. Decisions about change—especially those that are expected to have substantial consequences—should be based upon a broad range of considerations, including program operation, goal attainment, related effects, cause-effect relationships, and, where possible, cost-effectiveness.

The culminating activity of outcome assessment is communicating evaluation results. Outcome- and implementation-evaluation results should be communicated within the context of the ongoing interaction between the planning and evaluation team and those interested in the program (e.g., staff, parents, board members, students). Communication should be focused on facilitating program development and improvement.

Planning and Evaluation Content

Planning and evaluation content is the substance of planning and evaluation in special education; it is the methods, models, and activities that compose a particular planning and evaluation effort. As we stated earlier, the content of a particular planning and evaluation effort will vary as a function of both the phase in the planning and evaluation process and the service being focused upon. On the following pages we discuss the application of this general process to each of the five services that composes special education.

SUMMARY

This chapter has introduced a number of concepts central to our approach to special education planning and evaluation. The special education services delivery system was viewed as composed of five interrelated service areas—assessment, instruction, related services, personnel development, and administration—designed to provide an appropriate education for exceptional children and youth. Each service area is, in turn, made up of a series of specifically targeted programs. The special education services delivery system does not exist in isolation; it influences and is affected by other systems in the school district and community.

Planning and evaluation were seen as complementary processes meant to facilitate program development and improvement. Characteristics of good planning and evaluation include utility, feasibility, propriety, and accuracy.

The concepts of planning and evaluation and the special services delivery system form the basis of our special education planning and evaluation framework. The framework segments the planning and evaluation process into four phases— problem clarification, program design, program implementation, and outcome assessment—and suggests that this process is both applicable to all elements of the special services delivery system and generic in form; programs in each service delivery area can be planned and evaluated, and these activities can be conducted using the same general process. Second, the framework pictured planning and evaluation as a team effort, involving the collaboration of special educators and evaluators. Third, while the planning and evaluation process is generic, the specific models and methods used typically vary as a function of service delivery area and phase within the planning and evaluation process. Finally, planning and evaluation in special education was said to occur when the planning and evaluation process is applied to the special services delivery system.

2

PLANNING AND EVALUATING ASSESSMENT SERVICES

Assessment is an activity central to the appropriate education of children with special needs. Assessment provides the information upon which decisions of identification, categorization, program planning and placement, and program review are based. Assessment services are the range of programs and activities designed to gather data about individual students for purposes of educational decision making. Examples of such programs are community child find and in-school screening programs, preplacement evaluation, and periodic reevaluation.

We would also include under the rubric of assessment services such programs as IEP annual review and formative instructional evaluation (that is, the kind of evaluation any good classroom teacher routinely does over the course of the year), even though these are also part of classroom instructional service programs. The inclusion of these programs in the assessment service domain serves to emphasize the interrelationships among the various areas of special education services delivery discussed in Chapter 1; hence, the need for a systems approach to their planning and evaluation.

OVERVIEW OF ASSESSMENT SERVICES

Need for Assessment Services in Special Education

Assessment is the process of gathering and interpreting information about individual students for use in educational decision making. Data gathered through assessment programs are generally used in making two classes of decisions: service eligibility (that is, identification and categorization) and educational programming (that is, individualized program planning, placement, and program review).

That decisions of service eligibility and educational programming require accurate, objective information should be obvious: decisions based on inaccurate information can lead, at one extreme, to the stigmatization of children who are not special, and at the other, to failure to provide services to those truly in need (Bennett, 1981c). The seriousness of such decision errors is exemplified by a number of recent litigative actions brought against school districts that failed to insure the quality of information upon which service eligibility was based (e.g., *Larry P.* v. *Riles,* 1979; *Mattie T.* v. *Holladay,* 1979).

Individualized programs (IPs) also must be based on reliable, valid information.[1] The limited time available for IP development and the large number of children for whom IPs need to be developed demand that program-planning efforts be built upon a reasonably correct characterization of what a child knows and the types of conditions under which that child learns best.

Nature and Scope of Assessment Services

Assessment services are provided in the form of targeted programs meant to assist in making educational decisions about individual pupils (see Box 2-1 for a listing of common assessment programs). Community-oriented child find, in-school screening, and preplacement evaluation programs have traditionally served to answer questions of service eligibility; formative instructional assessment and IEP annual review have been directed toward educational planning. We believe, however, that assessment programs oriented toward one decision-making purpose should also, to the extent feasible, facilitate the other. This suggests that preplacement evaluation attempt to provide instructionally useful information and that formative instructional assessment and IEP annual review speak to the question of whether the classified child still requires special services.

Assessment services are typically provided in one form or another to all schoolchildren. Children throughout the school system are generally screened to determine whether they should be referred for special education preplacement evaluation. Those considered to be potentially handicapped are comprehensively evaluated, and, if classified, are assessed periodically over the course of their school careers.

The various assessment programs commonly found in schools are delivered by a wide variety of personnel. In-school screening programs require the involvement of regular education teachers and school specialists (e.g., the school nurse, school psychologist); community-oriented child-find efforts require the cooperation of members of the community (e.g., the physician, visiting nurse) in bringing potentially handicapped and handicapped children to the attention of school authorities. Preplacement evaluation programs are regularly staffed by such spe-

---

[1] We use the acronym IP to refer to individualized programs in general. The acronym IEP is used to denote PL 94-142's individualized education program. The distinction between the IP and IEP is fully explained in Chapter 3.

BOX 2-1 *SOME COMMON ASSESSMENT PROGRAMS*

Community Child Find: outreach effort primarily designed to locate handicapped children not currently receiving educational services. Child find efforts frequently involve media campaigns (TV, radio, newspaper) to encourage parents of unserved children to contact the school as well as arrangements with community agencies (e.g., public health clinics) to work with parents to obtain needed services for children.

In-School Screening: district level program to identify children in general education classes requiring comprehensive preplacement evaluation. In-school screening programs typically rely on teacher referral and district achievement testing programs as their primary identification mechanisms.

Preplacement Evaluation: district level program designed to gather information to be used in determining which referred children require special education and what their educational programs should consist of. Preplacement programs are generally conducted by a team of professionals using a variety of assessment methods.

Reevaluation: district level program to comprehensively reassess children currently receiving special education. Data from reevaluation programs are used in deciding if those children continue to need special services and the types of services required.

Annual Review: district level program to annually assess student progress toward achieving individualized program goals and develop a new individualized program for the coming school year.

Formative Instructional Assessment: classroom level program to track individual student progress on a routine basis (e.g., daily or weekly). The results of formative instructional assessment are used to adjust instructional methods and materials as necessary.

cialists as school psychologists, educational diagnosticians, and social workers, with medical personnel, audiologists, and speech, occupational, and physical therapists used on an ad hoc basis. Finally, formative instructional assessment involves the classroom teacher and IEP annual review, the teacher, school administrator, and the child's parents.

Difficulties in Providing Assessment Services

The most serious difficulty in providing assessment services in the schools relates to the very adequacy of assessment, as currently practiced, for informing those who make educational decisions about children. In particular, the adequacy of assessment for informing decisions about the identification of culturally different children and the utility of assessment for instructional programming have been strongly questioned.

The validity of assessment data for aiding decisions about the identification of culturally different children has been questioned primarily because there is a significant overrepresentation of minorities in special education, and in particular, in programs for the educable mentally retarded (Comptroller General, 1981). Such overrepresentation has been variously hypothesized to be due to bias in intelligence (IQ) tests (Mercer, 1973; Mercer & Lewis, 1979), bias in human decision making (Ysseldyke, 1979, 1980), and to a real need among lower socioeconomic groups for special, remedial, and compensatory education programs (MacMillan & Meyers, 1980; Reschly, 1981; Reynolds, 1981).

The problem of overrepresentation and the hypotheses of bias in assessment and decision making have been the focus of much debate: professional journals have devoted entire issues to the problem (e.g., see Prasse, 1980, and Reschly, 1979), a blue-ribbon panel from the National Academy of Sciences has studied it (Heller, Holtzman, & Messick, 1982), and the federal courts have litigated it (e.g., *Larry P. v. Riles,* 1979; *Parents in Action (PASE) v. Hannon,* 1980).

The major result of this continuing debate has been to highlight the complexity of the problem of minority overrepresentation. The federal courts, for example, have rendered contradictory decisions on the role of IQ tests in causing the problem (see *Larry P. v. Riles* and *PASE v. Hannon*), making eventual litigation before the United States Supreme Court likely. The true cause of minority overrepresentation in special education remains unknown (Comptroller General, 1981). The problem is most probably the result of many factors—social, administrative, cultural, and legal (Heller, Holtzman, & Messick, 1982). In any event, the problem continues to be an important one for federal, state, and local program directors saddled with the dual responsibilities of promoting equity and limiting the liability of the institutions for which they work.

The utility of assessment information for instructional program planning is a second problem frequently cited in the special education literature (e.g., Howell, Kaplan, & O'Connell, 1979; Jenkins & Pany, 1978) and experienced firsthand by many special education teachers. The problem has been tied to the content and orientation of commonly used measures, such as norm-referenced tests (Proger & Mann, 1973), the proficiency and performance of assessment personnel (Bennett, 1981c; Goodman & Bennett, 1982), and the lack of a solid theoretical and empirical base for linking individual child characteristics with instructional treatments (Salvia & Ysseldyke, 1981).

We believe that assessment programs can serve to adequately inform decisions of service eligibility and educational programming for handicapped children. However, the extent to which these ends are attained depends in no small way upon careful planning and ongoing evaluation. Planning a new assessment program, or reorganizing a currently operational one, requires first an understanding of the particular service delivery problem that the program is meant to address.

CLARIFYING ASSESSMENT SERVICE DELIVERY PROBLEMS

Assessing Service Delivery Needs

As has been discussed, assessment programs are generally designed to address service delivery problems relating to deciding who needs special education (service eligibility) and exactly what form that special education should take (educational planning). The existence of these service delivery needs is recognized and addressed by federal legislation, case law, and state education regulations. Hence, a common first step in clarifying assessment service delivery problems is an analysis of relevant education law and regulations.

In general, existing laws, such as PL 94-142, and regulations require schools to, at a minimum, have active child find, preplacement evaluation, IEP annual review, and periodic reevaluation programs. The specific requirements for the content and operation of these programs vary from state to state. We recommend as a first step in the clarification of any assessment service delivery problem a comparison of existing regulations and district programs. This is accomplished by reviewing the relevant state and federal regulations and listing all requirements for the content and operation of assessment programs. Next, existing district assessment programs, policies, and procedures are compared to regulatory requirements to identify gaps in services that should be the focus of program-design efforts.

The comparison of district assessment programs to education regulations often produces a number of interesting findings about a district's assessment efforts. One frequent result is the discovery that no explicit, written policies or procedures for assessment exist or that those that do exist are ambiguous or superficial. This in itself is an assessment problem; clear documentation of policies and procedures serves to describe the assessment program to parents and school-board members, communicate expectations for performance to the staff, and provide evidence to monitoring bodies (e.g., the state education department, U.S. Office of Civil Rights, the public advocate) that the district's policy and intentions with regard to student assessment are in keeping with the law.

A second frequent result of comparing district assessment programs and education regulations is the discovery that, at least as far as written district policies and procedures go, all required services are being provided. In the event that suspicion of problems in the delivery of assessment services still exists (e.g., because parents repeatedly complain about the accuracy of assessment results), a sensible next step in needs assessment is to observe portions of the program in action and to review samples of documents (e.g., assessment reports) produced by the program. Close investigation of this sort sometimes reveals discrepancies between written policy and the way the program is actually carried out (e.g., use of only a single measure in the evaluation of a child even though district policies clearly state otherwise). Such discrepancies suggest program needs that may become the focus of subsequent design efforts.

Assessing the Service Delivery Context

The context in which an assessment program is embedded is a critical factor in understanding both why an existing program is operating as it is and how successful a new or modified program is likely to be. Hence, assessing the context is an important element in clarifying assessment service delivery problems.

One useful approach to context assessment is suggested by the A VICTORY model (Davis & Salasin, 1975). A VICTORY is an acronym for a series of factors that appear to be related to program success. Box 2-2 defines the components of the A VICTORY model. Although all the elements of the A VICTORY approach are relevant to assessment programs, we take particular note of Obligation and Resistance.

BOX 2-2 *COMPONENTS OF THE A VICTORY MODEL*

FACTOR	DESCRIPTION
Ability	Capacity to carry out the program or change: staff, funds, space, sanctions, general resources.
Values	Predecisions, attitudes, beliefs, manners of operating held by various persons in the program being considered.
Idea	Information and sources and flow of information relevant to accommodating the program being considered in terms of solving problems and enhancing efforts.
Circumstances	Prevailing factors pressing for or detracting from the program's integration into the parent system or organization.
Timing	Synchrony of the program's installation with significant events occurring within the organization.
Obligation	Felt need by various people in the program being considered to do something and/or change in response to a perceived problem.
Resistance	Both frontstage and backstage fears of loss by people in the organization if the program being considered is adopted.
Yield	Rewards and benefits to program participants and clients as perceived by them.

Source: C. Hauser. Evaluating mainstream programs: Capitalizing on A VICTORY. Journal of Special Education, 1979, 13, 107-129. Derived from H. Davis and S. Salasin. The utilization of evaluation. In E. Struening and M. Guttentag (Eds.), Handbook of evaluation research (Vol. 1), pp. 652-654. Beverly Hills, CA: Sage Publications, 1975. © 1975 by Sage Publications, Inc. Used by permission.

Obligation.   As we have stated, a close look at district policies and operating assessment programs often reveals discrepancies between the two. Frequently, these discrepancies are the result of staff members' not feeling that existing policies prevent potential problems or serve otherwise important functions. Some districts, for example, have as policy the use of standard and percentile scores—in addition to grade equivalents—for reporting assessment results. This policy for reporting assessment results is, however, rarely followed in practice, because assessment personnel do not understand the problem the policy is attempting to ameliorate (that is, the widespread tendency to misinterpret grade-equivalent scores) and, hence, do not feel obligated to carry out this mandate.

Resistance.   Overt and covert resistance can also be a significant impediment to the success of an assessment program. Classroom teachers, for example, may have negative feelings about the district screening program because it creates additional work and interferes with class instructional time. These feelings may translate into carelessly completing the pupil-behavior rating forms required by the program or outright refusal to cooperate. That such resistance exists should be documented if the assessment service delivery problem is to be accurately described.

Describing the Assessment Service Delivery Problem

The assessment service delivery problem description is a brief summary of service delivery needs and relevant contextual factors identified during the problem-clarification phase (see Box 2-3). This summary documents the results of the problem-clarification phase and sets the stage for the second phase of the planning and evaluation process: designing the assessment program.

BOX 2-3   *AN ASSESSMENT SERVICE DELIVERY PROBLEM DESCRIPTION*

Service Delivery Need

 I. No systematic procedure for identifying kindergarten children needing special education evaluation currently exists in the district. State education regulations require such a procedure in all school districts. This procedure must be developed and implemented this school year.

Relevant Contextual Factors

 II. Ability

   A.   District staff does not have background in early screening methods or signs predictive of later school failure.
   B.   Approximately $5000 is available in the annual budget to fund an early screening program.

 III. Circumstances

   A.   School administration supports development of a systematic early screening procedure for kindergarten students, owing to the requirement for such a program in the state-education code.

 IV. Resistance

   A.   Child-evaluation staff members are concerned about the program because they feel they do not have the knowledge needed to carry it out and they feel they are already overburdened with current evaluation caseloads.

DESIGNING ASSESSMENT PROGRAMS

Our approach to planning and evaluating assessment programs is based upon the accreditation model (see Table 1-1). This model, often used in developing and evaluating university teacher-training programs, entails planning and evaluating programs with reference to explicit, conventionally recognized standards and criteria. The model is particularly well suited to planning and evaluating assessment programs because of the need for a strong foundation upon which to base and defend assessment programs and the ready availability of conventional standards and criteria.

Describing the Assessment Program
Purpose and Goals

The first major step in designing an assessment program is identifying the purpose the program is meant to serve. The statement of purpose should be based on the assessment service delivery problem description and be responsive to the needs expressed in that document. The purpose should communicate, in concise fashion, the general rationale for the program, its scope (proposed activities, client population, staff), and major outcomes. Here is an example of a program purpose for an in-school kindergarten screening program:

> The district screening program is part of the district's school and community child-find effort. The ultimate purpose of both the screening program and the child-find effort is to identify handicapped children as early as possible, so that appropriate educational services can be delivered. The program involves screening of kindergarten students by school staff in the sensory, physical, learning, and behavior areas, and results in a listing of students in need of further evaluation.

The explication of purpose is followed by a statement of the outcomes, or goals, the assessment program is intended to achieve. So, for example, the primary goal of the in-school screening program described above might be the following:

> The program will result in a list of students needing individual preplacement evaluation because they appear at risk for school-learning failure.

Care should be taken in specifying assessment program goals to note instances where goals and contextual factors identified through problem clarification appear incompatible. Discrepancies between goals and the existing context (e.g., a lack of trained staff to carry out the proposed program) should be explored so that information can be gathered on the feasibility of changing contextual factors. If such changes are not practicable (e.g., a trained staff cannot be obtained), the goals set for the effort will need to be modified.

Evaluating Assessment Program Alternatives

The alternatives chosen for evaluation are those that best fit the purpose of the assessment program and the goals it is meant to achieve. Alternatives should be evaluated on the basis of a number of factors, including resource requirements, fit with context, and the anticipated quality of the result. Resource considerations include those for staff, materials and equipment, and facilities. Contextual fit involves considering the match between district conditions and the requirements of each alternative. Finally, alternatives should be assessed with respect to the adequacy with which each is expected to achieve the goals of the assessment program.

Though we can advise on what to consider when evaluating assessment program alternatives, the final selection of a program alternative is a professional judgment best left to those familiar with local conditions. For example, kindergarten screening can be accomplished through a variety of alternative approaches. Among these are (1) teacher referral, where the kindergarten teacher subjectively decides whom to bring to the attention of the preplacement evaluation program, (2) pupil behavior rating, in which referral is made on the basis of the teacher's responses to a specific set of queries about each student's classroom behavior, and (3) individual screening, where the referral decision is based on the child's performance on a series of brief predictive measures.

Of these three alternatives, teacher referral is generally recognized as the least adequate in selecting students truly in need of preplacement evaluation. Teacher referrals are subject to many irrelevant influences, including socioeconomic status, race, and physical appearance (e.g., see Stevens, 1981; Tobias, Cole, Zibrin, & Bodlakova, 1982). As such, this approach often results in the inappropriate referral of students for special education evaluation.

Though it is generally less adequate in achieving common screening goals, there are instances in which teacher referral may be the alternative of choice. Consider, for example, the case of a district in which ability to adopt a screening program is low—because of a lack of funds or trained staff—and resistance to the program is high—because teachers and evaluation personnel are overworked. Under these conditions, both the pupil-behavior rating and individual screening approaches would likely produce less trustworthy results than teacher referral; in order to achieve their added benefit, both alternatives require trained personnel (to reliably rate behavior and administer tests), significant amounts of teacher and evaluator staff time, and nontrivial investments in materials. The teacher-referral approach, on the other hand, would require a minimal commitment from staff and the negligible cost associated with printing a referral form; demands on staff time would be minimal, with the only real requirements being some time for teacher training to reduce the subjectivity of referrals and time for teachers to complete the form and discuss the action with the school principal.

For decision makers, then, the task is not so much one of finding the all-around best alternative but, rather, locating the alternative that works best under the conditions existing in the school district.

Developing the Assessment Program Design

Following identification of the alternative to be used to fulfill the program purpose and goals, the written program design is developed. An assessment program design can be developed for an already operational program as well as for a program that is new and has yet to be installed. In either case, the written design serves to make explicit the expectations for the program's performance—be it a child-find, screening, preplacement evaluation, IEP annual review, or reevaluation program— and the criteria and standards against which it will be evaluated.

The major components of a program design were presented earlier as Box 1-2 and include a general statement of the *purpose* of the program, followed by specific statements describing program *implementation,* or operation, and the *outcomes,* or impact, the program is designed to achieve. The section describing the program purpose can simply incorporate the content developed earlier, in the design phase of the planning and evaluation process. This content (that is, rationale, scope, major outcomes) should be revised as necessary, to reflect any changes in the purpose made as a result of the choice of a specific program alternative (e.g., deciding that the community public-health service staff will participate in screening activities along with the school staff).

Program implementation, or operation, is described in the second section of the design. This section specifies how the program will achieve its purpose and goals. The section should include statements of preoperational program conditions (that is, the contextual factors necessary for the program to succeed), activities, duties and responsibilities of staff, scheduling, and variation across program sites (e.g., school buildings). Examples of implementation criteria for the kindergarten screening program described earlier are the following:

> Program clients will include all children currently enrolled in regular kindergarten classes in the school district.
> Program activities will include screening with the Snellen eye chart, pure-tone audiometer, and Pupil Behavior Scale.

Finally, the design is completed with the statement of the outcomes, or goals, the assessment program is intended to achieve.

The various statements that describe program implementation and outcomes become, in our approach, the standards and criteria that guide both operation and evaluation of the assessment program. Clearly, if this is the case, the adequacy of any assessment program built on the approach will depend in large part on the quality of the standards and criteria selected to guide the program. We therefore strongly recommend that assessment programs be based in large part upon *conventionally recognized* standards and criteria. Such standards, because they are typically developed through the input of a large number of individuals with a great diversity of expertise and experience, provide a solid, state-of-the-art foundation for district-level assessment programs, that, we believe, helps insure attention to such issues as fairness and instructional utility. In addition, because of their conventionality, the use of such standards provides a strong defense against charges of discrimination and arbitrariness in assessment that are increasingly brought against school districts (e.g., *Larry P.* v. *Riles,* 1979; *Lora* v. *Board of Education,* 1979; *Mattie T.* v. *Holladay,* 1979; *PASE* v. *Hannon,* 1980), and that are, unfortunately, in some cases true.

For assessment programs, conventional standards and criteria can readily be drawn from a number of sources. Sources of standards for assessment include education law and regulations, published professional standards, and expert judgment about what constitutes good assessment practice. Under the rubric of education law and regulations fall the Protection in Evaluation Procedures section of PL 94-142, similar language in the regulations for Section 504 of the Rehabilitation Act, and the education codes of most states. Box 2-4 presents the Protection in Evaluation Procedures section of the PL 94-142 regulations.

BOX 2-4   *PROTECTION IN EVALUATION PROCEDURES SECTION OF THE RULES AND REGULATIONS FOR PL 94-142*

PROTECTION IN EVALUATION PROCEDURES

§ 121a.530 General.

(a) Each State educational agency shall insure that each public agency establishes and implements procedures which meet the requirements of §§ 121a.-530-121a. 534.

(b) Testing and evaluation materials and procedures used for the purposes of evaluation and placement of handicapped children must be selected and administered so as not to be racially or culturally discriminatory.

(20 U.S.C. 1412(5) (C).)
§ 121a.531 Preplacement
            evaluation.

Before any action is taken with respect to the initial placement of a handicapped child in a special education program, a full and individual evaluation of the child's educational needs must be conducted in accordance with the requirements of § 121a.532.

(20 U.S.C. 1412(5) (C).)
§ 121a.532 Evaluation procedures.

State and local educational agencies shall insure, at a minimum, that:

(a) Tests and other evaluation materials:

(1) Are provided and administered in the child's native language or other mode of communication, unless it is clearly not feasible to do so;

(2) Have been validated for the specific purpose for which they are used; and

(3) Are administered by trained personnel in conformance with the instructions provided by their producer;

(b) Tests and other evaluation materials include those tailored to assess specific areas of educational need and not merely those which are designed to provide a single general intelligence quotient;

(c) Tests are selected and administered so as best to ensure that when a test is administered to a child with impaired sensory, manual, or speaking skills, the test results accurately reflect the child's aptitude or achievement level or whatever other factors the test purports to measure, rather than reflecting the child's impaired sensory, manual, or speaking skills (except where those skills are the factors which the test purports to measure);

(d) No single procedure is used as

the sole criterion for determining an appropriate educational program for a child; and

(e) The evaluation is made by a multidisciplinary team or group of persons, including at least one teacher or other specialist with knowledge in the area of suspected disability.

(f) The child is assessed in all areas related to the suspected disability, including, where appropriate, health, vision, hearing, social and emotional status, general intelligence, academic performance, communicative status, and motor abilities.

(20 U.S.C. 1412(5) (C).)

Comment. Children who have a speech impairment as their primary handicap may not need a complete battery of assessments (e.g., psychological, physical, or adaptive behavior). However, a qualified speech-language pathologist would (1) evaluate each speech impaired child using procedures that are appropriate for the diagnosis and appraisal of speech and language disorders, and (2) where necessary, make referrals for additional assessments needed to make an appropriate placement decision.

§ 121a.533 Placement procedures.

(a) In interpreting evaluation data and in making placement decisions, each public agency shall:

(1) Draw upon information from a variety of sources, including aptitude and achievement tests, teacher recommendations, physical condition, social or cultural background, and adaptive behavior;

(2) Insure that information obtained from all of these sources

is documented and carefully considered;

(3) Insure that the placement decision is made by a group of persons, including persons knowledgeable about the child, the meaning of the evaluation data, and the placement options; and

(4) Insure that the placement decision is made in conformity with the least restrictive environment rules in §§ 121a.-550–121a.554.

(b) If a determination is made that a child is handicapped and needs special education and related services, an individualized education program must be developed for the child in accordance with §§ 121a.340–121a.349 of Subpart C.

(20 U.S.C. 1412 (5) (C); 1414(a) (5).)

Comment. Paragraph (a) (1) includes a list of examples of sources that may be used by a public agency in making placement decisions. The agency would not have to use all the sources in every instance. The point of the requirement is to insure that more than one source is used in interpreting evaluation data and in making placement decisions. For example, while all of the named sources would have to be used for a child whose suspected disability is mental retardation, they would not be necessary for certain other handicapped children, such as a child who has a severe articulation disorder as his primary handicap. For such a child, the speech-language pathologist, in complying with the multisource requirement, might use (1) a standardized test of articulation, and (2) observation of the child's articulation behavior in conversational speech.

§ 121a.534 Reevaluation.

Each State and local educational agency shall insure:

(a) That each handicapped child's individualized education program is reviewed in accordance with §§ 121a.340–121a.349 of Subpart C, and

(b) That an evaluation of the child, based on procedures which meet the requirements under § 121a.532, is conducted every three years or more frequently if conditions warrant or if the child's parent or teacher requests an evaluation.

(20 U.S.C. 1412(5) (c).)

Source: U.S. Office of Education. Education of handicapped children: Implementation of Part B of the Education of the Handicapped Act. Federal Register, 1977, 42, 42474–42518.

Examples of published professional guidelines relevant to assessment are the American Personnel and Guidance Association's *Responsibilities of Users of Standardized Tests* (APGA, 1980) and the *Standards for Educational and Psychological Tests* (1974) developed by the American Psychological Association (APA), the American Educational Research Association (AERA), and the National Council on Measurement in Education (NCME). The APA-AERA-NCME *Standards* contains a section entitled, "Standards for Test Use," which is particularly relevant to the design of assessment programs in the schools. The revision of the 1974 *Standards* includes a chapter devoted exclusively to special education assessment. This chapter provides important guidelines for program development.

Expert opinion can be tapped through surveys of the professional literature and input from assessment consultants. Surveys of the professional literature can be facilitated through the use of such resources as the ERIC Centers on Handicapped and Gifted Children, housed at the Council for Exceptional Children (CEC) in Reston, Virginia; and Tests, Measurements, and Evaluation, at Educational Testing Service in Princeton, New Jersey. Additionally, *Diagnostique,* the quarterly journal of CEC's Council for Educational Diagnostic Services, represents an important professional resource devoted exclusively to assessment in special education.

In an effort to integrate information from these various sources, we recently published guidelines for preplacement evaluation based on existing law, professional codes, and expert judgment (Bennett, 1981a). Some of the more critical of these guidelines are presented in Box 2-5.

BOX 2-5 *SOME STANDARDS FOR PREPLACEMENT EVALUATION PROGRAMS*

I. Implementation

   A. The evaluation program should be staffed by a multidisciplinary team.
   B. Team members should be trained in individual assessment and meet state requirements for such practice.
   C. Team members should be knowledgeable about the nature, language, problems, and needs of the minority, sociocultural, and handicap groups they serve.

D.   Team members should encourage parental involvement in the assessment process.

E.   Team members should work to prevent irrelevant factors, such as race, sex, physical appearance, and suspected disability label, from inappropriately influencing the way in which they administer and interpret assessment tools.

F.   Assessment procedures should be selected to conform with the purpose(s) for which assessment is being conducted.

G.   Procedures should include observation of the child in the classroom setting.

H.   Procedures should be administered in the child's preferred language, in addition to the language of instruction if the two differ.

I.   Procedures should be used only for the purposes and with groups for which their validity and reliability is empirically supported.

J.   Procedures should be administered and interpreted in conformance with the directions of the producer.

K.   Procedures should include consideration of the child's family background, home environment, and the child's level of functioning within that environment.

L.   Procedures should relate to all areas connected with the suspected disability.

M.   More than one type of assessment procedure should be used to evaluate each characteristic of the child.

N.   Intelligence tests, if used, should be employed as predictors of achievement in the standard unmodified school curriculum, and not as measures of native, innate potential.

O.   Procedures should be administered so as to ensure that, to the maximum extent possible, impaired sensory, motor, and communication skills do not interfere with the assessment of other skills and abilities.

P.   The results of assessment should be stored, so as to insure confidentiality and compliance with all federal and state regulations.

II.   Outcomes

A.   Assessment results should be documented in a written report that at a minimum

1.   lists identifying data

2.   describes the reason for referral and the measures, procedures, and interventions used as a basis for referral

3.   lists the dates and purposes of assessment and the full names of all procedures used

4.   notes the language in which procedures were administered if other than English

5.   notes any departures from standardized procedure

6.   provides detailed information about the child's family, home environment, and functioning within that environment

7.   provides results of assessment in all areas related to the suspected handicap

8.   presents a detailed statement of the child's current levels of educational functioning, including a description of the types of tasks the child can and cannot perform

9.   reports results as estimates rather than exact indications of skill or ability

10. reports results from standardized measures in terms of percentile or standard scores from appropriate reference groups and not solely in terms of technically questionable metrics like grade and age equivalents

11. states whether and to what extent alternative explanations of performance (e.g., anxiety, motivation, failure to understand assessment task requirements) appear responsible for the obtained results

12. tells whether or not the child is thought to have a specific handicap and the basis for making that determination

13. includes each team member's certification that the report does or does not reflect his or her conclusions, with dissenting conclusions attached

14. lists the names and professional roles of all team members.

B.   The names of those individuals authorized to inspect results should be listed and a record of all accesses kept.

Conventionally accepted standards such as those denoted in Box 2-5 should be used, along with any relevant local standards, to fashion a comprehensive written design, or plan, for the district's assessment programs. The plan could take the general form used in Box 1-2, and include statements describing program purpose; specific criteria for selecting who is to be assessed; the materials, equipment, and facilities to be used; the sequence and timing of activities; the general procedures used to evaluate the program; and so on.

Evaluating the Assessment Program Design

Once the plan is drafted, it should be submitted to a small group of individuals for review. Those reviewing the plan might include the district superintendent; a sample of those who will work or are working in the program; a representative of the handicapped students' parents' organization; a minority parent; and the assessment consultant from the state education department, regional technical assistance agency, or institution of higher education. Reviewers should be asked to rate the extent to which the plan is *clear, comprehensive, internally consistent, compatible,* and *theoretically sound* or educationally meaningful. These characteristics are defined in Chapter 1.

IMPLEMENTING ASSESSMENT PROGRAMS

It is a fact of life that even the best-laid plans go awry. Given this fact, we suggest an approach to program implementation that we have found useful for installing new assessment programs or introducing modifications into already operational ones. The approach, identified by the acronym DURABLE, serves to foster program implementation and encourage evaluation by stressing the importance of frequent and purposeful interactions with staff. Such interactions serve to (1) communicate the parameters of the program, (2) provide information for use in modifying the program prior to and during implementation, and (3) develop a sense of ownership and investment in the program.

Facilitating Assessment Program
Implementation

The DURABLE approach consists of seven interrelated elements, six of which are primarily concerned with fostering program operation. The seventh DURABLE element, evaluation, serves the additional purpose of documenting the manner in which the assessment program is operating, and is discussed separately.

Discuss the assessment program with the staff. The purpose, implementation, and expected outcomes of the assessment program should be fully discussed with assessment personnel as well as with teachers and administrators affected by the program. Prior to or during these discussions, copies of the written program design should be distributed, so that the full scope of the program is clear to those who will be involved in it. Discussion of the assessment program should be led by staff members involved in designing the program, as opposed to general supervisory personnel, so that questions about specific program aspects can be accurately and knowledgeably answered.

Understand staff concerns about the assessment program. Understanding staff concerns often results from discussing the program. At other times, however, staff concerns are not voiced in an open discussion, and administrators must become aware of them through anonymous questionnaires, individual meetings, and other means. Attempting to understand staff concerns about the assessment program will let staff members know that their opinions are important and suggest to the administrator possible courses of action prior to program implementation. So, for example, members of the preplacement evaluation program staff may not understand the rationale for, and hence object to, a standard constraining the use of age and grade-equivalent scores in interpreting and reporting assessment results. This may suggest to the administrator a need to plan an in-service program on the inadequacies of these scores (see, for example, Bennett, 1982c, for a review of these problems) and the technical properties of various derived scores.

Reward staff members for their active involvement in the assessment program. Giving reinforcement to members of the program staff for contributing to assessment program development and for carrying out the program in a manner consistent with the program design is an important part of the DURABLE approach. Rewards may include such things as verbal praise for attendance at meetings where the program was discussed, mention in written staff evaluations of efforts to implement the program in keeping with design standards, and sharing with others examples of outstanding practices or methods of carrying out particularly troublesome standards (e.g., those relating to the assessment of functioning in the home environment).

Adapt the assessment program. Attempts to adapt the assessment program usually build upon information derived from *discussing* and *understanding,* as well as from *learning* and *evaluating,* described next. The intent here is to adapt program standards and/or operations, when necessary, according to information provided by the staff or by reviews of program operation. For example, given published research documenting a high incidence of clerical error in team members' scoring of cognitive tests (Miller & Chansky, 1972; Miller, Chansky & Gredler, 1970; Warren & Brown, 1973), it might be reasonable to include among the implementation standards for the preplacement evaluation program a requirement that the scoring of all tests be checked by a colleague. Most administrators, however, will quickly learn from interaction with the staff or through a review of program operation that such a standard is impractical, owing to the amount of additional time it would require. A sensible adaptation of the standard might be to require that every *n*th protocol— perhaps every fifth or every tenth—be checked instead.

Build positive expectations about the assessment program. Building positive expectations is especially important prior to and during the initial stages of program implementation. Program designers and administrators should communicate a sense of interest and enthusiasm about the program to the staff. The distribution of standards and criteria for an already operational preplacement evaluation program, for example, should be accompanied by statements from the special education director and program designers about how the new standards and criteria are expected to improve the program's ability to efficiently and effectively serve referred children, provide stronger protection for the district and for the evaluation staff against legal challenges, and call attention to the program as a model for other districts to emulate. From our experience, overt, but sincere, shows of enthusiasm by program directors go a long way toward developing interest and commitment to the program. Expecting the staff to be enthusiastic and committed to an assessment program in which administrators and designers show no interest is simply unrealistic.

Learn about potential assessment program pitfalls. Learning about potential pitfalls can occur at any time following assessment program implementation, and is an attempt to gain information about roadblocks to continued operation. For example, regular education teachers may begin to feel resentment about the amount of work involved in an in-school screening program that requires them to complete a behavior rating scale for each child in their charge. If not resolved, such resentment could result in scales being completed without care and, hence, in erroneous screening information.

Evaluating Assessment Program Implementation

The primary purpose of implementation evaluation is to determine the extent to which the assessment program is operating as planned. This information can be used both to document that important legal and ethical mandates are being complied with (e.g., mandates for fair assessment) and for program improvement. In the latter instance, implementation information is used to identify problem areas that might require adaptation of either program standards or operations.

For example, in a preplacement evaluation program that we helped to reorganize, implementation evaluation revealed few instances in which the adaptive behavior, or social functioning of the child within and outside the school environment, had been assessed. Because such assessment is held by many to be crucial to the fair evaluation of children thought to have mild mental retardation (Grossman, 1973), the district special education administrator deemed a modification, or adaptation, in program *operation* necessary. The administrator discovered, through discussions with her staff, that implementation of the adaptive-behavior standard would be facilitated best by an in-service program focused on the concept and techniques of adaptive-behavior evaluation.

A variety of methods can be used for the evaluation of assessment program implementation. These include observation, survey techniques (questionnaire and interview) and document or product review. Observational methods, because they are obtrusive, are generally not useful for evaluating such aspects of implementation as the performance of assessment program activities (e.g., the preplacement evaluation of a referred child). Rather, observational methods are more applicable to inspecting the contextual aspects of implementation, such as the condition of program facilities (e.g., examination rooms) and equipment (e.g., audiometers, test kits, and other evaluation materials).

Survey techniques can be employed to gather information about the qualifications and competencies of assessment personnel and about their perceptions of program implementation. Questionnaires and individual and group interviews can be used to assess, for instance, the extent to which members of the staff are knowledgeable about the nature, language, problems, and needs of various minority and handicapped groups (Implementation Standard I.E., Box 2-5); information derived from these techniques can then be used in planning staff-development efforts, an activity that we more fully describe in Chapter 6, Planning and Evaluating Personnel Development Services.

Questionnaires and interviews can likewise provide invaluable insight into staff (and parent) perceptions of assessment program implementation. These perceptions can be useful in identifying areas of operation that need to be more carefully studied or, in the case of targeted individual and group interviews (that is, structured discussions), for determining the underlying causes of a failure to carry out the program as planned.

The special services director of a district in our area utilized these techniques by distributing an open-ended questionnaire at the monthly meeting of the special education parents' organization. The questionnaire simply asked parents to comment briefly about the manner in which their children were assessed by the district's IEP annual review program and about how that program could be improved. Feedback from parents overwhelmingly suggested that parents felt they were capable of making a contribution to the annual review process (a program standard in the district) but that the school's staff did not welcome such offerings. With this information, the director held a number of targeted small-group interviews with the IEP annual review staff members to try to learn more about how they interacted with parents, why parents felt their participation was not encouraged, and how their perceptions could be changed.

Perhaps the most valuable and practical method for evaluating assessment program implementation is the document or product review. Because this method relies on documents produced as a result of assessment (e.g., reports, test protocols), the degree to which implementation evaluation interferes with the conduct of the assessment program is minimized, if not totally eliminated. The major drawback of this method, however, also relates to its distance from the actual conduct of assessment, in that the way in which the assessment program was carried out must be *inferred* from program documents.

A variety of documents can be reviewed to determine the extent to which an assessment program is being carried out in accordance with implementation standards and criteria contained in the program design. A sample of test protocols, for example, can be reviewed to determine the degree to which the administration and scoring procedures recommended by the producer were followed by preplacement evaluation personnel (Implementation Standard I.J., Box 2-5). That such procedures be correctly followed is essential, since failure to do so can significantly alter assessment findings and result in the provision of inaccurate data to decision makers (Bennett, 1981c; Warren & Brown, 1973). Box 2-6 presents a checklist that may be useful in the review of administration and scoring procedures common to stand-

BOX 2-6 *ASSESSMENT IMPLEMENTATION CHECKLIST: INSTRUMENT ADMINISTRATION AND SCORING REVIEW*

Instructions: Select a random sample of protocols administered to students served by the assessment program. Review each protocol in accordance with the questions below, placing a hash mark (!) for each protocol reviewed in the space under the appropriate heading (N/A for NOT APPLICABLE) for each item. Concentrations of hash marks in the 2 or 3 columns for any given item suggest specific areas of concern.

	ALWAYS 1	SOMETIMES 2	NEVER 3	N/A
1. Were subtests within a test begun with the appropriate item?				
2. Were basal levels correctly identified?				
3. Were items below basal credited?				
4. Were ceiling levels correctly identified?				
5. Were credited items correct?				
6. Were noncredited items incorrect?				
7. Were items above ceilings excluded from calculation of raw scores?				
8. Were raw scores correctly calculated?				
9. Were raw scores correctly converted to derived scores?				

	YES 1	NO 2	N/A
1. Was chronological age correctly calculated?			
2. Were raw scores correctly summed across subtests to arrive at a composite score?			

ardized measures employed in preplacement evaluation, reevaluation, and annual review programs.

In addition to test protocols, assessment reports can be examined as a means of gathering evidence about the implementation of assessment programs. Such reports can be used to suggest whether preplacement and reevaluation were conducted by multidisciplinary teams (Implementation Standard I.A., Box 2-5), procedures were consistent with the goals of assessment (Implementation Standard I.F., Box 2-5), family background and environment were considered (Implementation Standard I.K., Box 2-5), and so on. Box 2-7 depicts a checklist that can be used to guide implementation evaluation through reviewing assessment reports.

Finally, various administrative documents can be consulted to see if existing operational conditions match those specified as necessary for program functioning. Such documents as equipment invoices and cost reports can be compared to program budgets, and personnel records can be contrasted with design requirements for the number, type, and qualifications of the program's staff.

BOX 2-7 *ASSESSMENT IMPLEMENTATION CHECKLIST: ASSESSMENT REPORT REVIEW*

Instructions: Select a random sample of assessment reports. Look through each report for information suggesting answers to the implementation questions presented below. Answer each question by placing a hash mark (!) in the appropriate space (N/I for NO INDICATION) next to each item. Concentrations of hash marks in the 2 or 3 columns for any given item suggest specific areas of concern for which further information should be gathered through interview with program staff members or direct observation of program operations.

	GENERALLY	ONLY SOMETIMES	RARELY	N/I
	1	2	3	

1. Were assessment procedures appropriate given the purposes of assessment?

2. Were procedures administered in the child's preferred language?

3. Was evidence available supporting the appropriateness of measures for the group to which the child belongs?

4. Was more than one type of procedure used to assess each characteristic of the child?

5. Were IQ tests used as predictors of future achievement in the standard curriculum rather than indicators of innate ability?

	YES 1	NO 2	N/I
1. Was evaluation conducted by a multidisciplinary team?			
2. Was the student observed in the classroom setting?			
3. Were all areas related to the suspected disability assessed?			

	TO A REASON- ABLE DEGREE 1	ONLY SOMEWHAT 2	NOT AT ALL 3	N/I
1. Was the student's background and home environment considered?				
2. Was the child's level of functioning within that environment assessed.				

The discovery of discrepancies between assessment program implementation and program design should normally be followed up by investigation into the reasons for those discrepancies and the assessment teams or sites in which they are concentrated. (Isolating problems will be facilitated by sampling protocols or reports for review *within* teams or sites.) In the particular case where assessment program implementation does not seem to be in compliance with professional or legal standards, further investigation is critical. In these instances, interviews with the program's staff can be invaluable for isolating the reasons for such things as failure to use a multidisciplinary team, observe children in the classroom setting, or assess all areas related to the suspected disability. Failure to observe children in the class setting, for example, may be due to pupil absence, heavy caseloads, refusal of regular class teachers to permit observation, or staff ignorance of program standards. Because these diverse reasons have different implications for action, it is imperative that discrepancies be thoroughly investigated through interviews or direct observation before action is taken to improve performance or, alternatively, modify standards to make compliance with their intent more easily achieved.

EVALUATING THE OUTCOMES OF ASSESSMENT PROGRAMS

As noted in Chapter 1, the evaluation of program outcomes can be undertaken to provide information about a number of program aspects. With respect to assessment programs, we will discuss two types of outcome evaluation we consider critical, goal attainment and consumer reaction, and close by offering guidance on the communication of evaluation results.

Evaluating Goal Attainment

In the introduction to this chapter, we defined assessment as *the process of gathering and interpreting information about individual students for use in educational decision making.* Such a definition clearly implies that one of the primary goals of any assessment program is the production of high-quality *information* and responsible *interpretations* of that information.[2] In our approach, we attempt to guarantee the quality of assessment information and, to a lesser extent, its interpretation, by setting standards for gathering that information and by periodically evaluating the extent to which those standards are being faithfully carried out. We further attempt to ensure the adequacy of assessment information and interpretation by suggesting standards and criteria for the content of preplacement evaluation and reevaluation reports traditionally employed to communicate and preserve that information. Such reports typically provide the basis for determinations of pupil eligibility for special education, handicapping condition, educational program and placement, and progress toward achieving goals and objectives. As such, evaluation reports, and the information they contain, are of critical importance to the entire special education process. The extent, then, to which these reports meet the accreditation standards and criteria set for them is an important indication of the assessment program's success in achieving this critical goal.

The evaluation of assessment reports can take place at the same time that these documents are being reviewed for information about program implementation. Box 2-8 presents a checklist for the product review of preplacement evaluation and reevaluation reports. Note that the focus of evaluation here is on the quality of the reports themselves, *not* on what can be inferred from reports about the manner in which the assessment program was conducted.

Though quality of assessment program information is a critical goal for any assessment program, most programs will have additional goals specified as assessment program outcome standards. Evaluation of the extent to which these outcome standards have been met should be included as an integral part of any evaluation of assessment program goal attainment.

Evaluating Consumer Reaction

In addition to determining the extent to which assessment program outcomes are consonant with accreditation standards, sampling the perceptions of assessment program consumers (e.g., special education teachers, parents) and others familiar

---

[2] The quality of *decisions* based upon assessment information—in particular eligibility and placement decisions—is not, in our view, within the province of assessment. Such decisions should be made subsequent to setting instructional goals and objectives for students. Therefore, decisions of this type are most properly viewed as instructional decisions. Factors to consider in making these decisions are discussed in Chapter 3, Planning and Evaluating Instructional Services: Individualized Programs. Evaluating the results of this decision making is dealt with in Chapter 4, Planning and Evaluating Instructional Services: Group Programs.

BOX 2-8 *OUTCOME ASSESSMENT CHECKLIST: ASSESSMENT*
            REPORT REVIEW

Instructions: Select a random sample of assessment reports. Review
each report in accordance with the questions below, placing a hash
mark (¦) for each report in the appropriate space (N/A for NOT
APPLICABLE) next to each item. Concentrations of hash marks in the 2
and 3 columns for any given item suggest specific areas of concern.

	COMPLETELY	ONLY IN PART	NOT AT ALL	N/A
	1	2	3	

Identifying Data

1.   Is the child's name listed?

2.   Is the child's date of birth
     given?

3.   Is the child's home address
     specified?

4.   Are the names of the child's
     parents given?

Referral Information

1.   Is the reason for referral
     described?

2.   Is the referring agent
     identified?

3.   Are prereferral interventions
     attempted, documented?

4.   Are measures and procedures
     used as the basis for
     referral identified?

5.   Is the date of referral given?

	COMPLETELY	ONLY IN PART	NOT AT ALL	N/A
	1	2	3	

Procedures

1.   Is   the   date   of   assessment
     noted?

2.   Are   the   names   of   all
     procedures indicated?

3.   Is   the   language   in   which
     assessment was   conducted, if
     other than English, specified?

Results

1.   Is the child's developmental
     history described?

2.   Is the child's educational
     history detailed?

3.   Is the child's social history
     reported?

4.   Is the child's home
     environment described?

5.   Is the child's functioning
     within that environment
     specified?

6.   Are present levels of
     educational functioning
     reported?

7.   Are specific examples of the
     kinds of tasks the child
     can perform illustrated?

8.   Are specific examples of the
     kinds of tasks the child
     cannot do shown?

	ALMOST ALWAYS	ONLY SOMETIMES	NEVER	N/A
	1	2	3	

9.   Are results reported as
     estimates rather than exact
     indications of skill or
     ability?

10. Are results from standardized
     procedures given in terms of
     percentile or standard scores
     from appropriate reference
     groups?

	YES	NO		N/A
	1	2		

Conclusions

1.   Are alternative explanations
     of performance discussed?

2.   Are specific recommendations
     for instructional and/or
     behavioral interventions
     offered?

3.   Is a statement detailing
     whether the child is thought
     to have a handicap included?

4.   Is each team member's
     agreement or disagreement
     with the report's conclusions
     indicated?

5.   Are the names of all team
     members listed?

6.   Are the professional roles of
     all team members specified?

with the program can provide valuable information about both the intended and unintended effects of a program. For example, in a recent evaluation of a screening program, consumer reaction to the program suggested that parents were dissatisfied with the fact that the purpose of the program had not been clearly communicated to them, and preplacement evaluation team members were upset because they had not been consulted regarding the program's initial conceptualization and design. Unintended outcomes such as these obviously must be detected and addressed if program goals are to be achieved.

Consumer-reaction evaluation can, alternatively, reveal that program consumers are fully satisfied with the results of the assessment program. Such information can serve to bolster evaluation evidence obtained from other sources (e.g., product review) in making the case that an assessment program is producing high-quality information. On one occasion, for example, we were asked to help reorganize a preplacement evaluation program, with particular attention given to ensuring that the program treated minority students fairly. Drawing upon education law, professional codes, and input from the district staff and parents, we helped establish a set of standards and criteria for preplacement assessment to facilitate fairer treatment of minorities and a schedule for implementation and outcome evaluation. While data supporting the quality of preplacement evaluation information produced favorable results, the most convincing evidence reviewed by external auditors (e.g., state education department officials, representatives of the public advocate's office), we felt, was the positive reactions to the program gathered from parents of minority children classified as educable mentally retarded, a population over which concern for fair treatment has been prominent.

As may be evident, consumer-reaction evaluation is most expeditiously carried out through the use of survey methodology. Consumer-reaction surveys should include segments that are relatively unstructured, or open-ended, so that consumers are encouraged to comment on whatever aspects of the assessment program are of concern to them. Box 2-9 presents a sample Assessment Program Consumer-Reaction Questionnaire. This particular questionnaire will be most suitable for sampling special education teachers' perceptions about preplacement evaluation and reevaluation programs.

Data gathered through use of the questionnaire depicted in Box 2-9 can be quantitatively analyzed by calculating within items the proportion of individuals choosing each response. Consumer responses to open-ended questions can be organized by grouping comments according to the facet of the program to which they refer.

Communicating Evaluation Results

Information resulting from the outcome evaluation of assessment programs should be both informally shared with program staff and formally documented. The informal exchange of information should take place within the context of the ongoing communication built among the special services administration and pro-

BOX 2-9 *ASSESSMENT PROGRAM CONSUMER-REACTION QUESTIONNAIRE*

Our district preplacement assessment program is designed to provide
information for making decisions about which children need what types
of special instruction and related services. The improvement of this
and other district programs depends on regular examination meant to
identify program successes and problems. Your responses to the
following questions are requested for this purpose. There is no need
to write your name anywhere on this survey form. Thank you for your
cooperation.

1.   Is there anything about the assessment program that you
     particularly like? If so, please explain.

2.   Is there anything about the assessment program that you
     particularly don't like? If so, please explain.

Please answer the questions in the following section by placing the
number corresponding to your response in the appropriate space.

NOT AT ALL	ONLY SOMEWHAT	REASONABLY	VERY MUCH SO	EXTREMELY
1	2	3	4	5

___1.   Do you think that the assessment program provides information
        that accurately characterizes children's skills?

___2.   In your opinion, does the program provide information that is
        useful for teaching?

___3.   Do you think the program is fair to children of different
        racial/ethnic groups?

___4.   Are assessment reports easy to understand?

___5.   Do assessment staff members interact with teachers in a
        courteous manner?

___6.   In general, does the staff appear qualified to engage in the
        evaluation of children?

___7.   On the whole, does it appear that an adequate amount of time is
        devoted to the evaluation of children by the program?

___8.   Does the assessment staff appear to welcome input about the
        program?

___9.   In your perception, are assessment staff members generally
        willing to discuss their evaluations in order to help increase
        the utility of assessment results.

gram staff through the DURABLE approach. The findings of the outcome assessment should generally be discussed first with key members of the program staff on an individual or small-group basis, to get feedback about the sensibility of results, probable causes of identified deficiencies, and practical suggestions for remedial action. The results of implementation evaluation will frequently be helpful in identifying both the probable reasons why outcome standards were not met as well as the advisability of different remedial actions.

Initial discussions with key members of the program staff can be followed by a meeting with all program staff members to present outcome results. At this gathering, results should be communicated with an emphasis on those standards that the assessment program successfully achieved; the staff should be explicitly credited for its efforts in producing these results. Those standards that the program did not satisfy should also be identified, and likely causes and reasonable solutions discussed.

Outcome assessment results can be formally documented through means of a brief written report. This report serves first as a tool for program improvement; when viewed in conjunction with the written program design, it presents a historical picture of the assessment program that can be used to understand the program's successes and failures over time and to transmit these lessons to future program administrators and staff members. Second, the report documents what occurred; it documents that a particular set of assessment activities were actually performed and that an evaluation of these activities was carried out. These facts may prove important in demonstrating to a school board, state department, or public advocate that assessment programs were not only delivered but carefully monitored.

Because our primary evaluation focus is upon developing and improving programs, we suggest a report format that briefly notes the purposes, methodology, and results of outcome (and implementation) evaluation, and that highlights the recommendations for improving the assessment program. A comprehensive treatise characteristic of evaluations conducted to inform decisions involving the national funding and dissemination of programs is inappropriate, given the purpose for which we recommend the evaluation of assessment programs.

SUMMARY

This chapter has focused on the planning and evaluation of assessment services. For purposes of the chapter, assessment was defined as the process of gathering and interpreting information about individual students for use in educational decision making. The various decisions that assessment services are meant to facilitate were seen as falling into two major classes: service eligibility and educational programming. The targeted programs that typically compose the assessment service domain in school districts include community-oriented child find, in-school screening, preplacement evaluation, reevaluation, formative instructional assessment, and IEP annual review.

The approach taken to planning and evaluating assessment programs in this chapter is primarily built upon the accreditation model, in which conventionally recognized standards and criteria are integrated, along with information about program facilities, budgets, and so on, into a program design that is used to guide implementation and evaluation of the assessment program. Within the accreditation model, the DURABLE framework is used as a means of facilitating the smooth implementation and evaluation of new or reorganized assessment programs. Use of the DURABLE framework and accreditation model can, in our view, help to ensure that assessment programs achieve their primary goal—the provision of quality information about children—and that this information fairly characterizes all children and serves to enhance the instructional process.

PLANNING AND EVALUATING INSTRUCTIONAL SERVICES
Individualized Programs

The task of designing, implementing, and assessing the outcomes of an individualized program (IP) is rarely an easy matter. Whether the individualized program is an externally mandated one, such as PL 94-142's individualized education program (IEP), or another program designed to meet the special needs of an individual, issues are raised and problems encountered. These issues and problems include such questions as:

What should the nature and scope of the program be?
Where and how should the program be delivered?
How can the program's outcomes be meaningfully evaluated?
What information may be useful for making decisions about program revision or termination?

In this chapter, we discuss some practical planning and evaluation methods that can be used to address these questions successfully. In particular, we stress the need to understand the nature of individualized programming and its relationship to the larger special education services delivery system.

OVERVIEW OF INDIVIDUALIZED PROGRAMS

Need for Individualized Programs
in Special Education

The distinguishing facet of special education is without doubt the individualization of instruction and it is in fact this characteristic that can be used to trace the early roots of the discipline. The tailoring of education to the particular needs of the individual child is clearly seen in the work of such seminal educators as Jean Itard, Eduard Seguin, Maria Montessori, and Anne Sullivan. Itard, in particular, received recognition in his time for developing and providing one-to-one instruction to Victor, the "Wild Boy of Aveyron," in the early 1800s (Kauffman, 1981; Lieberman, 1982). Sullivan, of course, helped Helen Keller, a deaf-blind nonvocal child, become a literate and articulate individual and one of the more prominent persons of her time.

The work of these early special educators highlighted the potential value of individualized programming for teaching the handicapped. But it was not until the 1970s that the need for such an approach to the education of handicapped children and youth was given official sanction through the outcomes of litigation (e.g., *PARC* v. *Pennsylvania,* 1972), and finally through the passage of PL 94-142, the Education for All Handicapped Children Act of 1975. This federal legislation translated a concept rooted in the successes of the pioneers of special education into a national practice to be applied to the education of each and every one of the nation's handicapped students.

The value of the individualized approach—and the need for it—is based upon the belief that the needs of the handicapped are significantly different from those of the majority of children—and likewise sufficiently different from one another—that any more general approach to program planning would seriously fail to meet their needs. This philosophy has been recently generalized to the development of programs for other categories of students, in particular the gifted and talented and those in compensatory-education programs. The individualized approach is certainly logically defensible, and numerous case studies, such as those of Victor and Helen Keller, provide anecdotal support for its effectiveness. The benefit of the approach for handicapped students in general, however, has yet to be conclusively established (Carlberg & Kavale, 1980).

Nature and Scope of Individualized Programs

As has been suggested, an IP is an attempt to address the unique needs of an individual by means of a carefully developed plan of action. This plan of action, while tailored specifically to the individual, is not necessarily delivered in that manner; rather, elements of the program are implemented through a variety of intervention modes, including large- and small-group and one-to-one interactions.

The individualized program may also take many different forms. To special educators, the most familiar of these is undoubtedly the individualized education program mandated by PL 94-142. Other such programs include the individualized student instructional plan used in New Jersey compensatory-education programs, the individualized written rehabilitation plan, and the individualized service plan employed in community mental-health centers throughout the nation (Windle & Woy, 1977).

Central to understanding the nature of the individualized program is its relationship to the larger services delivery system. The relationship of the IP to the services delivery system and to other programs in that system is somewhat unusual. The IP can be perceived as both an overarching structure within which a series of other programs are embedded and as a component of other special education programs. For example, any given student's IP may reference more than one instructional program; Johnny Jones's IP may require placement in a resource-room program for one part of the school day, participation in a main-stream setting for another, and involvement in a group counseling program for yet another. The resource-room program in which Johnny Jones participates, however, is in part composed of a collection of IPs; the general goals that the resource program is meant to achieve are drawn from the individual goals of the students it serves.

The complexity of the special education services delivery system, then, lends different perspectives from which the IP can be viewed. Each of these perspectives has implications for how the individualized program is planned, implemented, and evaluated.

Difficulties in Providing
Individualized Programs

In planning an IP for a particular child, we will work from the perspective of the IP as an overarching program; that is, an organizing framework—or program design—for the educational services provided the handicapped child. From this perspective, the major problems encountered in providing IPs focus on content and include the following:

> What goals should compose the individualized program for a given child?
> What instructional and/or related service programs do these goals imply?
> Are these services best provided by the special services delivery system or by some other district intervention program?
> In which service delivery arrangements should these programs be delivered and in what modes (e.g., group versus one-to-one)?
> When and how should the program be carried out?
> How will the implementation and results of the program be evaluated?

The first of these questions, "What goals should compose the IP?" directly follows, as in the design of any program, from a clarification of the problem or need the program is to address.

CLARIFYING INDIVIDUALIZED
PROGRAM PROBLEMS

Assessing Service Delivery Needs

The educational needs of an exceptional student can be successfully clarified only to the extent that a sufficient base of data about the pupil's background and characteristics exists. The task of gathering this data base—a topic we have covered in much detail in Chapter 2—typically falls to the pupil-evaluation or child-study team.

Box 3-1 provides a framework that can be used to organize, for individualized program problem-clarification purposes, pupil data gathered by the child-evaluation team. The box divides planning data into five educationally relevant performance areas. These areas are affective, cognitive, academic, social, and physical.

In organizing pupil data, problem-clarification efforts should be directed toward identifying general intervention needs as well as pupil strengths. The determination that a need or strongpoint exists is always a professional judgment, one

BOX 3-1   *A FRAMEWORK FOR ORGANIZING INDIVIDUALIZED*
          PROGRAM PUPIL DATA

Affective
1. Attitudes
2. Motivation
3. Emotions
4. Self-concept

Cognitive
1. Reasoning and Problem Solving
2. Study Skills
3. Memory
4. Perceptual Abilities

Academic
1. Reading and Language Arts
2. Mathematics
3. Writing
4. Vocational Development

Social
1. Interpersonal Relations
2. Language Development
3. Cultural Background
4. Educational History
5. Family Background
6. Developmental History

Physical
1. General Health
2. Sensory and Motor Functioning
3. Specific Medical Conditions and Medications

that must be made in relation to some frame of reference. Three frames for making such judgments that may immediately come to mind are norm, criterion, and self-reference (Bennett & Maher, in press).

Norm reference. Normative reference frames are typically developed by giving a sample of educationally important tasks to a large number of individuals representative of the general school population. The range of performance within which *most* members of selected subgroups of that population (e.g., specific grade, age, ethnic, or socioeconomic groups) fall is then considered to be the standard for determining the extent to which the performance of a specific examinee is lacking. In general, performance can be said to be within the average range if it is comparable to the middle 68 percent—that is, between the 16th and 84th percentiles—of the subgroup to which an individual is being compared (Plas, 1977). So, for example, a fourth-grade child whose reading skills are observed to fall at the 10th percentile relative to those of other fourth graders would be considered below average in reading, whereas a fourth grader with skills at the 90th percentile would be viewed as particularly strong in this area.

A number of important factors should be considered in using norms for assessing individualized program service delivery needs and strengths. First, the measure for which norms are being reported should be examined to ensure that it assesses skills considered important by district educators. If it does not, a normative comparison will provide little information of value.

Second, the relevance of the norm group to the purpose of assessment should be evaluated (Goodman & Bennett, 1982; Seashore & Ricks, 1950). Norm groups may be organized according to ethnicity, grade or age, or geographic location, among other factors. If students are being assessed to determine their command of basic skills needed for success in a working world composed of diverse ethnic groups, then special ethnic norms are probably inappropriate, regardless of the racial background of the examinee. On the other hand, norms reflecting the unique ethnic makeup of a community would be more appropriate for the purpose of assessing student needs relative to chances for success in that immediate environment.

Subsequent to determining the relevance of norms, the extent to which the norm group actually represents the population it claims to represent should be evaluated. Because norms are almost without exception samples drawn from larger populations, the procedures used to select the normative sample and the characteristics of the final group should be reviewed. Some normative samples are "convenience" samples used solely because they were easy to obtain; the representativeness of such samples should be considered suspect. In general, "probability" samples, drawn in keeping with a systematic plan to obtain representativeness, are preferred, as are norms offering data favorably comparing the sample's characteristics to those of the population it is meant to reflect (e.g., sample characteristics are often compared to U.S. census data in an attempt to demonstrate the similarity between the normative sample and the U.S. population, thereby supporting the representativeness of the national norm group).

As might be expected, the use of normative frames of reference is not without its critics. One frequently raised criticism is philosophical: is it educationally meaningful or ethically defensible to compare the performance of individual children to that of others? Doesn't such comparison encourage unhealthy competition among students? Doesn't it guarantee the experience of failure to those low in ability? Wouldn't the performance of the individual student be more meaningfully compared to some skill standard or to the student's own previous performance?

These questions are certainly fair ones to ask. Their answers do not, in our view, necessarily make a good case for avoiding the use of normative frames for determining if learning needs and strengths exist. In the first place, comparing the performance of students to their peers makes particularly good sense in cases where limited remedial resources exist and our desire is to serve those children most in need. Second, success in our society is based upon the ability to compete for such things as jobs and other high-demand, low-supply commodities. It would seem to be grossly unfair to isolate students from competition in school, when they will inevitably have to face it upon entry into job or higher-education markets. Finally, we should note that even when not directly relevant, normative frames of reference are exceedingly difficult to avoid. As we shall see, even when making comparisons to a skill standard—such as 90 percent of math problems correct— the performance of others must be taken into account to give assessment results meaning.

Criterion reference.   A second method of ascribing meaning to performance is through criterion reference (Glaser, 1963; Popham, 1975). Using this approach, the performance of an individual is referenced, or compared, not to that of others, but rather to a set, or domain, of educationally important tasks (e.g., the 100 basic addition facts).

While criterion-referenced measurement is a popular and useful technology for instructional decision making (Bennett, 1982b), the use of this technology is not without its own peculiar set of problems. Perhaps the most critical of these difficulties is determining the mastery standard against which to measure pupil performance. What absolute standard should be used in determining whether a basic addition-facts deficiency exists? Should the standard be 70 percent of presented problems correct, or 80 percent? Or should the standard be 90 percent? What reasoning would lead to the choice of one of these standards over another?

The problem of defining an absolute competency standard is not intractable, but its solution requires professional time and effort, commodities in short supply in most school systems. The ideal means of attacking the problem is to call a pupil competent in an area if the pupil can demonstrate mastery of the skill to the degree required to move on to the next step in the curricular sequence. To be workable, this ideal solution requires: (1) a curricular sequence organized so that mastery of lower-level steps is in fact necessary for understanding of higher-level subject matter, and (2) mastery criteria that reflect the actual degree of skill necessary to succeed at the next curricular level. The effort required to develop and validate a comprehensive skill hierarchy of this type with empirically determined mastery criteria is, however, enormous, and far beyond the resources of even the largest school district. Not surprisingly, few empirically supported skill hierarchies exist (Bergan, 1981). As such, more practical approaches to the standard-setting problem will have to be employed if criterion reference is to be appropriately used as a means of determining individual needs and strengths.

One of the more workable methods for setting competency standards is the Angoff method (Angoff, 1971; Livingston & Zeiky, 1982; Zeiky & Livingston, 1977). This method requires assembling a group of content specialists (e.g., first-grade teachers) to make judgments about what types of tasks the minimally competent student should be able to perform and what the probability is that the minimally competent student will perform each individual task correctly. So, for the case of first-grade students, a group of first-grade teachers would be asked to specify the types of tasks that such students should be able to perform in various content areas (e.g., reading, math, language). The group might, for example, agree that students in the last part of the first grade should, among other things, generally be able to add and subtract single digit numbers, have a basic sight vocabulary, and know a number of rudimentary reading decoding rules.

Next, the group would be asked to come to consensus on the probability that the minimally competent student would correctly perform each of a series of tasks drawn from these critical skill domains. The group might, for instance, decide that the minimally competent first grader would have a 1.00 probability of getting $1 + 1$ correct but only a .60 probability of getting $5 + 3$ correct. The competency standard for each skill area is then set to the sum of the probabilities of the items representing that content domain. A ten-item sample of addition problems with correct probabilities of .90, .70, 1.00, .90, .80, .60, .50, .90, 1.00, 1.00 would have a competency standard of eight of the ten problems correct. Box 3-2 presents a worksheet for setting mastery criteria using the Angoff method.

A second common method for choosing competency criteria is the Contrasting Groups method (Livingston & Zeiky, 1982; Zeiky & Livingston, 1977). This approach is similar to the Angoff method, in that teachers are initially asked to define the types of tasks that the competent student should be able to perform. Instead of subjectively assigning probabilities to individual tasks, the next step in the Contrasting Groups method is to present the tasks to a group of students known to be masters of the content (e.g., second or third graders) and a group known to be nonmasters (e.g., beginning first graders). The competency cutoff can then be set, as shown in Figure 3-1, at the point that maximally differentiates the two groups.

Self-reference. A third type of standard that can be used in determining educational need is self-reference. This type of reference underlies the common practice of profiling and involves the intraindividual comparison of skills and abilities. One common method of using self-reference for needs determination begins with an examination of a student's pattern of skills and abilities. Students with large discrepancies between predicted achievement based on cognitive ability

BOX 3-2 *JUDGE'S RECORDING FORM FOR THE ANGOFF METHOD*

Test Title:

Judge's Name:

Question Number	Estimated Probability	Question Number	Estimated Probability
1		16	
2		17	
3		18	
4		19	
5		20	
6		21	
7		22	
8		23	
9		24	
10		25	
11		26	
12		27	
13		28	
14		29	
15		30	

SUM =

Adapted from Manual for Setting Standards on the Basic Skills Assessment Tests, by M. Zeiky and S. Livingston.   Princeton, N.J.: Educational Testing Service, 1977.   Copyright 1977 by Educational Testing Service.   Used by permission.

tests and observed achievement, or with discrepancies among the various achievement areas, are identified as needing special services, typically as learning-disabled students. Their specific educational strengths and needs are those areas that are significantly more and less well developed than most other skills in their profiles.

Self-reference does, of course, imply the use of either normative or absolute frames for giving meaning to each of the measurements that compose an individual's profile. Unless each of these measurements shares a common normative or absolute scale—that is, unless both reading and mathematics tests, for example, have been normed on the same population or have had absolute mastery standards set using the same group of content judges—it will not make sense to compare the performance of a student on one measure to that on another measure.

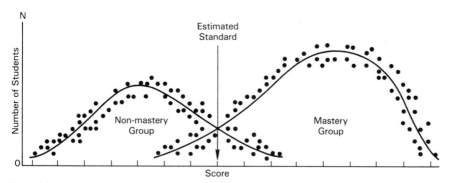

From <u>Manual for Setting Standards on the Basic Skills Assessment Tests</u> by M. Zeiky and S. Livingston. Princeton, N.J.: Educational Testing Service, 1977. Copyright 1977 by Educational Testing Service. Used by permission.

FIGURE 3-1 *SETTING COMPETENCY STANDARDS USING THE CONTRASTING GROUPS METHOD*

The determination of educational needs and strengths on the basis of self-referenced discrepancy is a hazardous endeavor, which we generally do not recommend. The major pitfall encountered in using this approach lies in the unreliability of differences (Thorndike, 1963, 1973; Thorndike & Hagen, 1977): the difference between two measures of ability or achievement is almost always substantially *less* reliable than either of the measures alone. This is owing to the fact that the unreliability contained in each measurement is combined in the difference between them. Many of the differences in achievement and ability observed in individual student profiles will, then, be artifacts of measurement as opposed to accurate representations of the student's actual pattern of skill development. In using profiles, we therefore recommend focus on those areas of ability or achievement that are low or high relative to some normative or absolute mastery standard and discourage more than passing attention to all but the most obvious intraindividual differences (Angoff, 1982).

In sum, a number of different reference frames for determining the existence of individualized program service delivery needs and strengths exist. Our general recommendation is to use multiple reference frames, to the extent possible, in making these determinations (Bennett, in press). The contention that a need or strongpoint exists can be most confidently made when both criterion and normative comparisons support that diagnostic judgment.

Assessing the Service Delivery Context

For the case of individualized programs, context assessment takes on a somewhat different character than that generally employed in special education planning and evaluation. Rather than using the A VICTORY model to look at aspects of the general district environment, we instead suggest focusing on the educational context in which the pupil is experiencing difficulty. As with student data, this information should be drawn from preplacement evaluation reports and should include a description of the structure of the educational setting (e.g., physical organization of the classroom), characteristics of the teacher and students (e.g., teaching style, functional levels of students), and the initial and alternative interventions attempted and their results.

Describing the Individualized
Program Problem

The results of context assessment should be combined with the descriptions of pupil background, needs, and strengths to form what we will call the Pupil Data Base. This data base is critical in the next planning phase, designing individualized programs.

DESIGNING INDIVIDUALIZED PROGRAMS

During the design phase, planning and evaluation efforts are directed toward development of an operational program for the individual pupil. This program is typically developed by a team of professionals, including a school administrator capable of committing resources to the program, a teacher familiar with the pupil's educational performance, and the pupil's parents. The program is formulated around a general purpose and a specific set of goals and objectives meant to address the needs of the individual pupil.

Describing Individualized Program Purpose,
Goals, and Objectives

The purpose of the individualized program is not often explicitly considered in special education practice; there is, for example, no legal mandate for including a statement of purpose in the IEP. We believe that the general reason for providing an individualized program for a pupil should be made explicit if the goals of that program are to be consistent with aspirations shared by parents and school officials for that student. We therefore recommend developing a short rationale consistent with pupil needs as a first step in designing the individualized program.

For example, pupil needs and aspirations might suggest that the purpose of an individualized program for a deaf high-school student be directed at improving verbal abilities necessary for success in college. For a severely physically handicapped student, on the other hand, the purpose might be oriented more toward providing the functional skills needed for independent living. For a mildly handicapped elementary-school student, it might be to develop the academic and social skills needed to succeed unassisted in the regular class environment. In any event, a statement of purpose provides a sense of direction to the individualized program design process that might otherwise be absent.

Goals and objectives represent the outcomes that professionals will be working toward achieving with a given pupil. Goals represent general statements that serve as the targets of instruction and related services. As general statements, program goals will not usually be directly observable or measurable.

We use the term "objectives" to refer to specific statements that indicate progress toward achieving a particular goal. Objectives, therefore, describe observable, measurable phenomena that can be used as benchmarks or indicators of pupil progress. For individualized programming purposes, we suggest that development of objectives be guided by the following questions:

Who?
Will do what?
Under what conditions?
To what level of proficiency?
Within what time frame?

An example of an individualized program purpose, goal, and accompanying objectives is provided in Box 3-3.

BOX 3-3   *INDIVIDUALIZED PROGRAM PURPOSE, GOAL, AND OBJECTIVES*

```
Purpose:    To give Johnny the skills needed to succeed in the regular
            education class without special assistance.

Goal:   To improve reading skill.

Objectives:

    1. Upon end-of-year outcome assessment, Johnny will show evidence

       of maintaining his standing compared to his normal age peers

       by obtaining a Total Reading percentile score on the Woodcock

       Reading Mastery Tests within no less than 2 standard errors of

       the score obtained at the time of program initiation.

    2. Upon end-of-year outcome assessment, Johnny will be able to

       read words from Dolch list flash cards appropriate for Grade 1

       students with an accuracy rate of 8 words pronounced correctly

       for every 10 words presented.

    3. Upon end-of-year outcome assessment, Johnny will be able to

       say the sounds made by each of the r consonant blends (e.g.,

       br, tr, cr, fr, gr, pr) when these are presented in the

       initial position in words belonging to the at, ap, and up

       families with an accuracy rate of 9 blends correct for every

       10 presented.
```

Goals for an individual pupil should be selected based upon the program purpose and needs reflected in the Pupil Data Base. One goal should be developed to address each general area of need consistent with the program purpose. Though goals designed to address other needs can also be developed, the individualized program should focus on the purpose it is meant to serve. Programs primarily meant to prepare students for independent living and employment, for example, should emphasize functional-living and vocational skills as opposed to academics. Box 3-4 shows the relationship between pupil needs, program purpose, and goal statements.

Once a goal has been established for each general area of need, a set of objectives should be written for each goal. The type and number of objectives set for each goal area should be based on a variety of factors including the characteristics of (1) the goal area, (2) the pupil, and (3) the program. Each of these considerations deserves some discussion.

BOX 3-4 *RELATIONSHIP BETWEEN PUPIL NEEDS, PROGRAM PURPOSE, AND GOAL STATEMENTS*

```
Pupil Needs:

    I. Academic

        A. Mary has not yet developed the mathematics skills
           normally mastered by middle first grade, such as the
           ability to name all the single-digit numbers and count
           the number of objects in a group.

   II. Social

        A. Mary often has difficulty getting along with her
           classmates.  She frequently makes insensitive remarks and
           often inadvertently bumps into children while moving
           around the class.


Program Purpose:

    To give Mary the skills needed to succeed in the regular
    education class without special assistance.


Goal Statements:

    I. Academic

        A. To improve Mary's basic mathematics skills.

   II. Social

        A. To improve Mary's interpersonal skills with peers.
```

Characteristics of the goal area. Two general content characteristics that have implications for choosing goals are difficulty and organization. It is a fact that some types of content are easier to teach—and to learn—than others. For example, it is generally easier to teach mathematics skills than it is to teach students to feel more positively about themselves. This is true because mathematics is a more easily organized domain and because we know more about teaching mathematics, have more materials available for its instruction, and do not usually have to worry as much about the interference of home environment with our efforts. In other "hard-to-teach" and "hard-to-learn" areas, we may need to be somewhat more modest in selecting objectives.

In addition to difficulty, content organization affects the selection of objectives. As we mentioned in our discussion of standard setting, defensible organizational schemes do not exist for many content domains; for the area of reading comprehension, there is no one generally agreed-upon sequence of skills that can be used in choosing objectives for indicating progress. In these domains, program planners will need to rely upon their own professional judgment in developing skill hierarchies or in selecting from the various logical schemes that have been proposed (see Wallace & Larsen, 1978, for examples of logically derived scope and sequence charts for various content areas). For some domains, in particular basic mathematics skills, defensible hierarchies do exist (e.g., see Gagne & Briggs, 1979). In these domains, it is relatively easy to select particular objectives to serve as benchmarks for a single goal.

Characteristics of the pupil. Four pupil characteristics have implications for setting objectives: position in the skill sequence, past learning rate, home environment, and handicapping condition. For those content areas that can be easily sequenced, the choice of objectives will be influenced by the student's current position in the skill hierarchy; the objective selected is generally the one directly following those the pupil has already mastered. Position in the skill sequence also has implications for setting target dates for achieving objectives. This is because some portions of the domain will inevitably be more difficult—that is, take longer to master—than others. For example, it is commonly known that some basic multiplication facts are harder to learn than others: the nines table is more difficult than the tens.

The speed with which the pupil has learned similar content is a second important student factor in setting objectives. Obviously, more ambitious and numerous objectives within a goal area can be set for the pupil whose previous rate of learning has been more rapid than that of other special students.

Third, the extent to which the student comes from a family environment that is committed to the student's growth and emotionally supportive of it should be taken into account. We can be more confident that a child will achieve the objectives we set if we know that the efforts we make at school will be complemented by similar efforts at home. In general, the individualized programs for such students should reflect this optimism by containing objectives that may imply a more demanding program than usual.

Finally, the appropriateness of an objective is also partially a function of the pupil's handicapping condition. For instance, a mathematics problem-solving objective that requires instruction to focus on the solution of written word problems might be inappropriate for a severely reading-disabled student. Care should be taken to set objectives so that instructional requirements do not demand more of the student than the student can reasonably be expected to bear.

Characteristics of the program.   Characteristics of the program important to objectives selection include the program purpose and the extent of previous special services. The program purpose will frequently imply the choice of some objectives over others. For example, many special students have a goal to improve basic reading skill. The objectives for this goal should differ, however, for a program designed to give a mildly handicapped high-school student the skills needed to function independently and one meant to prepare an elementary-school child to succeed in the regular class. Objectives for the high-school student might concentrate on consolidating such functional skills as sight recognition of "survival" words (e.g., "danger," "no smoking," "exit," "police"), reading common applications and forms, and recognizing road signs and other driving-related vocabulary. For the younger child, objectives would likely focus on age-appropriate sight words (e.g., "the," "said"), development of basic decoding strategies (e.g., consonant and short-vowel sounds), and other skills necessary for keeping pace in the regular class environment.

The extent of special services already provided is a second program characteristic relevant to choosing objectives. The amount of effort previously spent attempting to achieve a particular goal can help to suggest how difficult it will be to achieve similar goals in the future. Objectives for pupils who have been the beneficiaries of years of specialized effort and have made little progress despite that effort should probably be less demanding than those for students being considered for special instruction for the first time.

Evaluating Individualized
Program Alternatives

Once goals and objectives have been chosen for a pupil, the most appropriate set of instructional and related service programs to address those goals and objectives needs to be identified. Determining the appropriate programs is best accomplished on a goal-by-goal basis. As a result, for many exceptional pupils, the IP will consist of a number of special and regular education programs. Program alternatives for the IP should be drawn from the array of special and regular education services commonly available both inside and outside the school district. Some of these alternatives include:

regular class
regular class with related services (e.g., counseling, social work, occupational therapy, physical therapy, audiology, team monitoring)
regular class with part-time remedial services (e.g., compensatory education, supplemental reading)
regular class with resource room
special class within district
special class in another public-school district

    special class with related services
special day school
special residential school
home instruction

While the choice of which program is appropriate for a given goal is clearly a matter of professional judgment, some basic guidelines can be given. First, to the extent possible, the programs assigned to address goals for a given child should be ones that have proven successful at addressing similar goals for similar children in the past. Programs that have been unsuccessful in remediating particular goals with specific populations constitute inappropriate, restrictive environments for students from those populations even if they are closer to the regular class environment than the alternative (Cruickshank, 1977a, 1977b). The goals of instruction for some children require placement in isolated programs such as the special class or residential school, and for such children, the appropriate least-restrictive environment is this program alternative.

A second guideline for selecting programs is to split the pupil's IP among more than one program wherever it is clear that no single program can adequately satisfy all goals assigned to a student. Such assignments are often necessary for IPs containing specialized goals such as those commonly addressed by the various related services or by specialized programs of instruction (e.g., vocational education). Split assignments like these may place the student in-district part of the time and out-of-district for the remainder of the school day. The benefits of such assignments clearly must be weighed against their costs, in particular instructional time lost to travel.

A final point relevant to the selection of program alternatives is this: if the goals for a given child can be adequately achieved without the benefit of special education services, then special programs should *not* be recommended and the student should *not* be classified as exceptional. This suggestion runs somewhat counter to practice, in that once a child is diagnosed as handicapped, that child is commonly provided some type of special education service. Our approach, which is consistent with the Rules and Regulations of PL 94-142 (U.S. Office of Education, 1977b), does not consider a child to be handicapped *unless* that child needs the assistance of the special services system. By focusing on the functional needs of children, this approach should reduce the all-too-common error of classifying children as exceptional when they are not. In addition, specific remedial suggestions for *all* children subjected to the pupil evaluation and planning process are provided because specification of goals and objectives is accomplished *before* making a placement decision. We think this sequence of activities makes the pupil-evaluation process work more for the benefit of the children it is meant to serve.

Once individualized program recommendations have been agreed upon, efforts should be directed toward working out the nitty-gritty details of program placement. These include (1) an estimate of the time period over which services are expected to be provided (e.g., six months; one year), (2) the persons responsible for providing those services and the locations and times during which they will be delivered, and (3) recommendations for the modes (i.e., individual, group), methods, and materials that might be used to achieve each objective.

Recommendations for methods and materials are best worked out in cooperation with those responsible for providing the actual services. We suggest that recommendations be offered for nonspecial program placements also. We believe this to be particularly important to regular education teachers, who often have little familiarity with the problems of handicapped children and their management in the regular class environment. Recommendations will also be of use to regular educators in cases where the goals set for a recently referred and evaluated child do not seem to warrant special services. In these cases, some guidance must be given the regular education teacher if the child is to be kept from being referred again.

In formulating recommendations for service provision, we also suggest that planning-team members take care to communicate that the recommendations developed are guidelines, and not mandates that dictate how a child must be taught. Some professionals are more comfortable and achieve better success with some methods over others; final judgment about intervention strategy might be best left with the individual service provider. However, if, after a reasonable period of time, progress is not being made, those responsible for monitoring the case should push for use of the intervention methods originally recommended.

Developing the Individualized
Program Design

The individualized program design is described in a written document, which for special education purposes has typically taken the form of the Individualized Education Program. In Chapter 1, we suggested a detailed outline that could be used for the design of a variety of special education programs (see Box 1-2). This program structure was designed to make explicit the complexities of large-scale programs, such as a preplacement evaluation program or a resource-room program, in which numerous staff members and students are involved. For purposes of individualized programming, however, this structure is of limited value; it includes some elements of little general relevance to individualized programming (e.g., developmental and operating budgets) and omits some critical considerations (e.g., pupil needs).

For individualized program planning, we offer a simplified adaptation of our generic program-design structure (see Box 3-5). In viewing Box 3-5, you will notice that the bulk of our discussion up to this point has been devoted to developing the first three components of the IP: the Pupil Data Base; Purpose, Goals, and Objectives; and Services. You will also notice that while this structure differs in its specific composition from our generic design outline, it shares with that outline all basic planning and evaluation elements; the simplified outline includes a statement of purpose, implementation information in the form of Services and Review Guidelines sections, and a description of expected outcomes (i.e., goals and objectives). Finally, the simplified design is consistent with the requirements of PL 94-142; all elements required by the law's rules and regulations for the IEP are included.

The fourth section of our IP design is titled Review Guidelines. This section

BOX 3-5 *COMPONENTS OF THE INDIVIDUALIZED PROGRAM DESIGN*

I. Pupil Data Base

   A.   Educational needs and strengths
      1. Affective
      2. Cognitive
      3. Academic
      4. Social
      5. Physical

   B.   Relevant background characteristics
      1. Social
      2. Physical

   C.   Educational context
      1. Structure of setting in which student is having difficulty
      2. Teacher and student characteristics
      3. Interventions tried

II. Purpose, Goals, and Objectives

   A.   Purpose
   B.   Goals and objectives
      1. Affective
      2. Cognitive
      3. Academic
      4. Social
      5. Physical

III. Services

   A.   Instructional and related service programs
   B.   Service delivery arrangements (i.e., settings)
   C.   Goals and objectives to be addressed by each program
   D.   Professionals responsible for providing each program
   E.   Anticipated duration of services
   F.   Recommended modes (i.e., group, one-to-one), methods, and materials for achieving each objective

IV. Review Guidelines

   A.   Implementation evaluation
      1. Staff
      2. Methods
      3. Criteria
      4. Schedule

   B.   Outcome evaluation
      1. Staff
      2. Methods
      3. Criteria
      4. Schedule

sets forth a brief but explicit plan for gathering information about the extent to which the program was actually carried out and the degree to which program goals and objectives were achieved. We will offer some suggestions for the composition of this section here, saving a more detailed treatment of implementation and outcome evaluation for subsequent portions of this chapter.

The guidelines for program review should specify the staff, methods, criteria, and schedule for conducting both individualized program implementation and outcome evaluation. We recommend that one person, such as the case manager, be given general responsibility for coordinating both implementation and outcome evaluation. Specific responsibility for carrying out implementation evaluation is probably best divided among a number of planning-team members who can usually gather this information in the course of their routine contact with the student's teacher and other service providers. Outcome-evaluation responsibilities can be shared by all of those involved in delivering services to the pupil; each provider should be asked to continually gather evidence about the extent to which goals and objectives are being achieved.

Methods for implementation and outcome evaluation fall into four general categories: tests, observations, document or product reviews, and surveys (i.e., questionnaires and interviews). We will discuss these methods in more detail later in the sections on program implementation and outcome assessment.

The criteria for determining whether an individualized program is being implemented or an objective achieved should be embedded in the program description and the objective, respectively. Criteria for determining whether a program is being implemented include the promised services, responsible service providers, schedule, and the areas of focus described in program goals and objectives. Standards for judging goal attainment are the norm- or criterion-referenced competency levels that are an integral part of any well-written objective.

The final component of the program-review guidelines is the review schedule. In general, implementation review should be conducted on a regular basis, so that problems in carrying out an individualized program can be rapidly identified and corrected. Outcome assessment is generally conducted at the end of a logical programming period; in the case of the IEP, this assessment should be conducted in preparation for the mandated annual review, held at the end of the school year or on the anniversary date of the previous program plan.

Evaluating the Individualized Program Design

Before an individualized program is implemented, it is good practice to review its design, so that any errors or inconsistencies can be identified and corrected. The individualized program design is reviewed in light of the general criteria used for the evaluation of any program design: clarity, comprehensiveness, internal consistency, compatibility, and theoretical soundness.

Clarity. With respect to the individualized program, clarity refers to the extent to which each section of the program (i.e., Data Base; Purpose, Goals, and Objectives; Services; Review Guidelines) and all elements within each section are clear to those responsible for carrying out the program. For instance, program objectives should describe observable, measurable phenomena and possess explicit criteria for mastery; service descriptions should likewise identify exactly what will be provided, when, and by whom; review guidelines should identify evaluation responsibilities, methods, and schedules.

Comprehensiveness. In evaluating comprehensiveness, the primary concern should be to ensure that all elements of the individualized program have been included and that no particular state- or federally-required components are absent.

Internal consistency. Reviews of the plan's internal consistency should center upon the interrelationships of the plan's elements to one another. For example, clear ties should exist between data-base needs and purpose, purpose and goals, goals and objectives, and goals and the services to be provided.

Compatibility. Compatibility relates to the fit of the individualized program with other district programs. Reviewers should check to see that the individualized program does not call for the delivery of services in places or at times during which they cannot be provided. Review guidelines should also be carefully assessed, to ensure that implementation-evaluation and outcome-evaluation plans do not take unreasonable amounts of staff time from other critical duties or otherwise interfere with the conduct of ongoing programs.

Theoretical soundness. The final consideration in reviewing the individualized program design is theoretical soundness or educational meaningfulness. This criterion particularly applies to the needs identified in the Pupil Data Base, and to the program purpose, goals, and methods and materials. For example, pupil needs in areas whose relevance to education has been seriously questioned, such as auditory or visual memory (Salvia & Ysseldyke, 1981), should be critically reviewed. The same type of critical assessment should be done for controversial treatment methods, such as those optometric and perceptual-motor stratagems sometimes recommended for the treatment of learning disability (e.g., see Ad Hoc Working Group, 1982).

Box 3-6 presents a scale that can be used in reviewing the individualized program design. We recommend that the scale be completed independently by at least two of the team members developing the IP. Items to which one or more low ratings are assigned can be used to suggest areas in which the design may need to be improved.

BOX 3-6   *INDIVIDUALIZED PROGRAM DESIGN REVIEW SCALE*

DIRECTIONS: This scale is designed to guide review of the
individualized program-design document. Please read each question and
refer to the design document before formulating your response. Mark
the number corresponding to your response in the space next to the
question. Your assistance in completing this review scale will help
ensure the quality of the individualized programs developed in our
school district.

Completely	Very Much So	To a Reason- able Degree	Only Somewhat	Not at All
5	4	3	2	1

Clarity and Comprehensiveness

____1. Are pupil strengths identified?
____2. Are pupil weaknesses given?
____3. Are relevant background characteristics specified?
____4. Is the educational context in which the pupil is experiencing
       difficulty described?
----5. Is the general purpose of the program listed?
____6. Do objectives describe what behaviors the student is expected
       to master?
____7. Do objectives define the conditions under which those behaviors
       are to be displayed?
____8. Do objectives possess explicit mastery criteria?
____9. Are the programs to be provided, identified?
___10. Is the service delivery arrangement specified in which each
       program will be provided?
___11. Is the schedule for providing each program given?
___12. Are the professionals responsible for delivering each program
       identified?
___13. Are the goals and objectives given that each program is
       targeted toward achieving?
___14. Are the individuals responsible for implementation review
       specified?
___15. Are implementation review methods listed?
___16. Are criteria for determining the success of program
       implementation included?
___17. Is a schedule for implementation review given?
___18. Are the individuals responsible for outcome evaluation
       specified?
___19. Are outcome evaluation methods listed?
___20. Are criteria included for determining if outcomes have been
       achieved?
___21. Is a schedule for outcome evaluation given?

Internal Consistency

----1. Is the program consistent with pupil needs?
----2. Are goals generally consistent with the program's purpose?
____3. Are goals directly related to needs identified in the pupil
       data base?
____4. Are objectives directly tied to goals?
____5. Are programs designated for delivery related to specific goals
       or objectives?
____6. Are programs designated for service delivery appropriate for
       addressing the goals and objectives toward which they are
       targeted?
____7. Are recommended materials related to specific objectives?
____8. Are suggested strategies related to specific objectives?
____9. Are outcome-evaluation methods appropriate for measuring
       attainment of the types of goals and objectives specified?

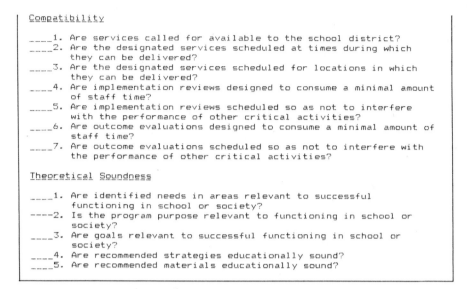

IMPLEMENTING INDIVIDUALIZED PROGRAMS

The primary intent of the program-implementation phase is to insure that the individualized program is carried out according to plan. Toward this end, planning and evaluation activities in this phase center upon (1) facilitating implementation and (2) evaluating the extent to which the individualized program is carried out.

Facilitating Individualized Program Implementation

In Chapter 2, we presented the DURABLE approach as one means of encouraging the implementation of a program according to plan and illustrated the application of that method to assessment programs. In this section, we will consider the use of those components of the DURABLE approach most relevant for carrying out individualized programs.

Discussing.   As applied to individualized program implementation, discussing involves meeting with those personnel responsible for carrying out various aspects of the program. The initial purposes of this meeting are to (1) make all providers aware of the content of the student's program (i.e., Data Base; Purpose, Goals, and Objectives; Services; Review Guidelines) and (2) encourage the coordinated delivery of services to the student. Individuals present at the implementation meeting should include the case manager, those slated to provide direct instructional and related services to the pupil, and any evaluation-team members acting as consultants to the individualized program.

Understanding. The second purpose of the implementation meeting is to identify and understand any concerns that providers have about the individualized program as it is constituted. In our experience, concerns are frequently raised about the appropriateness of goals and objectives, the schedule for providing services, or about evaluation plans. Regardless of the validity of the concern, the case manager and program designers should do their best to see the problem from the service provider's point of view, making any reasonable accommodations necessary to alleviate it. In those situations where the staff disagreed with elements of a program, we have consistently found implementation was facilitated when the reasons for program decisions were made clear and staff members were made to feel that their feelings and opinions were sought and considered.

Adapting. This DURABLE component comes into play in both the initial implementation meeting and after delivery of the individualized program has begun. The focus here is on modifying elements of the program that prove impractical or inappropriate.

Past experience has shown us that program objectives in particular require adjustment. Objectives set during program development often are found to be too easy or too difficult once work with a student has begun. Modifying objectives that are considered too easy is a relatively straightforward task. Objectives already mastered by the student can be noted as such on the program plan and new objectives added to that goal area. Objectives felt to be too difficult should *not* be removed from the program plan. Instead, intermediate objectives should be inserted in the plan and the schedule for achieving the original objectives altered to reflect the expectation that mastery will be achieved at a later date. In those few cases where an objective or entire goal area is judged to be completely inappropriate for the student, an addendum should be attached to the plan, noting the date, reasons, and individuals responsible for making the modification.

Learning. Learning focuses exclusively upon detecting sources of resistance and other practical problems that may inhibit delivery of the individualized program. Particular problems that should be watched for include pupil absence, case overloads that prevent teachers or other specialists from fully meeting their responsibilities to a student, and lack of knowledge about the specifics of the plan. The results of learning should suggest courses of action, such as adapting the student's program, discussing the program with the provider and understanding the individual's concerns, and if necessary, withholding rewards.

Evaluating Individualized
Program Implementation

In keeping with the notion that evaluation is an integral part of program planning, we first introduced the topic of individualized program implementation review in our discussion of design. At that time, we stated that the individualized program design should make explicit the staff, methods, criteria, and schedule for conducting implementation, or process, review. It may now be helpful to discuss individualized program implementation review in more detail.

For program-improvement purposes, implementation review focuses on identifying problems hindering operation of a program so that these problems can be promptly corrected. Additionally, this review serves to document what was delivered. This documentation, while useful for accountability, can be subsequently employed in conjunction with outcome information to identify elements of the program thought responsible for specific positive or negative effects. Box 3-7 presents a series of questions designed to focus implementation review.

The pitfalls commonly encountered in gathering the information called for in Box 3-7 revolve for the most part around staffing, methods, criteria, and scheduling concerns.

BOX 3-7   *QUESTIONS FOR FOCUSING IMPLEMENTATION EVALUATION OF THE INDIVIDUALIZED PROGRAM*

Evaluation Questions

1. What programs are being provided in connection with the IP?
2. Toward what goals is each program working?
3. On what date did the provision of each program begin?
4. How frequently is each program being delivered?
5. Are the programs, goals, duration, and frequency of delivery consistent with those specified in the program design?
6. If delivered services are not consistent with those described in the program design, what events have led to departures from the original plan?
7. Toward what objectives is each program working?
8. What methods and strategies are being employed to achieve each objective?
9. Are the objectives of each program being achieved on schedule?
10. If objectives are not being achieved as planned, what types of problems are impeding goal attainment?
11. Do any particular methods or materials seem to be working very well or poorly with this student?

Staffing.   The major staffing problem encountered is almost always one of time. Special education staff members are many times taxed to the limit by their direct service responsibilities; adding new labor-intensive tasks is often impractical. We firmly believe, however, that the time invested in individualized implementation review is worthwhile if the evaluation is well conducted and the results utilized.

If staff members are indeed near the breaking point, our first suggestion is to focus attention on only a *sample,* or subset, of the total population of individualized programs provided by the district. The size of this sample should be determined by the amount of staff time that can be spared. For program-improvement purposes, we recommend that the programs chosen for inclusion in this review sample be ones for which there is a reasonable suspicion of difficulty; for example, as signaled by repeated complaints from a teacher about a student's performance. If no such programs can be found, then programs can be randomly chosen.

In addition to limiting the number of programs chosen for review, we suggest dividing evaluation tasks among a number of individuals. This recommendation has two important effects. First, it limits the amount of time any one individual must devote to the implementation-review process. Second, and perhaps equally important, it tends to increase the reliability of data gathered for implementation review. This is true to the extent that (1) some overlap in the evaluation tasks assigned to individuals for a case exists and (2) these tasks are carried out and reported independently.

For example, we might assign the review of one element of Johnny Smith's individualized program—math resource-room services—to both his school psychologist and his social worker. In doing this, we could ask Ms. Jones, Johnny's resource-room teacher, to forward her lesson plans and samples of Johnny's work to our reviewers. We could further ask one reviewer to interview Ms. Jones about Johnny's program. Upon receiving the results of these two separately conducted reviews, we would compare them to see how divergent they were. If significant disagreement was apparent, we would speak with each reviewer, first independently, and then together, to see if the cause of disagreement could be identified and if either reviewer's judgment should be disregarded (e.g., in the case that one individual declares a general dislike of Ms. Jones). Finally, we would pool, or average, the results to derive a combined judgment that, in the long run (i.e., over many similar evaluations), will be more reliable than either reviewer's judgment alone.

Methods.   A second area of potential difficulty in carrying out individualized-implementation review relates to the choice of data-gathering methods. Earlier, we stated that implementation- and outcome-evaluation methods fell into four general categories: tests, observations, document or product reviews, and surveys (Bennett, 1981b). Testing, the first of these methods, is primarily an outcome-evaluation tool and as such is of limited use in process review.

Of greater utility for implementation review is observation. Observation is particularly well suited to those cases where problems in service delivery are evident and witnessing those difficulties firsthand appears necessary before remedial action can be taken (e.g., in the case of a personality conflict between teacher and child or when a child presents behavior difficulties). In addition to the fact that it is very time-consuming, the major disadvantage of observation is its reactivity, the distorting effect of the observer on the typical behavior of those observed. The result of this reactivity is that the program sample observed by the implementation reviewer may not be representative of normal program operation.

The document or product review is an indirect but valuable method of evaluating the delivery of an individualized program. The method is indirect in that the reviewer must *infer* from a document or product that a particular program was (or was not) provided. In using this method, we would, for example, look through the attendance book and lesson plans of the resource specialist to determine if the pupil came to resource class and if instructional plans were consistent with the pupil's individualized program objectives. In addition, we might wish to examine samples of any written classwork or homework the student produced, such as completed phonics worksheets and answers to reading comprehension questions—again, to determine if work completed was consistent with stated program objectives.

The last implementation-review method we should mention is the survey. With this method, the teacher or related service specialist is asked, via questionnaire or interview, to describe the program given the student. Surveys provide the opportunity to gather a wide range of information about implementation and hence should contain questions that probe along a number of dimensions. Questions for inclusion in an implementation-review survey can be based upon those suggested in Box 3–7, presented earlier.

As a general rule, we suggest using interviews in only the limited number of cases where serious implementation problems are suspected. In these cases, the interview can be employed to clarify and explore solutions to any implementation problems that exist. Use of the interview on a basis any more widespread will usually require more staff time than most districts can spare.

To the extent feasible, it is generally good practice to use more than one type of method in conducting implementation review. All data-gathering techniques are flawed in the sense that they present a view of reality that is both somewhat off target, or invalid, and somewhat imprecise, or unreliable (Cronbach & Associates, 1980). As in assessing pupil needs, using a variety of techniques for gathering information will generally result in a more accurate representation of individualized program implementation.

Criteria. A third aspect of implementation review that sometimes causes problems relates to the criteria for determining whether an individualized program is being implemented according to plan. Such criteria should, of course, be built into the original program design and include explicit specification of the services to be delivered, the schedule for delivery, those responsible for service provision, and the methods and materials to be used. Program designs that do not completely specify these elements of the individualized program should not be allowed to pass beyond design review; a program that is not explicit enough to evaluate is not explicit enough to carry out.

In comparing the manner in which an individualized program is being carried out to the criteria set for its implementation, particular care should be taken to avoid negatively judging a program simply because it has departed from its design. For example, a special education teacher may come to the conclusion that the Orton-Gillingham method specified for teaching phonics skills to Johnny Smith is simply not working, and may switch to a more linguistically based approach, such as Glass Analysis. The teacher's reasons for this switch can be discussed, to ensure that some systematic method is being used to choose and evaluate the success of different strategies with Johnny. In addition, the date and rationale for the switch should be documented, so that a record of the interventions provided is maintained.

In short, departures from the program design do not necessarily mean that an individualized program is being improperly carried out; they should, however, signal the need for closer examination to determine if in fact any serious problem exists.

Scheduling. The last potential problem area related to implementation review is scheduling: how frequently and when should process review be performed? Our feeling, stated earlier, is that review of individualized programs should be undertaken on a regular basis, so that difficulties encountered in delivering programs can be readily identified and addressed. To achieve this end, teachers and other members of the staff responsible for carrying out the program should *informally* check implementation monthly or bimonthly, by comparing the IP and the services they are actually providing. Significant discrepancies or problems should be communicated to the case manager, who can arrange for these programs to be more closely reviewed.

With respect to the time of year when formal review should routinely occur, we recommend that this evaluation generally be part of the annual review of individualized programs required by PL 94-142. In this way, implementation of most programs will be formally checked at least once a year. For those districts that routinely perform their annual reviews at the end of the school year, implementation evaluation can be carried out at this time; in other districts, annual review, and hence process evaluation, will be undertaken on the anniversary date of the IP's last formulation.

ASSESSING THE OUTCOMES
OF INDIVIDUALIZED PROGRAMS

The assessment of individualized program outcomes is undertaken to determine if a program has been successful and how that program should be changed to more fully benefit the student. A familiar example of outcome assessment of this type is the IEP annual review routinely carried out by school districts in accordance with the rules and regulations of PL 94-142.

Four interrelated questions that can be used to guide individualized program outcome assessment are:

Have program goals been achieved?
What reactions do consumers have to the program?
Was goal attainment caused by programs delivered through the IP?
How should the program be changed?

The basic plan for conducting outcome assessment should be constructed during development of the review-guidelines section of the individualized program design. In discussing the development of this plan, we briefly noted four elements to which attention should be paid: staff, methods, criteria, and schedule. We will now discuss these considerations and the questions that focus outcome assessment in more detail.

Evaluating Goal Attainment

In our view, the primary emphasis of outcome assessment for individualized programs should be placed upon determining the extent to which program goals have been achieved. This determination is essential if intelligent decisions about program modification are to be made.

Staffing. Good teachers and related service professionals constantly evaluate the progress of the children they serve. Therefore, the primary data-gathering responsibilities for determining if program objectives have been achieved are most logically divided among those working with the student. Additional information on goal attainment can be gathered by parents, especially when objectives related to behavior outside the school (e.g., adaptive behavior, self-help skills, social interaction) are included in the individualized program plan.

Methods. As has been stated, the extent of progress toward a goal—such as "to improve basic reading skill"—is judged according to the degree to which the objectives comprising that goal are achieved. So, for example, Johnny would be regarded as making progress toward this reading goal if he were able to demonstrate mastery of such individualized program objectives as those presented in Box 3-3.

As can be seen from Box 3-3, the methods used for gathering information about goal attainment can be embedded in the objectives indicating student progress toward a particular goal. This is true for each of the objectives in Box 3-3, which imply that Johnny will, in the first case, be tested with a formal reading-achievement test, and in the second and third cases, be informally assessed to determine the extent to which he has mastered his sight words and consonant blends.

Table 3-1 suggests general categories of method that might be appropriate for evaluating progress toward different types of goals. For example, formal and informal testing strategies may be used to document progress toward academic goals in areas such as reading and mathematics; in mathematics, reviews of classwork and homework products can also be employed. Movement toward affective goals, on the other hand, might best be assessed through methods more amenable to the measurement of emotions and attitudes, such as observation and interview and questionnaire surveys. Reviews of different instruments for measuring goal attainment in special populations can be found in Salvia and Ysseldyke (1981), Lambert (1981), and in the Buros's *Mental Measurements Yearbooks;* guidance in constructing new measures can be obtained from Thorndike and Hagen (1977) and Cronbach (1970).

A number of pitfalls in using these different methods should be recognized, and, if possible, actively protected against. These pitfalls exist with regard to both formal, standardized measures, such as norm-referenced tests, as well as with such informal tools as unstructured teacher observation.

TABLE 3-1   Methods Appropriate for Evaluating Different Types of Goals

	METHOD				
GOAL AREA	TEST	OBSERVATION	INTERVIEW	QUESTIONNAIRE	PRODUCT REVIEW
Affective					
1. Attitudes			x	x	
2. Motivation		x	x	x	
3. Emotions		x	x	x	
4. Self-concept			x	x	
Cognitive					
1. Reasoning	x		x		x
2. Study Skills	x				
3. Memory	x	x			
4. Perceptual Abilities	x				x
Academic					
1. Language Skills	x	x	x		
2. Reading	x	x			
3. Mathematics	x	x			x
4. Writing	x	x			x
5. Vocational Skills	x	x			x
Social					
1. Interpersonal Relations		x	x		
Physical					
1. General Health		x	x		
2. Sensory/ Motor	x	x			x

The most common pitfall we have found in evaluating goal attainment is the tendency to evaluate mastery using content that may not validly reflect the objective being measured. The content or behavior sample chosen for assessment of an objective may be an invalid representation of the objective in a number of ways. First, the measure selected or developed to assess goal attainment may contain items that fall outside the domain or realm of content called for by the objective —as in the case of the word "approach" in relation to the *r*-blend objective presented earlier (the *r* blend in "approach" is medial, not initial, as specified). Second, the group of items or behaviors used to judge mastery may be incomplete or unbalanced—as when *cr* words are accidentally omitted from mastery testing (the *cr* is also specified by the objective), or when all blends are represented but not in reasonable proportions (e.g., 10 *fr* words and one *cr* word).

To protect against the pitfall of using a measure that does not validly reflect the objective, we suggest three precautions. First, use program goals and objectives as the basis for developing or selecting assessment tools. Second, try to arrive at some defensible rationale for the distribution of items required for proper measurement of the objective. In the case of the *r*-blend objective, each blend specified by the objective might ideally be represented in proportion to the frequency with which it appears in the English language, or, alternatively, how frequently it is used in words employed by a particular basal-reading series; in those instances where a reasonable basis cannot be found, equal proportions of items are probably best used. Finally, if a measure has been developed, carefully review all the items to make sure each matches the objective; also, check the item sample to see that (1) all parts of the domain specified in the objective are represented and (2) all segments are employed in reasonable proportions.

A second common pitfall in measuring the outcomes of individualized programs is the tendency to use too limited a sample of behavior (e.g., too few items) for assessing each objective. This pitfall is related to the notion of unreliability. It is conceptually similar to basing your impressions of an individual on the results of a single brief encounter that you alone have had. Judgments of personal characteristics should generally be made on the basis of considerably more exposure; behavior during longer encounters and under different conditions should be considered, as should the opinions of others familiar with the individual, before coming to a judgment.

As with enduring personality traits, measurements of individualized program outcomes should show evidence of stability—at least for the short term—if they are to be considered reliable representations of a pupil's achievement. That is, performance should be relatively consistent across different samples of items testing the objective, on different days, and with different examiners if it is to be accepted as accurate.

The problem of employing too few items might best be illustrated using the objective of focusing on the mastery of *r*-blend words, mentioned earlier. The population, or number, of all English words containing this blend is finite but undoubtedly quite large. If Johnny has mastered the use of this blend in the initial position, then he should be able to read the large majority of words incorporating it—that is, exclusive of those containing other more advanced characteristics he may not yet have learned—by applying his knowledge of the *r* blend to these words. The most sensible way of testing Johnny's mastery of the *r* blend is to present him with a number of words containing this consonant combination. However, Johnny has undoubtedly learned many of those words by rote, as a function of practicing the blend during instruction. If we decide to test Johnny's mastery of the objective with an inadequate sample—say, five words taken from a popular diagnostic reading test—we may by chance end up with some words that Johnny has committed to memory. Johnny may also get lucky and guess the correct pronunciation of a few words. The result of these chance occurrences is a not-very-dependable estimate of Johnny's mastery of the objective, one that may lead to an incorrect judgment on the success of his program and on subsequent emphases for reading instruction.

The obvious protection against this type of unreliability is to use as many items as practicable in assessing mastery of an objective. For cases in which the results of an incorrect decision are not severe and can be easily reversed—such as for mastery of the *r* blend—a *minimum* of five to ten items per objective should be used (Berk, 1980). For situations where the consequences of making an incorrect decision are more serious, or the decision is less easily reversed, a *minimum* of 10 to 20 questions is more appropriate.

A second way in which a behavior sample may be too limited is in terms of the time, or occasion, on which it is collected. Johnny may well have mastered the *r* blend—or maintained his standing in reading relative to his age peers in the Woodcock norm group—but if his attention is elsewhere on the day he is tested —because of inattention, fatigue, or lack of motivation—he will likely fail to demonstrate the progress he has made. The best protection against this potential problem is simple: test the child's mastery on at least two different occasions and average the results. If possible, use different samples of items on each occasion—for example, alternate forms of the Woodcock—so that both errors due to the particular sample of items used and those resulting from the time of testing can be protected against.

One final way in which a sample of behavior may be too limited relates to those responsible for its observation and documentation. This source of error is typically negligible in the use of well-constructed, commercially available standardized tests, where acceptable answers and the conditions under which they must be given are clearly defined. It is a significant problem, however, in most teacher-made tests and unstructured observations of behavior.

The problem is perhaps best illustrated for an objective requiring a student to spend at least 80 percent of classroom reading time engaged in on-task behavior. Evaluation of the student's achievement of the objective can be achieved by observing samples of the student's behavior during those periods scheduled for reading practice. The teacher can watch the child for a limited number of fixed-length periods (e.g., five three-minute periods) and record the amount of time spent by the child on reading as a basis for calculating the needed proportions. The problem typically encountered in the use of such procedures is that different teachers—or observers—tend to perceive the same behaviors differently. So, for example, one observer might consider the student to be on task if the child remains on the same page of the reader for three minutes. Another, assuming that Johnny is daydreaming, may not.

The most straightforward protection against this problem is twofold. First, clearly specify the behavior to be exhibited by the student, and the conditions under which it is to be performed, as part of individualized program objectives. This may make for rather long and detailed objectives, but it will reduce ambiguity and improve the accuracy of subsequent outcome assessments.

Second, to the extent practicable, have a second individual—such as a classroom aide—*independently* take part in the outcome assessment. This individual may observe the student demonstrating the target behavior at the same time as the teacher or may repeat outcome assessment at a later time. In either case, the judgments of both observers should be independent, to keep the perceptions of one from influencing the judgment of the other. After both observations have been completed and judgments independently formulated, conclusions should be shared and, if unusually discrepant, discussed to discover the sources of disagreement. Finally, the conclusions of each observer should be averaged to form a single pooled assessment of the extent of mastery.

The protections we have offered to increase reliability—that is, limit the influence of error owing to the particular sample of items chosen for assessment, the occasion on which it occurs, and the examiner performing the evaluation—can be easily combined. This combination can be achieved by simply repeating assessment on a second occasion using a new sample of items administered by a different examiner, the results, again, to be pooled with those of the original assessment. The resulting pooled estimate will, in general, be more dependable than any single mastery estimate.

The measurement of an individual's skills and abilities is clearly no simple matter; many opportunities for invalidity and unreliability exist. To minimize the effect of these difficulties, we have suggested a number of protections. These protections do *not* guarantee accurate assessment; they merely raise the *likelihood* of collecting accurate results. Judgments of goal attainment based on assessment results are best regarded as tentative, subject to reconsideration and revision as more information is gathered about a particular student's skills and abilities.

Criteria.   Criteria for measuring goal attainment should be specified as part of the program-design process and should be embedded in the objectives composing a particular goal. In assigning criteria, every effort should be made to select educationally defensible reference frames and standards. Criterion reference is implied when an objective focuses upon mastery of a clearly defined class of behaviors (e.g., the 100 basic addition facts) to which performance can be unambiguously related. Mastery standards for such objectives (e.g., 90 percent correct performance) can be based on the typical performance of students who have already been instructed in, or who have mastered, a particular skill; on the judgments of a group of subject-matter experts (e.g., math teachers) about the level of proficiency required for movement to the next step in the curriculum; or on field-based research about the likelihood of mastering higher-level objectives given proficiency in preceding ones.

Normative reference is sensible in those instances where comparison of a student's performance to that of some relevant group is deemed important and where a global measure of progress toward achieving a goal is desired. For example, if the purpose of a student's program is to facilitate transition into the mainstream, or otherwise make that student more like his or her normal peers in terms of academic skills or social behavior, then it is defensible to compare the performance of that student in global content areas (e.g., reading achievement) to the performance of those in regular classes (Goodman & Bennett, 1982). For other students, such as the severely handicapped, the more relevant comparison may be not with the performance of normal students but with the progress typically made by students with the same handicap receiving a similar type of intervention.

Normative standards can be operationalized in a number of ways. One such individualized program evaluation standard is movement in a goal area from similarity with a less-sophisticated group of children to that with a more-sophisticated group. Movement up a scale defined by groups of children with various levels of sophistication can be easily measured for mildly handicapped pupils (that is, those not drastically different from the general education population) working toward relatively common academic goals. For such cases, we recommend *individual* administration of a group-standardized test such as the Sequential Tests of Educational Progress (Educational Testing Service, 1980) or the California Achievement Tests (CTB/McGraw-Hill, 1979).[1] These measures have a number of advantages over the individualized tests commonly used in special education. Among these advantages are that they are generally more carefully constructed, their norms are based on larger samples and are therefore likely to be more accurate, their subtests are typically longer and therefore more reliable, and they usually contain out-of-level norms, permitting functional-level testing and interpretation (see MacGinitie, 1978, pp. 43–46, for a discussion of functional-level testing).

With such tests, the metric commonly used to track movement from similarity with one group to that with another has been the grade-equivalent scale. This scale, however, suffers from so many inadequacies that its use in educational assessment has generally not been recommended (see Bennett, 1982c for a comprehensive review of the problems inherent in this metric). In fact, use of grade- and age-equivalent scores has been advised against by a number of professional organizations, including the International Reading Association, the American Psychological Association, the National Council on Measurement in Education, and the American Educational Research Association (International Reading Association, 1980; *Standards for Educational and Psychological Tests,* 1974).

Instead of grade equivalents, we recommend use of the expanded-score scales commonly found on most well-constructed group-achievement tests (e.g., see MacGinitie, 1978, pp. 37–38, 40). Such scores, which go by a variety of names, including scale scores, extended-scale scores, and standard scores, are intended to vertically span—as do grade equivalents—the range of achievement measured by all levels in a given test series.

To determine if a child has made progress moving up this scale, one of the group-achievement tests should be administered at the beginning of the program and again at the time of outcome assessment. The pre- and posttests should, if at all possible, be from the same level in the test series, so as to prevent pseudo-gains owed to errors in the calibration or linking of levels. Finally, the level of the test

---

[1] The test should be administered following all directions provided in the test manual. The administration is individual only in the sense that the child takes the measure alone and not with a group. Failure to follow administrative procedures (e.g., reading items to the child) will make comparison of the child's performance to the test's norms unmeaningful.

series chosen should be commensurate with the student's functional level, so that the majority of test items are neither too easy nor too hard.

Standard scores from pre- and posttesting should be compared to see if any observed gain exists. If so, the difference between pre- and posttest scores should be compared to the minimum amount required to conclude that a real gain has occurred. This minimum threshold can be found in most test manuals (see, for example, Prescott, Balow, Hogan, & Farr, 1978, p. 53). When it is not, it can be calculated through the following formula, offered by Thorndike and Hagen (1977):

$$Sm(\text{diff}) = \sqrt{Sm_1^2 + Sm_2^2}$$

where $Sm(\text{diff})$ is the standard error of measurement for the difference, Sm_1^2 is the square of the standard error of measurement for the pretest (found in the test manual), and Sm_2^2 is the square of the standard error of measurement for the posttest (also found in the test manual). If the difference between pre- and posttest scores exceeds the standard error of measurement for the difference, we can be fairly confident that progress up the scale has been made; if the observed difference exceeds *two* times the standard error, we can place a higher degree of confidence in inferring progress. Box 3-8 presents an example of calculating and using the standard error of measurement for differences (see Salvia & Ysseldyke, 1981, for further examples of using this statistic to evaluate observed score differences).

BOX 3-8 *EVALUATING THE SIGNIFICANCE OF OBSERVED GAIN SCORES*

```
Name:    Terry Smith

Test:    Metropolitan Achievement Tests Survey Battery:   Mathematics


Pretest scale score   (Form JS) =   262       Sm = 30.5

Posttest scale score (Form JS) =   300        Sm = 30.5

Observed scale score difference = 300 - 262   = 38



                                --------------------------
                                |
                                |       2            2
                Sm(diff)    =   |   30.5   +    30.5
                                |
                              \ |


                Sm(diff) =    43.13



Sm(diff) = 43.13 > Observed difference = 38. Therefore no.dependable
difference can be said to exist.
```

A second, more difficult, normative criterion for goal attainment is maintaining standing compared to a relevant peer group (e.g., normal peers of the same age, other profoundly retarded students receiving the same intervention program) over the period of time the program is delivered. Achieving this criterion indicates that the student is making sufficient progress to keep up with his or her peers at the same initial skill level; in other words, the student is not losing any ground. This criterion may be particularly important for programs designed to prevent skill regression, such as summer programs for severely handicapped students or interventions for children with degenerative diseases.

In cases where the peer group of interest is the general education population and the goal of interest is a common academic one, maintenance of standing can be assessed using group-achievement tests. To evaluate maintenance of standing, a group measure should be administered individually at the beginning of the program and at the time of outcome assessment, again preferably using the same level of the test for both sittings. If the percentile scores resulting from the two testings are the same or the posttest percentile is greater than the pretest score, we can be relatively confident that standing has been maintained and the program objective achieved. If, however, the pretest percentile score is greater than the posttest score, those scores should be converted to standard scores and the difference between them tested for chance occurrences in the same manner as stated earlier. If the difference between pre- and posttest scores exceeds two times the standard error of measurement for the difference, we can be very confident that standing has *not* been maintained and the objective not achieved. This does not necessarily mean that no progress has been made; it simply means that whatever progress was made was not at a rate commensurate with that of other children having the same standing at the time of the pretest.

A final and still more stringent progress standard that can be readily implemented using commercially available standardized tests is a *gain* in standing relative to a peer group. This criterion may be particularly important in instances where an eventual return to the mainstream setting is planned. Such a return presumes that the student will be able to function in that setting with little or no support—that is, that the student's standing in important goal areas is generally similar to those of students in the mainstream setting.

Achievement of this standard is evaluated in much the same way as that of the maintenance-of-standing criterion. Here, however, the difference between pre- and posttest scores is evaluated using the standard error of measurement for the difference only if the posttest percentile is *greater* than the pretest percentile. In this instance, the percentile scores are converted and the difference between the converted scores is calculated. If this difference exceeds the minimum value given in the test manual for significant differences—or if it exceeds the standard error of measurement for the difference—we can conclude with a fair degree of confidence that a gain in relative standing was made and that the objective based on this criterion was achieved.

As has been suggested, the three normative criteria for achieving objectives we have discussed are most easily applied to those cases for which commercially standardized measures are available. These criteria also can be applied in situations where local norms exist. In some cases—for example, those involving the outcome assessment of severely handicapped students—the absence of national norms will necessitate the ongoing collection of local normative data if a reasonably sound base for using normative criteria is to be developed.

Scheduling. Data relevant to the progress children are making toward achieving program goals should be collected as many times over the course of a program as is practicable. Clearly, the frequency with which such data can be collected will vary according to a variety of factors, including whether an objective requires gathering data through standardized tests or through some other, less demanding means. Because continuous progress monitoring can suggest modifications in the methods and materials used to achieve an objective, it is frequently found to be an integral part of the instructional routines of good teachers. In fact, such approaches to the education of exceptional children as precision teaching (Howell, Kaplan, & O'Connell, 1979) explicitly incorporate the repeated measurement of progress as an essential element of the teaching process.

The results of repeated measurements of progress routinely gathered by teachers over the course of a program can be formally documented and employed as part of the evidence submitted to support goal attainment. Figure 3-2 presents

FIGURE 3-2 *USING REPEATED MEASURES OF PROGRESS TO DOCUMENT GOAL ATTAINMENT*

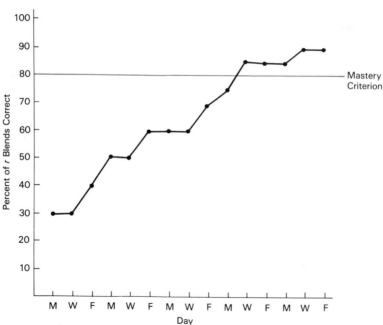

a graph showing the results of repeated assessments of Johnny's progress toward achieving mastery of the *r* blend. The gradual growth suggested by the curve and the repeated measurements indicating standing above the mastery criterion provide a more convincing argument that the objective has in fact been achieved than would the results of a single postprogram assessment.

Evaluating Consumer Reaction

The primary consumers of individualized programs are parents and students. Evaluating parents' reactions to the program serves to test the value or "social validity" (Kazdin, 1977) of individualized program results. In addition, exploring consumer reaction aids in uncovering unintended effects and gives an indication of the consumer's overall view of the IP.

Staffing.   For purposes of consumer reaction, we recommend that responsibility for data collection reside with the case manager. This is because in our experience program consumers, such as parents and students, are generally more comfortable, and more direct in, responding to questions about the program when asked by individuals other than those delivering services to the child.

Methods.   The most straightforward means of determining the reactions of parents and students to a program is simply to ask. Box 3-9 presents an example of a questionnaire meant to sample parents' reactions to the individualized program. Questionnaires such as that presented in Box 3-9 are best used to gather data on the reactions of parents *in general* to the programs provided their children. In these cases, the proportions of parents choosing each option for each individual question can be computed across the group of parents, providing an indication of specific IP areas that need to be looked at more thoroughly.

BOX 3-9 *INDIVIDUALIZED PROGRAM CONSUMER-REACTION QUESTIONNAIRE*

DIRECTIONS: This questionnaire is meant to gather your reactions to the individualized program provided your child.   Please read each question and mark the number corresponding to your feelings about the part of the program referred to.   Your opinions will help us improve the services we provide your child and are very much appreciated.

Totally	Very Much So	To a Reasonable Degree	Only Somewhat	Not at All
5	4	3	2	1

_____1. Did school staff encourage you to participate in developing the individualized program for your child?
_____2. Did school staff seem to understand your child's good points?
_____3. Were your child's educational weaknesses understood by school staff?
_____4. Was the general purpose of your child's individualized program suited to your child's needs?
_____5. Were the goals selected for your child appropriate?

```
____6.  Was the school your child was assigned to satisfactory?
____7.  Was the class your child was placed in appropriate?
____8.  Were the materials used to achieve the goals set for your child
        suitable?
____9.  Were the methods used to teach your child appropriate?
___10.  Did the professionals assigned to instruct your child do a
        good job?
___11.  Were the efforts of school staff to keep you informed about
        your child's progress satisfactory?
___12.  Was the amount of input you had in making decisions about your
        child's education appropriate?
___13.  Was the progress your child made satisfactory?
___14.  Was this progress made in areas you consider important?
___15.  Were the school's efforts to evaluate the effectiveness of your
        child's individualized instructional program satisfactory?


THANK YOU FOR YOUR TIME AND COOPERATION IN FILLING OUT THIS FORM!
```

For those instances in which the reactions of an individual child's parents are desired (e.g., when a parent has previously expressed concerns about the quality of a program), a telephone or personal interview may be the method of choice. This method is particularly attractive because it allows feelings to be probed and interesting or ambiguous comments to be pursued. The protocol, or guiding framework, for the interview can be informal, though it is generally a good idea to lend the session some structure by having a preformulated set of questions designed to elicit relevant perceptions of the program. The questionnaire presented in Box 3-9 can be used as a source of ideas for interview questions.

Criteria. Because few districts can realistically be expected to address every problem perceived by program consumers, we suggest ordering questions concerning specific program elements (e.g., sensitivity of staff to parent concerns, quality of materials, subject-matter knowledge of staff) according to the proportion of parents responding negatively to the item. Priorities for administrative action can then be assigned based upon these orderings, with those elements perceived most negatively by consumers addressed first.

When the reactions of a single consumer, such as an individual parent, are the subject of interest, ordering the seriousness of concerns raised should be undertaken as part of the interview process. The results of this ordering can then be used in a way similar to that already suggested.

Scheduling. Because consumer-reaction evaluation can help identify successful and unsuccessful elements of an individualized program, reactions should ideally be gathered for all programs as part of outcome assessment. Few districts, of course, have the resources for such extensive data-gathering. In keeping with our own pragmatic beliefs, we recommend that, at the least, consumer-reaction evaluation be scheduled for those programs for which there is a suspicion of difficulty. In cases where no such suspicions exist and resources permit, consumer reactions can be gathered for a random sample of individualized programs. The result of this sampling will be—depending upon sample size and instrument quality—a more or less reasonable representation of general reaction to the individualized programs provided students by the school district.

Evaluating Cause-Effect Relations

Establishing that a particular IP intervention (e.g., a resource-room program) is the actual cause for increased achievement is, to say the least, a very tricky business. Many conditions independent of the IP can effect goal attainment; from positive changes in the home environment that result in improved behavior despite a poorly implemented counseling program, to a private after-school tutor whose incompetent approach dooms IP resource-room reading goals to failure. Yet, knowledge of the relationship between IP interventions and observed effects is critical if decisions to continue particular programs are to be based upon effectiveness and not the happenstance of external events.

Firm statements about the causes of program results are best based upon carefully controlled experimental research using large samples of students. Because the conditions necessary to support such research are rarely available in special education (e.g., random assignment to interventions, large samples), the methods we recommend will be more suggestive than definitive in attributing cause to effect.

Staffing.   Data relevant to the relationship between IP programs and effects can be gathered by the case manager from program providers and by providers from students. Students represent a source of evaluation data that is too often ignored; yet they often can offer valuable input as to whether an intervention is working for them.

Methods.   In our discussion of evaluating goal attainment, we stated that taking repeated measurements of pupil progress was one useful means of documenting the achievement of program objectives. Repeated measurements can also be used to evaluate cause-effect relations. One of the more practical examples of employing repeated measurements for this purpose is the time-series design (see Figure 3-3).

In the time-series design, baseline data relevant to a particular outcome—for instance, increasing the incidence of on-task behavior through a token-reinforcement stratagem—is repeatedly gathered before intervention is implemented and again once intervention begins. If the data show a steady baseline *and* an increase in progress toward achieving the objective once the program has been implemented, then the program can be viewed as the probable cause of achieving the target objective.

For establishing cause-effect relations, the time-series design has a number of limitations. Among other things, it does not control for normal pupil growth, for other programs that may be teaching the same skills (e.g., private tutoring), or for changes in the nature of the content being taught (e.g., the content related to

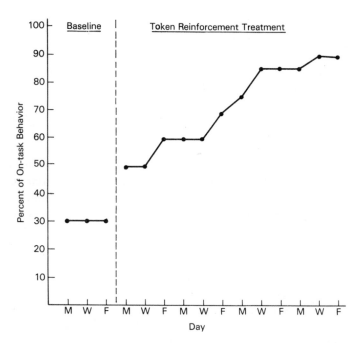

FIGURE 3-3   *USING SINGLE CASE DATA TO ATTRIBUTE PROGRAM EFFECTS TO INSTRUCTIONAL METHODS*

an objective may vary in difficulty from one subtopic to the next, as is true for the multiplication tables). These problems can to some extent be protected against by attempting to rule out the existence of competing explanations for program effects. Other programs being provided the pupil should be reviewed and parents contacted to discern if similar interventions are being delivered; the times at which content changes occur should be checked against time-series results to determine if concommitant increases (or decreases) in achievement are evident.

Criteria. In the time-series approach depicted in Figure 3-3, a number of conditions related to the nature of baseline and intervention results help to support cause-effect inferences. By definition, baseline data are gathered before intervention begins. A stable baseline throughout the preintervention period helps support the contention that the intervention is responsible for observed effects. A stable baseline provides an initial consistent picture against which to compare the effects of a subsequent intervention.

Because cause and effect normally occur close together in time, a perceptible increase (or decrease) in responding when the intervention is first introduced also supports the inference that a program is responsible for an observed effect. A sudden rise over baseline considerably *after* the intervention is introduced weakens the case for a cause-effect relationship. This pattern opens the door to outside influences as the cause of the observed effect.

A final condition supporting cause-effect relations is evidence of continued increases, or otherwise high levels of responding, throughout intervention. This pattern supports the cause-effect inference because of the close temporal relation between continued delivery of the intervention and continued results. Inconsistent response to an intervention reduces the interpretability of time-series data; observed effects may be because of any number of conditions not directly related to the program itself (e.g., errors in data collection, lucky guessing, inconsistently taken medication).

To the extent that time-series data deviate from these ideal baseline and intervention criteria, the judgment that an IP element is responsible for achieving a particular program goal is all the more difficult to support. Further discussion of employing time-series and other approaches to support cause-effect inferences is presented in Chapter 5, Planning and Evaluating Related Services; in Howell, Kaplan, and O'Connell (1979); and in Deno and Mirkin (1977).

Scheduling.   Information about the effectiveness of program elements should be gathered by interveners on a regular basis. Teachers and related service professionals can collect time-series data, through precision teaching techniques, as part of the intervention process (Howell, Kaplan, & O'Connell, 1979). These data should be forwarded to the case manager for review at the same time that documentation of progress toward goals and objectives is offered.

Determining How a Program Should Be Changed

The question of how an individualized program should be changed is, at its most basic level, a matter of program design: developing a revised individualized program to meet the needs of the student as determined by outcome assessment. In this sense, the planning-and-evaluation process is brought full circle; the relevant questions are the same as those that direct development of any individualized program:

What goals should compose the individualized program for a given child?

What instructional and/or related service programs do these goals imply?

Are these services best provided by the special services delivery system or by some other district-intervention program?

In which service delivery arrangements should these programs be delivered and in what modes (e.g., group versus one to one)?

When and how should the program be carried out?

How will the implementation and results of the program be evaluated?

The answers to these program-development questions should be based on the results of goal attainment, consumer-reaction, and cause-effect evaluations. Data from these three outcome-evaluation activities should be reported to program designers to help suggest new goals and objectives, changes in the program desired by consumers, and potentially effective interventions for future use.

SUMMARY

This chapter has discussed planning and evaluating individualized programs. We have viewed the individualized program as a general program category—one popular example of which is PL 94-142's IEP—that functions as an overarching framework for organizing the numerous educational and related service programs typically provided the exceptional student.

Our suggestions for clarifying individualized program problems have centered upon the need for gathering and organizing data describing the educational needs and strengths, relevant background characteristics, and educational environment of the student. In the needs-determination process, we have stressed the importance of setting explicit and defensible criteria against which to compare student performance.

In the area of planning, we have suggested a modified design for the individualized program that is consistent with the mandates of PL 94-142 and our own generic design structure. We have also, in contrast to the common planning practice of first determining service eligibility and then specifying program goals, advocated the development of program goals as the basis for assignment to a special education program.

With respect to individualized program implementation, one of our primary concerns has been facilitating the delivery of services by the various professionals working with handicapped pupils. Communication, coordination, and regular monitoring of program implementation, through such mechanisms as the DURABLE framework, are essential if maximum effects are to be achieved.

In discussing outcome assessment, the final element of the individualized program planning-and-evaluation process, four key questions were suggested. These were related to the achievement of goals, reactions of consumers, relationship between IP interventions and program effects, and necessary program modifications. The final outcome-evaluation question, relating to the modifications needed, brought the individualized program planning-and-evaluation process full circle, by raising anew questions of problem clarification and program design.

PLANNING AND EVALUATING INSTRUCTIONAL SERVICES
Group Programs

Group programs are the primary means of educating exceptional pupils. Group programs are based upon recommendations contained in the individualized programs of these students, and are provided through special classes, regular classes, resource rooms, and other arrangements. Group programs address goals of academic achievement and functional living and are essential to the efficient operation of the special services system.

Providing group programs is a complex endeavor. The task requires cooperation between and among regular and special educators, coordination of individualized and group programs, and evaluation of group rather than individualized program outcomes. In this chapter, we discuss those planning and evaluation methods that can facilitate the delivery of group programs to special students.

OVERVIEW OF GROUP PROGRAMS

Need for Group Programs
in Special Education

School districts typically have limited resources to deliver services to handicapped children. For example, teachers have little time to develop the diverse skills needed to address the wide range of handicaps children possess. In addition, districts can afford to buy only so much equipment and material for teaching different content areas.

The primary means of maximizing these limited resources is to organize children with similar learning needs into group programs. Assigning students with similar learning characteristics to a group program permits the teacher to concentrate professional-development and instructional-planning efforts on a manageable range of educational activities. For example, the teacher working with blind students can focus on teaching pupils to physically negotiate their environment and other skill development needs unique to this population. The teacher of the deaf, on the other hand, typically centers intervention upon communication, the primary learning need of this group. Few teachers would have the time to master the strategies and materials necessary for teaching both of these diverse populations.

Nature and Scope of Group Programs

A group program is an organized configuration of resources designed to achieve a set of academic or functional-living goals for two or more pupils. Group programs take their form from recommendations contained in the individualized programs of exceptional children and are considered to be the primary means by which IPs are implemented in school districts (Kennedy, 1982).

There are various types of group programs. Each type can be characterized by its service delivery arrangement and modes of instruction. The service delivery arrangement is the place where the program is physically carried out. The three most common group program service delivery arrangements appear to be the special class, the resource room, and the regular classroom (Paul, 1981). Group programs, however, can be delivered in other arrangements, such as in the home, a vocational training center, or a residential school.

Two instructional modes can be employed in a group program: the one-to-one mode and the group mode. In the one-to-one instructional mode, a pupil interacts on an individual basis with an instructor. This mode is used when required staff are available and when the IP specifies that intensive one-to-one instruction is critical to the progress of the child.

The group mode is characterized by the teacher's working with two or more pupils concurrently. This mode is probably the most frequent way in which special instruction is delivered (Sage, 1981). In addition to being an efficient delivery mechanism, the group mode is thought to have social advantages. The modeling of appropriate academic and social behaviors by classmates and teachers, as well as group discussion and problem solving, seems to enhance the learning of pupils with special needs (Spivack & Shure, 1974; Strain & Kerr, 1981).

A variety of group programs exist as part of a special services system. These include resource-room reading programs, special class programs for the severely handicapped, and shared-time vocational-school programs. One type of group program not commonly recognized as such is home instruction. Home instruction can be considered a group program because it serves a cluster of children with common educational needs; that is, the group of pupils confined to home or hospital settings. In most instances, the one-to-one mode of instruction is employed because individual students are confined to their own homes. The group mode, however, might be utilized for children with similar needs residing on the same ward in a hospital.

Difficulties in Providing
Group Programs

A range of difficulties usually is encountered when providing group programs. Prior to the start of the school year, those exceptional pupils whose IPs recommend group programs must be identified, and the identified pupils organized into meaningful instructional target groups. Once target groups have been determined, decisions must be made about what new group programs need to be designed and what existing ones can be expanded to include other students. Important problems here include specifying group-program goals that validly reflect individualized goals of pupils and identifying interventions that might satisfy those goals.

Deciding how to evaluate the outcomes of group programs also requires considerable attention and skill. Problems encountered include delineating appropriate evaluation questions and selecting practical methods and procedures to answer those questions. For example, questions of cost-effectiveness invariably are raised by different audiences, such as board of education members concerned with the growing costs of special instruction. Properly posing questions of cost-effectiveness and designing an evaluation to answer those questions is no easy undertaking. Deciding how to report the results of evaluation to school and community constituencies can be equally troublesome.

In the remainder of this chapter, we discuss methods and procedures for planning and evaluating group programs that address the foregoing kinds of difficulties and concerns.

CLARIFYING GROUP SERVICE
DELIVERY PROBLEMS

Our approach to planning and evaluating group programs draws upon the systems and goal-based models (see Table 1-1). The systems model focuses attention on interactions of the elements within a group program as well as its interactions with other programs. This systems emphasis is particularly important because the primary elements that comprise a group program—pupil IPs—play a major role in most phases of the group planning-and-evaluation effort.

The goal-based model also has important implications for group programs. Among the elements we borrow from this model is the philosophy that group programs must have explicit goals and objectives (over and above those contained in pupil IPs) if they are to be purposefully run and meaningfully evaluated. Without such goals and objectives, a coherent group service delivery effort will be unlikely to occur.

Assessing Service Delivery Needs

Building upon assumptions derived from the systems and goal-based models, we base the assessment of group service delivery needs on a review of pupil individualized programs. This review is meant to identify those pupils whose IPs recommend group programs and to provide information for assigning pupils to instructional target groups.

Identifying pupils. Review of pupil-individualized programs should concentrate on obtaining the following kinds of information:

Administrative classification of the student (e.g., emotionally disturbed, mildly handicapped)

Academic and functional-living goal areas recommended for instruction (e.g., reading, motor skill development)

Types of objectives delineated in each goal area (e.g., reading comprehension, manual dexterity)

Type of group program and instructional mode recommended (e.g., resource-room reading program with one-to-one instruction)

Frequency of instruction (e.g., five days per week)

Anticipated duration of instruction (e.g., September–June)

Location of instruction (e.g., Washington Elementary School)

Once information for each pupil has been gathered, it can be summarized in a matrix format, such as the one presented in Table 4-1. The horizontal dimension of the matrix denotes the goal areas for which instruction in a group program has been recommended. The vertical axis refers to the types of group programs to be delivered. The intersection of the horizontal and vertical dimensions of the matrix results in 15 cells into which the numbers of pupils needing different types of group programs can be placed. For example, cell A1 indicates that 9 pupils need reading

TABLE 4-1 Matrix for Summarizing Group Service Delivery Needs[a]

	GOAL AREA				
TYPE	READING (A)	MATH (B)	LANGUAGE ARTS (C)	VOCATIONAL EDUCATION (D)	PHYSICAL EDUCATION (E)
Special Class (1)	9	12	17	18	9
Resource Room (2)	14	13	16	0	0
Regular (3)	16	11	14	15	12

[a]A pupil may be counted in more than one cell in certain instances, such as where a pupil is recommended for a special-class reading program (cell A1), a resource-room language-arts program (cell C2), and a regular classroom physical-education program (cell E3).

instruction in a special class arrangement; cell C3 suggests that 14 students require placement in a regular language-arts program.

The matrix in Table 4-1 provides a general overview of group service delivery needs for a school or school district; it helps in the *initial* organization of pupils for group programs. Depending upon the specificity of information desired, the matrix can be further elaborated. For example, the horizontal dimension could be expanded to include more specific or additional goal areas. Likewise, the vertical dimension might include listings of more program types, modes of instruction, or school buildings where programs are to be delivered.

Determining instructional groups. When initial identification of pupils needing group programs has been made, instructional target groups are further refined. First, those pupils identified as needing a particular type of group program can be divided into specific instructional target groups or classes. Dividing pupils into such groups is based on information contained in their individualized programs as well as information found in their cumulative files. The information of most relevance consists of the current needs and strengths of the pupils in the academic and functional-living areas where group programs have been recommended; individualized goals and objectives; suggested modes of instruction; and other program requirements (e.g., that a pupil be grouped only with others who exhibit certain behavioral characteristics).

Assessing group service delivery needs concludes with a review of the composition of each target group. This review involves considering whether each group is appropriate, given apparent similarities of instructional need and related learning characteristics. If it is determined that one or more pupils are not suitable for a particular target group, changes in group composition should be made at this time.

Assessing the Service Delivery Context

The context of group programs should also be considered when describing the service delivery problem and when designing new group programs. Three organizational readiness factors of the A VICTORY model (see Box 2-2) of particular importance are ability, values, and timing.

Ability. Assessing the school's ability to allocate resources for group programs involves gathering information about the group programs currently delivered to exceptional pupils, as well as the personnel, facilities, equipment, and materials that might be made available for new program efforts. Context information about organizational ability can be obtained through document review. In this procedure, the program design of each existing group program is reviewed to determine:

Number and types of existing group programs serving exceptional pupils
Resources that comprise these programs (i.e., staff, methods, materials, facilities, and so on)

Number and classifications of handicapped pupils who have participated in these programs in the past

Reactions of consumers to these programs

Outcome-evaluation information about goal attainment, cause-effect, relations, related effects, or cost-effectiveness

This document-review procedure can be conducted on a yearly basis. The information obtained can be compiled in a Group Program Resource Directory, which can be used throughout the district as a guide to existing group programs.

Values. Assessing how the school staff feels about educating exceptional pupils can be accomplished via a questionnaire or structured interview procedure. Using these methods, administrative and instructional staff members who are or may become involved in group programming for exceptional pupils can be asked the following kinds of questions:

Does your program include exceptional pupils?

If so, what is your opinion of the benefits that those pupils have derived from the program (e.g., increased academic skills, socialization with normal peers)?

For what kinds of exceptional pupils is this program appropriate, and why?

If you were to include exceptional pupils in this program in the future, what concerns would you have about instructional programming or related issues?

Timing. Assessing the factor of timing involves identifying events or opportunities in the school and community that may affect group program delivery. If it is determined that the conditions are appropriate for instituting a new group program, program-design efforts can proceed accordingly. However, if it is considered impractical to install a new program, then planning and evaluation activities may need to be curtailed, with other program options being considered (e.g., expanding an existing program).

Timing can be assessed by reviewing permanent products, such as minutes of board of education meetings or program budgets, as well as by holding informal discussions with school personnel and board officials. In employing these methods, information is sought about recent or current events and opportunities, such as the following:

Budget revisions or cutbacks that may signal fewer funds for new programming efforts in the district

Unanticipated award of state or federal funds that may allow addition of new programs

Changes in central office staff (e.g., new superintendent) or school administrators (e.g., new school principal) that may affect sanction and support for a new group program

Opportunity to obtain funds through newly available grant programs

Public support from interest groups (e.g., teachers association, parents of exceptional children) for better educating handicapped children

Once context information about ability, values, and timing has been gathered, it can be used along with information about the need for group programs to describe the extent of the service delivery problem.

Describing the Group Service
Delivery Problem

In describing a group service delivery problem, a comparison is made between a current state of affairs (e.g., a number of pupils require special instruction in particular goal areas) and a desired state of affairs (e.g., a group program that offers instruction in the identified areas). If the comparison reveals a discrepancy between existing and desired states—for instance, that no such group program with room for those pupils currently exists—a group service delivery problem is indicated.

As the basis for subsequent planning, a written problem-clarification statement should be developed. Such a statement can be used to communicate information about the group service delivery problem to school administrators (e.g., principal) and others (e.g., school-board members) responsible for deciding to proceed with program-design efforts. The statement should briefly describe the problem and note any relevant context information. An example of such a statement is the following:

> In Jones School, 20 pupils classified as learning-disabled have been identified as needing resource-room instruction in mathematics with a focus on developing basic skills. Currently, no such group program exists in the school, though financial and staff resources to support such an effort are available. For next school year, a group program to meet this need should be designed.

DESIGNING GROUP PROGRAMS

Describing Group Program Purpose,
Goals, and Objectives

A group program's statement of purpose should be consistent with the need for the program determined during problem clarification. This need, in turn, should be consistent with goals and objectives expressed in the individualized programs of students selected for the group program.

Box 4-1 presents examples of statements of purpose for a resource-room mathematics program and an adaptive physical-education program. These statements illustrate important aspects of each program: rationale, scope (i.e., modes of instruction to be provided, target group, service delivery arrangement, and staff), and expected results.

Once the purpose of the program has been determined, group program goals are derived. These goals reflect important knowledge, skills, and attitudes to be acquired by members of the instructional target group. Group program goals guide development of program objectives, selection of instructional resources, and assess-

BOX 4-1 *STATEMENTS OF PURPOSE FOR TWO GROUP PROGRAMS*

The purpose of the middle-school resource-room program is to provide small-group instruction in basic mathematics to students with special needs. The program is intended to improve pupils' addition, subtraction, multiplication, and division skills, so that they can develop the foundation for subsequent functional mathematics skills (e.g., those related to money and measurement). The program will be staffed by state-certified teachers of the handicapped.

The purpose of the elementary-level adaptive physical-education program is to provide mildly handicapped pupils with gross-motor-skill instruction. The program is intended to improve skills in running, throwing, catching, jumping, and balancing, so that pupils can more effectively negotiate their environment and enjoy recreational activities. The program will be staffed by a state-certified physical therapist and special education teacher.

---

ment of program outcomes. Examples of group program goals derived from the statement of purpose for the resource-room mathematics program (Box 4-1) are

> To develop basic math computational skills
> To foster a positive attitude toward mathematics

Examples of goals for the adaptive physical-education program (Box 4-1) are

> To develop small gross-motor skills
> To foster appreciation of physical recreation

Group program objectives are employed to direct instructional activity and to assess the degree to which group goals have been attained. Such objectives can be formulated in a number of ways. In one approach, objectives are written to reflect the average percentage goal attainment for individualized program objectives related to a group goal. For example, if the group goal of a resource-room mathematics program is "to improve basic math computational skills," the group program objective might be:

> Upon end-of-year outcome assessment, pupils will attain an average of 75 percent of their individualized program objectives in the basic goal area of math computational skills.

This approach does, of course, assume that objectives contained in student's individualized programs are clearly specified. Review of a sample of these programs should be undertaken to ensure that this is indeed the case.

In another approach, group program objectives are written to reflect a desired average level of performance for pupils in a *common* skill area. For example, for the mathematics goal previously described, one objective might be:

> Upon end-of-year outcome evaluation, pupils will be able to demonstrate proficiency of the basic addition facts by achieving an average of 70 percent correct on a written test of 30 horizontally and vertically presented examples in a 15-minute period.

The choice of which format to use for writing group objectives is best based on the commonality of the individualized programs brought by participating pupils. If pupils generally share very similar objectives (e.g., a number of pupils in the same program have the same objective: to master basic addition facts), the latter format may be preferred. If, however, large variance exists in pupil objectives for a goal area (the proficiency levels and conditions under which mastery is to be determined vary widely), then the first format would probably be more appropriate.

In setting objectives for group programs, commercially available standardized achievement tests may be incorporated in the objectives as measures of goal attainment. Incorporation of norm-referenced measures is most appropriate when an instructional target group includes mildly handicapped pupils, when the purpose of the program is to improve functioning relative to normal peers, and when program outcomes reflect skill development in achievement areas tested by such measures (e.g., reading, language arts, mathematics). In choosing such measures, it is important to consider the (1) appropriateness of achievement-test content relative to group program goals and objectives, and (2) technical adequacy of the test.

Assessing technical adequacy may frequently prove to be a difficult task. Measures are not valid and reliable in and of themselves, but rather are such when used for specific purposes and populations. The data needed for determining technical adequacy must therefore come from investigations of the behavior of those measures with *handicapped* groups. Unfortunately, most instrument manuals present data collected from *general* populations (e.g., regular education students). In addition, although independent investigators are conducting increasing numbers of studies with specific handicapped groups, few available resources have summarized this research in a way that allows the practitioner to easily judge the adequacy of particular measures for evaluating the goal attainment of specific handicapped groups.

A second problem that may be encountered in selecting tools to measure the achievement of group program objectives is that well-constructed tools for assessing some special populations do not exist. This is particularly true for low-incidence populations such as the deaf, blind, deaf-blind, and severely retarded. Major test publishers have little motivation to develop measures for use with these populations because the likelihood of their recouping development costs for such tools is very slight. Further, federal agencies and foundations have not generally supported such development efforts.

The lack of readily accessible technical data and tools specifically constructed for use with the handicapped will frequently make developing and measuring program objectives difficult. These problems can be addressed in several ways. Where promising measures can be identified, published and unpublished research literatures can be searched for technical adequacy studies. If no studies can be located, it may be possible to undertake a local investigation of the effectiveness of the measure. When no workable measure can be found, efforts might be best directed at developing new measures.

In any case in which the availability of quality measures is at all in doubt, multimethod strategies should be employed (Bennett, in press; Cronbach & Associates, 1980). In the absence of proven measures, the use of a number of unproven tools may provide significant information if results from the various measures all point, even if only weakly, to achievement of a particular outcome.

Finally, measures possessing levels of reliability that would normally be considered low for individual assessment should not automatically be discarded (Joint Committee, 1981). These measures can often be used for *group* assessment purposes because measurement error dramatically decreases as the size of the group being evaluated is increased (Stanley, 1971). This means that measures of unknown or relatively low precision can be used, given that moderate-size samples are available for outcome assessment.

For further discussion of considerations relevant to test selection and review see Chapter 3, Planning and Evaluating Instructional Services: Individualized Programs; Madaus, Airasian, Hambleton, Consalvo, and Orlandi (1982); and Hambleton and Eignor (1978).

Evaluating Group Program Alternatives

Evaluating alternatives for satisfying group program goals and objectives involves two elements. Initially, the resources that might be included as part of the program are identified and organized into configurations representing different group program alternatives. Second, the advantages and disadvantages of each alternative are considered, and a selection is made.

Several questions can be used to assist in identifying resources and alternatives. These are:

What human resources might be used to provide the group program (e.g., teachers, aides, peer tutors, consultants)?

What technological resources might be employed to enhance instructional goal attainment (e.g., instructional methods, materials, activities)?

What informational resources might be necessary to operate the program (e.g., written policies, procedures)?

What physical resources might be used for the program (e.g., buildings, rooms)?

What financial resources might be available to support program development and operation (e.g., local funds, private funds)?

In gathering information to answer these questions, various people may be interviewed and permanent products reviewed. For example, directors and supervisors of special education from other school districts with group programs focusing on similar goals and target groups might be contacted. Educational and psychological literature can be reviewed, particularly the data bases of the Educational Resources Information Center (ERIC) and *Psychological Abstracts,* to identify programs that might be viable alternatives. Technical assistance can be sought from state education agencies and from university resource specialists. Finally, special and regular educators can be asked to "brainstorm" and list as many alternatives as possible in terms of human, technological, informational, physical, and financial resources. Table 4–2 displays summary information about two alternatives for a group program designed to provide supplementary reading-skills instruction for learning-disabled elementary school pupils in mainstream classes.

After program alternatives have been outlined, the advantages and disadvantages of each competing option should be considered. Two procedures can be employed for doing this. The first procedure incorporates a rating scheme such as the one seen in Box 4–2. The procedure is meant to facilitate the comparison of program alternatives across a variety of critical dimensions including resource requirements and expected outcome results.

A second procedure for considering the advantages and disadvantages of program alternatives is the Nominal Group Technique (NGT), a program-planning

TABLE 4–2 Two Alternatives for a Supplementary-Reading-Skills Program

	PROGRAM ALTERNATIVES	
PROGRAM RESOURCES	RESOURCE ROOM	CROSS-AGE TUTORING
HUMAN	1 special education teacher (6 hours per day)	12 high-school tutors (1 hour per day per tutor)
	2 teacher's aides (6 hours per day per aide)	1 teacher supervisor (4 hours per day)
TECHNOLOGICAL	Small-group instruction	One-to-one instruction
	Daily performance feedback to pupils	Supervisor monitors and assists tutors to perform instructional activities
	Use of programmed reading materials	
INFORMATIONAL	Written procedures for monitoring pupil progress	Written procedures for functioning of cross-age tutors
	Written procedures for providing performance feedback to students	
PHYSICAL	1 classroom (6 hours per day)	3 small rooms or carrels in one room (4 hours per day)
FINANCIAL	Salary of 1 teacher for 180-day school year ($16,000)	Salary of supervisor for 4 hours' supervision per day over 180 days ($10,000)
	Salaries of 2 teacher's aides for 180-day school year ($11,000)	Material and supplies for 180-day school year ($500)
	Materials and supplies for 180-day school year ($500)	
	TOTAL COST = $27,500	TOTAL COST = $10,500

BOX 4-2 *QUESTIONS FOR RATING A GROUP PROGRAM ALTERNATIVE*

<u>Directions</u>: Review the group program alternative in accordance with the rating scheme and questions below. Place a numerical rating of 1, 2, or 3 for each question in the space provided to the left of each question. At the bottom of the page and on the reverse side, add any comments you care to make about the alternative being considered.

Title of Alternative: _____

Name of Rater/Position: _____

Date: _____

RATING SCHEME

Unlikely	Possibly	Likely
1	2	3

_____ 1. Can the staff for this group program alternative be made available?

_____ 2. Can this program be implemented without staff training?

_____ 3. Can the program be implemented by the anticipated starting date?

_____ 4. Will the instructional target group respond positively to the kind of instruction required by the alternative?

_____ 5. Can the necessary instructional materials be obtained?

_____ 6. Will the program be sanctioned by appropriate school officials?

_____ 7. Can the physical space needed for the alternative be made available?

_____ 8. Can the financial resources required by the alternative be made available?

_____ 9. Will this program alternative facilitate achievement of program goals?

<u>Comments About the Alternative</u>:

procedure initially developed for use in business and industrial settings (Delbecq, Van deVen, & Gustafson, 1975). In adapting the NGT for group program planning purposes, each member of the program-planning team ranks each alternative as to its probability of achieving program goals. Once this task has been accomplished, each member is asked to state the reasons for his or her rankings. After these reasons have been stated, the group seeks to obtain consensus on a program alternative. If consensus cannot be reached, the decision can be referred to a third party (e.g., director of curriculum).

Developing the Group Program Design

Developing the group program design is the process of putting the program into a form that can be implemented. This process can be facilitated through a set of development questions. Box 4-3 presents these questions along with the activities they imply for development of a high-school resource-room mathematics program. Information resulting from the development questions and activities should be included in a written program design, along with statements of program purpose, goals, and objectives developed earlier. The design should follow the generic structure presented in Box 1-2.

BOX 4-3 *DEVELOPMENT QUESTIONS AND ACTIVITIES FOR A HIGH-SCHOOL RESOURCE-ROOM MATHEMATICS PROGRAM*

Development Questions	Development Activities
1. What instructional staff must be hired or reassigned?	1. Three full-time certified resource teachers must be hired; two aides reassigned.
2. Are program consultants required?	2. One evaluation consultant from the research and evaluation unit must be assigned one day/month.
3. What staff training will be needed? When? By whom?	3. Teacher and aides must be trained in behavior management during summer by school psychologist.
4. What materials and equipment must be acquired?	4. Allocate one overhead projector for instructional purposes; order math-textbook series.
5. Who must be informed about the program?	5. Staff must receive orientation from principal; parents of target pupils must get briefing from staff.
6. What policies, procedures, or eligibility criteria need to be written?	6. Procedures for selecting pupils for resource placement must be established.
7. What sanctions are needed for the program to operate?	7. Eligibility criteria need to be approved by superintendent.
8. What budget needs to be established?	8. Develop line-item budget using district format.
9. What budget approval is needed?	9. Budget must be presented to superintendent for review and school board for approval at next meeting.
10. What physical facilities must be assigned?	10. Three classrooms at the high school must be allocated.
11. What renovations must occur prior to implementation?	11. New lighting fixtures must be installed.
12. Who will write the program design?	12. Supervisor of special education.

Evaluating the Group Program Design

Box 4-4 provides some sample questions that can be used to guide evaluation of a group program design. The questions follow from the five major design specifications discussed in previous chapters: clarity, comprehensiveness, internal consistency, compatibility, and theoretical soundness.

BOX 4–4 *SAMPLE QUESTIONS TO GUIDE EVALUATION OF A GROUP PROGRAM DESIGN*

Clarity and Comprehensiveness

1. Has an instructional target group been described?
2. Has a group program purpose been stated?
3. Have group goals and objectives been described?
4. Have program staff qualifications been specified?
5. Have instructional methods, materials, and activities been described?
6. Has a program budget been delineated?
7. Has an evaluation plan been included that details procedures for implementation and outcome evaluation?
8. Have physical facilities been indicated?

Internal Consistency and Compatibility

1. Do group goals and objectives reflect the program's purpose?
2. Are instructional methods, materials, and activities consistent with program goals?
3. Do methods, materials, and activities seem appropriate for the characteristics of the target group?
4. Is the program scheduled at times or in places that conflict with other district programs?
5. Are the resources required to support the program available?
6. Does the program respond to the group service delivery need originally identified?

Theoretical Soundness

1. Is the purpose of the group program generally consistent with improved functioning in school or society?
2. Do group program goals and objectives imply educationally valuable outcomes for the target group in question?
3. Are suggested methods and activities sound?

IMPLEMENTING GROUP PROGRAMS

Facilitating Group Program Implementation

In order for a group program to be implemented as designed, its purpose, activities, and implementation criteria must be made known to those special and regular educators who are to staff it. Also, personnel from other educational programs with which the group program needs to be coordinated must be so informed. Three elements of the DURABLE approach can be applied to facilitate group program implementation: discussing, understanding, and learning.

Discussing. School principals, classroom teachers, and related specialists (e.g., counselors) can be informed about program goals, objectives, and instructional activities at faculty or small-group meetings. Sometimes, as a result of discussing, it may become clear that the staff requires additional training on how to implement the program in the required manner. For example, it may be determined that staff members need assistance in planning instruction in the one-to-one mode. This information should be fed into the personnel development planning and evaluation process (see Chapter 6), with training activities undertaken as soon as possible.

Understanding.   Once the group program has been implemented, teachers can be offered individual and group consultation to help understand and respond to their concerns about the program. Individual meetings can be scheduled periodically to discuss specific problems encountered in carrying out the program (e.g., scheduling difficulties, delays in receipt of necessary instructional materials and equipment) and how these problems might be resolved. In addition, a support network can be established, in which teachers and administrators meet regularly to share concerns and ideas about how to improve group program delivery.

Learning.   Learning involves gathering information about potential program pitfalls. For example, discussions with teachers may suggest that they are not proficient in applying the instructional methods required by the program. If left uncorrected, this deficiency would impact negatively on the program. The information learned about this potential program pitfall should be utilized to provide a training experience to put the program back on course.

Evaluating Group Program Implementation

Evaluating the implementation of a group program serves to describe how a program was carried out. Implementation evaluation can identify problems in program operation needing immediate attention. Further, its results can be compared to the written design to assess the extent to which the program is functioning as planned and the reasons for any discrepancies between actual and intended operation.

Evaluation of group program implementation is best undertaken at regularly scheduled intervals during the time that the program is occurring. In this way, information can be gathered and reviewed on a regular basis throughout the program's life, rather than only once, at the program's conclusion. For example, the implementation of a year-long resource-room program can be evaluated during each half of the school year; a program of a shorter duration, such as a 20-week-drug-education effort, might be assessed on a quarterly basis.

Three questions can help focus evaluation of group program implementation. These questions are:

Did the appropriate pupils receive the group program?

Which activities, methods, and staff members were used to provide instruction?

What instructional content was emphasized?

Determining if the appropriate pupils received the program.   Several methods can be used to obtain information about whether the appropriate pupils received the group program. For example, a review of pupils' attendance records can be undertaken to determine how many members of the designated instructional target group actually attended the program. Low attendance rates would suggest that the need for the group program was not being met and that an outcome assessment of that program would likely be a wasted effort, since the program did not have a chance to affect the intended pupils.

A second method for evaluating whether the appropriate pupils received the program is to compare those receiving the program with another group enrolled in a program appropriate for more or less advanced students working in the same goal area(s). For example, those pupils receiving a resource-room reading program should be perceptibly different on some dimension relevant to program placement (e.g., reading skills, ability to work independently) from students in a reading program delivered in a more isolated environment, such as a special class. If criteria *ir*relevant to placement *are* entering into the process of assigning pupils to programs, then it may *not* be possible to differentiate students in different programs on relevant dimensions, such as reading. Further, it may be possible to distinguish those groups on dimensions that are clearly irrelevant to program placement, such as race or physical appearance. The implication of such a finding is that only part of the intended target group received the program; other appropriate pupils were excluded from the program on seemingly questionable bases.

The statistical method used to investigate differences in populations receiving the program is termed multiple discriminant analysis (Veldman, 1967). Applying multiple discriminant analysis will normally require the services of a professional evaluator or statistician. Examples of its use for determining differences among groups receiving different special education programs are found in Singer (1978) as well as in Hansche, Gottfried, and Hansche (1981).

Whenever implementation evaluation reveals a failure to reach part or all of the intended target group, additional investigation is implicated. Such an investigation should consist of reviewing placement criteria, interviewing the staff to determine how criteria were applied, and talking with pupils to determine why they failed to attend the program. Results of this investigation may suggest the need to modify or clarify placement criteria, revise program schedules to avoid conflicts with other pupil obligations, and so on.

Describing activities, methods, and staffing.   Interview, questionnaire, and observational methods can be used to gather information about what activities, methods, and staff were involved as part of a group program. Information obtained about these variables can be used to determine if the program is proceeding as planned, or to formulate hypotheses at the time of outcome assessment about which program processes and inputs are responsible for particular outcomes.

The primary guide for describing activities, methods, and staffing is the implementation section of the program design. An example of this section for a middle-school resource-room reading program is presented as Box 4-5. The information contained in the design can be used to guide observation of the program or to generate questionnaire or interview items for presentation to teachers and other program staff members. A set of sample questions generated from this program design is presented in Box 4-6.

BOX 4-5 *IMPLEMENTATION INFORMATION FROM A PROGRAM DESIGN FOR A MIDDLE-SCHOOL RESOURCE-ROOM READING PROGRAM*

Nature of Methods, Materials, and Activities

1. Small-group instruction in reading, using the school district's high-interest/low-level reading series.
2. Use of flash cards for acquisition and reinforcement of sight words.
3. Use of reading-workbook exercises.
4. Use of written and verbal feedback to pupils on their work.

Roles, Responsibilities, and Relationships

1. Written daily lesson plans prepared by the resource-room teacher.
2. Pupils provided an explanation of the day's objectives at the beginning of each work session.
3. Teacher's aide assists teacher by working with pupils during individualized work periods.
4. Teacher meets regularly with each pupil's special or regular class teacher.

Sequence and Timing of Instructional Activities

1. Class sessions run in hourly increments from 9:15 A.M. to 2:45 P.M., Monday through Friday.
2. Quiz given at the beginning of each Monday session.
3. Didactic presentation of material normally precedes individualized work session, so that tasks can be clarified and the stage set for individualized activities.

BOX 4-6 *SAMPLE QUESTIONS ABOUT PROVISION OF A GROUP PROGRAM*

Nature of Methods, Materials, and Activities

1. How frequently were high-interest/low-level materials used?
2. To what extent were flash cards used to foster sight word-recognition skills?
3. When were reading-workbook exercises employed?
4. How often were pupils given written or verbal feedback on their class performance?

Roles, Responsibilities, and Relationships

1. Were daily lesson plans prepared?
2. Were pupils given an explanation of each day's lesson?

3. How was the teacher's aide involved in providing assistance to pupils?
4. How frequently were meetings held between resource-staff members, special class, and regular class teachers?

Sequence and Timing of Instructional Activities

1. Did class sessions occur as scheduled?
2. Were quizzes routinely given at the beginning of each Monday class session?
3. How frequently did didactic sessions precede individualized activities?

As an adjunct to asking the types of questions presented in Box 4-6, teachers can be asked to keep a program-implementation log. Information about the methods and activities used in the program can be recorded in the log on a regular basis and compared to design specifications.

Determining instructional content emphasis. The focus of this final implementation evaluation concern is determining if the content emphasized in delivering the group program is consistent with the nature and relative importance of the goals set for the effort. Information relevant to this question can be gathered through product or document review. Teachers' lesson plans, for example, can be examined to determine the type of content planned for instruction and the amount of coverage assigned to different domains. This information can be supplemented through review of student classwork and homework samples.

The results of implementation evaluation often suggest discrepancies between a group program design and its operation. The identified discrepancies may exist in a variety of areas, including the student population served, activities, methods, staffing, instructional content, and other elements indicated in the program design. The existence of discrepancies between design and operation signals the need for looking into the reasons for deviation and for seriously considering whether the actual operation of the program is really less desirable than that originally planned. If not, the most responsible decision may be to permit the program to continue to operate as is while revising the design to bring it into line with operations.

ASSESSING THE OUTCOMES
OF GROUP PROGRAMS

Assessing the outcomes of group programs is regarded as a relatively undeveloped yet important aspect of special education program evaluation (Cronbach, 1982; Dunst, 1979; Kennedy, 1982). Positive outcome results can justify the continued existence of a group program, can serve as a basis for requesting resource support for program expansion, and can help identify the most worthwhile parts of the program. Negative outcome results may suggest a need for a variety of program-design or operational improvements as well as the possibility of termination.

With respect to assessing group program outcomes, we will discuss three relevant questions. These are:

To what extent have the goals of the group program been attained?
Was the group program responsible for program outcomes?
Was the group program cost-effective?

Evaluating Goal Attainment

An evaluation of the attainment of group program goals attempts to answer such questions as the following:

Have the goals of the resource-room mathematics program been achieved?
Have the goals of the special classroom social-skills program been met?
Have the goals of the regular classroom biology program been realized for mainstreamed pupils?

Several approaches can be employed to evaluate group program goal attainment. These are the (1) postprogram assessment, (2) preprogram-postprogram assessment, (3) time series, and (4) norm-referenced approaches.

Postprogram assessment. The postprogram-assessment approach involves measurement of goal attainment at one prespecified time, usually at the conclusion of the program (e.g., end of the school year), or at the end of a certain phase of the program's operation (e.g., completion of an instructional unit). For example, a middle-school resource-room mathematics program might have the following goal and associated objective:

To improve knowledge of mathematics concepts.
    By the end of the year, pupils will attain an average of 80 percent of their individualized program objectives in mathematics concepts.

In using the postprogram-assessment approach to evaluate attainment of this goal, information would be collected at the conclusion of the program about the extent to which each target-group pupil attained his or her individualized mathematics-concepts objectives. Those data then would be used to calculate the average level of goal attainment for the group. If the 80 percent criterion stated in the group objective was reached, the goal would be considered attained and the group program could be judged as having the desired effect. The size of the program effect—that is, the degree of goal attainment above or below the expected level of effect (80 percent)—could also be calculated.

The postprogram-assessment approach is relatively easy to employ, provided goals and objectives have been adequately described. The approach, however, results in data obtained only at one point in time during the course of a program. Therefore, judgments about amount of pupil progress toward goals and objectives relative to other points in time, such as prior to program implementation, cannot be made. The postprogram-assessment approach, although enabling a judgment about the degree of goal attainment, is weak in terms of determining if the program produced the results. Since data prior to program implementation are not available, it is possible that pupils may have acquired some of the information reflected in program goals before the program was even begun.

Preprogram-postprogram assessment. The preprogram-postprogram–assessment approach is an extension of postprogram assessment, in that goal attainment is measured at two points in time, prior to program implementation (baseline) and at the conclusion of the program or some phase of it. To illustrate preprogram-postprogram assessment, consider the following goal and objective taken from a group reading program delivered in a special classroom:

> To increase reading decoding ability.
>> By the end of the school year, pupils will increase their accuracy in decoding consonant-vowel-consonant (CVC) words by reading 40 words randomly selected from the reading curriculum's CVC list with an average accuracy rate of 75 percent.

In order to assess attainment of this goal, a baseline level of pupil functioning (that is, in terms of accuracy in pronouncing CVC words) would be established to ensure that the goal is appropriate; pupils should neither have already achieved the goal nor be so far from it as to make its attainment unrealistic. For example, using the small-group reading-program goal and objective just delineated, a preprogram, or baseline, level of pupil functioning might reveal that the average correct rate in reading 40 CVC words to be 15 percent. At the conclusion of the program, if the postprogram measurement revealed an average accuracy rate of 80 percent, the goal would be judged attained.

Assuming that group program goals and objectives are clearly stated, the preprogram-postprogram–assessment approach is relatively easy to employ; measurement of goal attainment occurs at only two points in time. The advantage of this approach to evaluating goal attainment over postprogram assessment is the addition of the baseline measurement, which allows an early judgment as to the appropriateness of the goal for the target population. The preprogram-postprogram-assessment approach does not, however, allow definitive conclusions to be drawn about the program's role in causing the observed effects.

Time-series approach. The time-series approach can be considered an extension of preprogram-postprogram assessment. In the time-series approach, measurement of goal attainment occurs at frequent intervals throughout the course of the program. Goal-attainment data can be collected a number of times prior to program implementation, while the program is in operation, at the program's conclusion, as well as at points following the program's termination. The time-series procedure, therefore, results in multi-wave data rather than data gathered only at one or two points in time. The approach is particularly useful for evaluating the attainment of group programs possessing goals that describe improvement in *rate* and *amount* of pupil achievement. Examples of such goals are:

> To improve the oral reading rate
> To increase the number of written social studies assignments completed.

Figure 4-1 illustrates data collected by means of the time-series approach for a resource-room reading program for mildly handicapped students. One of the program's goals and one of the objectives listed under that goal was:

> To improve reading speed.
> Over the course of the program, pupils will increase their reading rate to an average of 30 words read correctly per minute.

The data presented in Figure 4-1 suggest that pupils participating in the resource-room program began the reading intervention with a relatively low rate of reading speed but were able to approximate the minimal criterion set for goal attainment and maintain that level through the intervention's conclusion. Additional data collected after the program shifted focus to other reading goals indicate a drop in reading speed. Thus, time-series data suggested that the group program goal was achieved and that continued efforts may be needed to consolidate program effects.

The time-series approach provides more information about program-goal attainment than either postprogram or preprogram-postprogram assessment. The time-series approach allows more confidence to be placed in the appropriateness of goals as well as in goal attainment and maintenance after program termination. The approach also allows somewhat more confident inferences to be made about the degree to which the program caused observed effects. More detailed informa-

FIGURE 4-1   *DATA GATHERED THROUGH THE TIME-SERIES OUTCOME-EVALUATION APPROACH FOR A RESOURCE-ROOM READING PROGRAM*

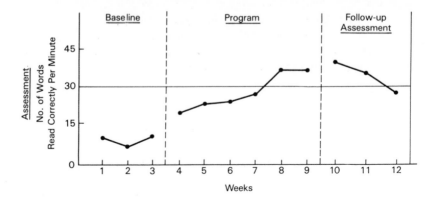

tion on the use of time-series data for evaluating educational programs can be found in Chapters 3 and 5, as well as in Kazdin (1976), Gottman and Glass (1978), and Murphy and Bryan (1980).

Norm-referenced approach. The norm-referenced approach involves comparing the progress made by an instructional target group toward program goals and objectives with a national or local norm group. The norm-referenced approach appears most suitable for evaluating the goal attainment of group programs for mildly handicapped pupils, such as regular-class mainstream and resource-room programs. The approach is applied to such programs since a defensible goal of programs for the mildly handicapped is to help these pupils become more like their normal peers in terms of knowledge, skill, and social development (Goodman & Bennett, 1982). Thus, comparison to a norm-group representative of the regular education population is reasonable.

In employing the norm-referenced approach, target pupils are pretested at the beginning of the group program and again at its conclusion. In this sense, the approach is similar to the preprogram-postprogram assessment, discussed earlier. The methods for determining goal attainment, however, are decidedly different.

To determine the degree of goal attainment in the norm-referenced approach, the actual *pre*test standard score of each target group pupil is used to generate an *expected post*test score. Next, mean pretest and expected posttest standard scores are calculated for the group. Following administration of the posttest, the actual posttest mean is calculated and the difference between it and the expected mean is tested for statistical significance by means of a *t*-test for correlated samples (Winer, 1971). Since the programs provided norm-group students presumably aspire to the general outcomes measured by the test—well-constructed standardized tests are designed to measure outcomes common to a great majority of school districts —the existence of a significant positive difference between actual and expected posttest score means suggests that the program did a better job attaining these goals than the typical program. The extent of this edge can be expressed in terms of the norm group through the *ES* (effect size) statistic, which is the significant difference divided by the standard deviation of the norm group (Sechrest & Yeaton, 1982).

Table 4-3 presents data for mainstreamed mildly handicapped pupils for whom a goal of a group program is to foster language-arts skills comparable to those of regular education students. Data presented in the table are scores from a test of language arts with content closely matching the goals of language-arts instruction for the district. The expected posttest scores, displayed in the middle column, are generated by looking up each pupil's pretest percentile, locating that percentile in the test manual's end-of-year norms table, and reading the corresponding standard-score value.

The norm-referenced approach is advantageous in that it is relatively easy to carry out; only one group is assessed, and testing can often be done in conjunction with the district's regular, standardized testing program. The approach, however, is subject to a number of caveats. First, the content of the measures used must, as

TABLE 4-3   Data Gathered through Norm-Referenced Outcome Evaluation
for a Mainstream Language-Arts Program

PUPIL	ACTUAL PRETEST STANDARD SCORE	EXPECTED POSTTEST STANDARD SCORE	ACTUAL POSTTEST STANDARD SCORE
1	50	60	80
2	40	42	46
3	45	51	47
4	60	63	69
5	45	48	59
Mean	48	52.8	60.2

Difference between expected and actual posttest standard score means = +7.4

in any evaluation of goal attainment, match the outcomes the group-instructional program is meant to achieve. Second, the tests employed must be administered during the time intervals stated in the test manual, usually in early fall, midyear, or late spring. Third, background differences between the instructional target group and norm group should be considered. If the two groups are dramatically different in terms of cognitive, cultural, linguistic, or other characteristics, then the approach may not be appropriate. Finally, the approach assumes steady growth in learning throughout the school year; empirical support for this linear growth assumption has, however, been lacking (see Linn, 1979, 1981). Because of these limitations, we suggest the norm-referenced approach be used in conjunction with one of the other approaches discussed, rather than as the only method for evaluating goal attainment.

Evaluating Cause-Effect Relations

Determining whether a group program was responsible for observed outcome results involves ruling out factors *other* than the program itself as likely causes of the effects. Two means that can be readily employed for evaluating cause-effect relations are the comparison-group and regression approaches. The time-series approach, which can also be used to evaluate cause-effect relations in group programs, is discussed in the cause-effect relations sections of Chapter 5, Planning and Evaluating Related Services, and Chapter 3, Planning and Evaluating Instructional Services: Individualized Programs.

Comparison-group approach.   The comparison-group approach involves comparing the performance of students in a special program with that of similar students in a less specialized program designed to achieve the same instructional goals. If the pupils receiving the special group program achieve a higher degree of goal attainment than the comparison pupils, the special group program would appear to have had an effect over and above that produced by the less specialized alternative. The degree of confidence that can be placed in the special program as cause of this "special" effect is determined by the extent to which plausible competing explanations for the effect can be ruled out.

Evaluating cause-effect relations using the comparison-group approach is facilitated if both the instructional target and comparison group are similar prior to program implementation in terms of learning outcomes and related learning characteristics. The version of the comparison-group approach that best assures the initial equivalence of groups is the randomized-group design (Campbell & Stanley, 1966; Cook & Campbell, 1979). This design requires the *random* assignment of pupils to two or more alternative group programs. Random assignment facilitates— though it does not guarantee—the placement of similar types of students in each program, so that differences in effects cannot be attributed to the characteristics of students placed in a particular program.

The randomized-group design is the method that will enable most of the competing explanations for program effectiveness to be ruled out. We are of the opinion, however, that use of the randomized-group design is not practical for evaluating group programs serving exceptional pupils; assignment of pupils to a group program should be based upon each pupil's individualized program, and not on the technical requirements of evaluation design. Since random assignment of exceptional pupils to alternative program conditions is not generally feasible, an intact group of pupils thought to be similar to the instructional target group on important characteristics (e.g., general ability level, specific skill levels) may be used.

Employing the comparison-group approach involves several activities. First, the group program and its target population are identified along with a comparison group and program thought to be appropriate. For example, two reading programs for learning-disabled children, one delivered in a resource room and one in a mainstream classroom, might be identified. Second, the pretest measures prescribed in group program goals and objectives are administered, under similar conditions, to all pupils in both programs. Measures that do not closely match program goals may also be administered, to assess characteristics relevant to educational performance (e.g., general ability) or areas in which related effects may occur (e.g., self-concept). If analysis of any of these data reveal significant differences among program groups prior to program implementation, appropriate adjustments in pretest scores can sometimes be made (more information on statistical methods used to make such adjustments can be found in Winer, 1971).

A third activity in carrying out the comparison-group approach is to evaluate the implementation of each program, so that important similarities and differences in program content can be detected and considered as possible explanations for differences in outcome results. Fourth, at the conclusion of the program's period of operation (e.g., the end of the school year), posttest data are collected for students enrolled in both programs. These data are then analyzed, using inferential statistics, to determine if differences in outcome results between the programs being compared are statistically reliable (that is, not due to chance). Table 4–4 sum-

TABLE 4-4 Some Inferential Statistical Procedures

DATA TYPE	PROCEDURE	PURPOSE	EXAMPLE OF QUESTION ASKED
Score	t-Test	To determine whether a significant difference exists between two groups	Did students in the resource-room program perform better on a test of achievement given at the end of the year than pupils who were in the same program last year?
	Analysis of variance	To determine whether a significant difference exists between pretest and posttest scores	Did a significant change take place over normally expected gains during the course of the year?
		To determine whether significant differences exist among 3 or more groups	Is student achievement affected by cutting instructional time from 60 minutes to 50 minutes or 40 minutes?
		To determine what factors account for outcomes of a particular program	Are gains in student achievement due primarily to teaching methods, to time allotted for instruction, or to the presence of aides in the classroom?
Ordered	Sign Test	To determine whether a significant change has taken place between two different testing times	Did students express a more positive attitude toward school after a special unit on value clarification?
	Rank Sums Test	To determine whether there is a significant difference between two groups	Are students ranked differently on aggressive behavior in school A as compared to school B?
	Kruskal-Wallis Test	To determine whether significant differences exist among 3 or more groups	Do the self-concepts of pupils with varying degrees of exposure to special education differ from one another?
	Friedman Test	To determine significant differences when 3 or more common measurements are made on the same persons over time	Do students' perceptions of their teacher change over the course of a semester?
Categorical	Chi-square (X^2)	To test deviation of obtained frequencies against some a priori set of expected frequencies	Did parents make favorable responses significantly more times than could be expected by chance?
		To determine whether there is a significant relationship between two variables	Are parents with children in school more likely to favor a tax increase election than persons not having children in school?

Source: Adapted with permission from the Evaluation Improvement Program. Program Evaluator's Guide. Sacramento: The California State Department of Education, 1979.

marizes some of the more common inferential statistical procedures used to test the significance of the differences observed between the groups being compared for cause-effect as well as other outcome-evaluation purposes. The table indicates the test statistic appropriate for different types of outcome data (that is, score, ordered, categorical), the different purposes for which the statistic may be used, and examples of the types of outcome-evaluation questions to which the test might be applied. The formulae for these statistics, the conditions under which they can be appropriately applied, and directions for their application can be found in most introductory statistics texts.

The sixth activity is undertaken when a determination has been made that the special group program has had an effect over and above the program to which it is being compared. This activity involves making a judgment about whether the added effects observed for the group program were caused by it or whether other nonprogram factors may have been responsible. The group of pupils receiving the alternative program is used in this activity as a reference point in ruling out such factors. The focus here is on determining (1) whether a nonprogram factor appears to be a plausible explanation for the effects, and (2) whether the factor was operating with equal intensity in the comparison group as well.

Cook and Campbell (1979) provide an extensive discussion of external factors that can be considered and possibly ruled out when the comparison-group approach is employed. Among the factors Cook and Campbell suggest as possible competing explanations for program effects are:

Historical Events—those unrelated events concurrent with the group program that contribute to pupils' achieving program goals (e.g., home or after-school tutoring received by target-group pupils and not by comparison-group pupils)

Pupil Maturation—growth of pupils in a goal area simply as a function of increasing age, and as a result, becoming more knowledgeable about instructional content (e.g., target-group pupils may have matured faster than those in comparison group)

Testing Sensitization—improved facility with posttest tasks because of familiarity with test items (e.g., target-group pupils may have been given practice lessons using test items)

Instrumentation—apparent effect owed to measuring program goals with pre- and posttest instruments whose scores do not share a common underlying scale

Statistical Regression—pseudo-effect due to the movement, or regression, of students on a posttest because of their assignment to the program on the basis of low pretest scores

Pupil Mortality—situation where an observed effect is due to differences in the outcome levels attained by those pupils who drop out of the program before outcome assessment occurs, as compared to those pupils who remain in the program

Group Selection—situation where outcome differences are due to achievement differences in the groups upon entering the programs

Program Imitation—situation where treatments delivered by two nominally different programs end up being the same, thereby obviating the value of the outcome comparison

Compensatory Rivalry—pseudo-effect owed to the comparison group's desire to outperform pupils receiving the group program

Resentful Demoralization—lowered achievement in the comparison group because of feelings of rejection at being excluded from the group program

The ability to make a confident judgment that a group program was responsible for program effects depends on the extent that the foregoing factors can be ruled out as the cause of the added effect observed for the special program.

Regression approach. The regression approach is best employed when part of a larger population of exceptional pupils can be assigned to a program on the basis of their performance on some set of relevant educational measures. For example, a population of mildly handicapped pupils might be placed in a resource-class program on the basis of low performance in mathematics and given a few hours' additional instruction per week. The effectiveness of this additional mathematics instruction can be evaluated using the regression approach.

The regression approach derives its name from a statistical procedure called *regression analysis* (Campbell & Stanley, 1966). The approach is implemented by first gathering pretest data from a population of students (e.g., all mildly handicapped high school students). The measures used should closely match the goals of the program for which pupils are being selected. Those who fall below a designated cutoff point on the measure or set of measures (i.e., those who have not achieved the goals the program is intended to foster) are assigned to the program. As the program is delivered, its implementation is evaluated, so that the exact nature of the treatment can be described. At the conclusion of the program period, pupils in both groups are posttested, using the same set of measures employed for pretesting. These data are used to construct regression equations for each group. From the equations, regression lines that summarize the relationship between pre- and posttest results within each group are drawn (see Figure 4-2). The regression line for the high-scoring group (that is, the group that did not receive the program) can be projected downward (see dotted line, Figure 4-2). This downward projection provides an estimate of how *low*-scoring students would have done on the pretest and posttest had they *not* received the program. A difference between the no-program expectation and the *actual* low-scorers' regression line can be taken as an indication that the program was responsible for the observed effect.

The regression approach has a number of limitations that should be recognized. One such limitation is that assignment of pupils to the target program and comparison group must be based primarily on pretest score, or on some composite such as a combination of teacher ratings and test scores. This requirement allows little latitude for professional judgment in making placement decisions and is often objectionable to the school's staff and to parents. Another important limitation is that the approach prohibits the transfer of pupils between target and comparison programs after initial placements have been made, a fact obviously not in the best interests of pupils needing program changes. Third, extrapolating the performance of the comparison group to estimate how the treatment group would have per-

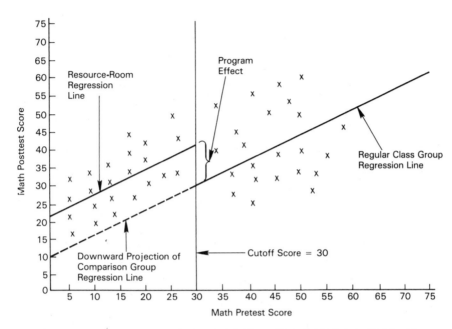

FIGURE 4-2 *DATA GATHERED THROUGH THE REGRESSION APPROACH
FOR A HIGH-SCHOOL RESOURCE-ROOM PROGRAM
AND REGULAR CLASS COMPARISON PROGRAM*

formed without the special program is dangerous because such extrapolations are often inaccurate. Finally, the regression approach involves complex statistical assumptions and procedures. It is best used with a relatively large comparison group (at least 30) and under the direction of an experienced statistician or professional evaluator.

Evaluating Cost-Effectiveness

Evaluating the cost-effectiveness of group programs has been a topic of concern for many special education administrators, advocates, and policy makers. The topic is important to advocates and policy makers who need evidence to justify continuing or increasing the levels of support devoted to special education. These levels, according to some, run as high as $20 billion per year (Hartman, 1981). Others, responsible for the actual delivery of services, are under constant pressure to spend available funds wisely by getting the greatest "bang for the buck."

In evaluating cost-effectiveness, a group program (e.g., a resource-room reading program) is compared to another group program (e.g., special-class reading program) with respect to costs and outcomes. A group program is said to be cost-effective if it results in a greater degree of goal attainment than the program to which it is compared and if the costs of the group program are less than, or the same as, the other option.

There has been considerable discussion about methods and procedures for evaluating cost-effectiveness of large-scale, federally funded educational and mental-health programs (see, for instance, Levin, 1975; Levine, 1981; Rossi & Freeman, 1982). This discussion has centered on the importance of evaluating cost-effectiveness by using experimental designs and methods that, unfortunately, cannot practically be used in most special education settings. There has been virtually no published information detailing practical, trustworthy methods for cost-effectiveness evaluation of special education programs. In fact, some professionals and groups—for example, the AERA Task Force on Special Education Program Evaluation (Kennedy, 1982)—have gone so far as to consider evaluating the cost-effectiveness of special education programs inappropriate and impractical in most school districts.

In this section, we discuss methods and procedures useful for (1) considering when it may be appropriate to undertake a cost-effectiveness evaluation; (2) analyzing costs; (3) conducting an evaluation; and (4) making judgments about cost-effectiveness. The methods and procedures discussed, although illustrated with respect to group programs, are also applicable to cost-effectiveness evaluation of related service and personnel development programs.

Considering the appropriateness of a cost-effectiveness evaluation.   A number of factors need to be considered in deciding whether it may be appropriate to undertake a cost-effectiveness evaluation. First, the group program and the alternative program to undergo cost-effectiveness evaluation must be reviewed, in particular the length of time each has been in existence. For example, if a special-class supplemental reading program utilizing teacher aides had been in existence for several years, while the alternative program utilizing microcomputers is newly designed and implemented, a cost-effectiveness evaluation at the end of the coming year might be premature. In this situation, although two programs have been identified, it may be best to delay the cost-effectiveness evaluation for a year, in order to give the new program an opportunity to work its "bugs" out and for any novelty associated with the program's innovative delivery system to subside.

If the two programs do appear comparable in terms of their stage of development, the goals and objectives of the programs should be reviewed. For cost-effectiveness evaluation to be meaningful, the goals and objectives of the group program and the alternative one should be similar; if they are not, then it should be presumed that the programs are working toward different outcomes and the evaluation of their cost-effectiveness vis-à-vis each other is inappropriate.

Assuming comparability of goals and objectives, the similarities of the instructional groups in terms of current need and related learning characteristics should be reviewed. This comparison can be made with extant educational data, such as data describing the number of goals already attained and standing on achievement tests, as well as other educational performance measures. If the groups are initially different in terms of instructional levels, the appropriateness of conducting a cost-effectiveness evaluation should be questioned, as any observed difference in outcome results might be solely due to initial group differences. Initial group differences can in some instances be statistically adjusted; such adjustments are, however, complex.

In addition to program history, goals and objectives, and initial pupil characteristics, there exists a fourth important element in determining the appropriateness of conducting a cost-effectiveness evaluation: program size. It is generally recommended that groups be equal in size and include at least 30 members (Kenny, 1975). Smaller group sizes will not provide adequate "statistical power" for detecting any differences that might exist in the outcomes produced by the programs (Reichardt, 1979).

Finally, a cost-effectiveness evaluation presumes comparison of programs that differ in terms of resources and activities. If group programs being compared are found to employ similar staff, methods, materials, settings, and schedules, conducting a cost-effectiveness evaluation may be inappropriate. Under these circumstances, programs would, in essence, be compared to themselves, rather than to alternative approaches to achieving the group outcomes of interest.

Analyzing program costs.   The next element in conducting a cost-effectiveness evaluation is to analyze program costs. Program costs can be determined—preferably with the help of a business administrator or other professional familiar with cost analysis—using a line-item accounting structure such as the simplified sample one presented in Box 4-7. As seen in Box 4-7, the various resource items that might comprise a program are listed. For each item, the dollar figures assigned can be categorized as developmental or operational costs. A developmental cost is incurred prior to program implementation and should reflect a one-time expenditure necessary for the program to begin operation. For example, group program developmental costs might include expenditures for initial staff training, program-development consultation, equipment purchases, and renovation of instructional facilities. An operational cost is incurred once the program has been implemented, and involves ongoing expenditures necessary for the program to operate. For example, staff salaries, fees for equipment rental, and supply expenditures all fall under the rubric of program operating costs.

The distinction between developmental and operational costs is particularly important in situations where a decision must be made to continue fewer group program alternatives than the number currently operating. In such a case, the important costs to consider in evaluating cost-effectiveness are those associated with continuing each program—that is, the operational costs. Developmental costs have already been "sunk," and unless differences exist between alternatives in the developmental amounts that can be recovered (e.g., through renting classroom space), these costs may be considered moot.

Developmental costs do become important in those cost-effectiveness situations where the evaluation question revolves around which of a number of group program alternatives to expand to other settings within the school or district (e.g., extending a microcomputer-based supplemental reading program to all resource

BOX 4-7 *SAMPLE FORMAT FOR ANALYZING A PROGRAM'S RESOURCE COSTS*

Title of Program: _____

Date of Analysis: _____

Cost Evaluators: _____

RESOURCE ITEM	COSTS	
I. Personnel	Developmental	Operational

A. Administrative
    1. Director
    2. Supervisor
    3. Secretarial
    4. Other		

B. Staff
    1. Teachers
    2. Teacher-Aides
    3. Consultants
    4. Other		

II. Facilities
  A. Buildings (e.g., Rental)
  B. Rooms (e.g., Renovation)
  C. Maintenance
  D. Other		

III. Materials
  A. Books
  B. Supplies
  C. Equipment
  D. Desks
  E. Other		

IV. Transportation
  A. Bus Driver Salaries
  B. Bus Maintenance		

V. Information
  A. Public Relations
  B. Data Processing
  C. Other		

classes). In this case, the developmental cost of expanding each alternative is important and should be considered along with operational costs in conducting the cost-effectiveness evaluation.

Conducting a cost-effectiveness evaluation. Properly conducting a cost-effectiveness evaluation requires information regarding the implementation and goal attainment of the programs being compared. Evaluating program implementation documents what was actually provided to pupils in each group and allows differences among the alternatives to be verified. Evaluating the goal attainment of the programs being compared gives an indication of which program was best at achieving the common outcomes of interest, or which had the greater effect.

For outcome-evaluation purposes, the comparison-group approach, described earlier in the discussion of evaluating cause-effect relations, should be used. As stated, this approach allows for both comparing effects across programs and for a moderate degree of confidence in inferring that differences in observed effects are the result of the program alternatives themselves. To strengthen this inference, attempts should be made to rule out as many external reasons as possible. Thus, conclusions about effectiveness should be viewed as tentative statements that "make a case" for one group program alternative as the cause of greater goal attainment—or greater effects—than others.

Judging cost-effectiveness. Determining whether a particular group program is cost-effective involves considering the costs and effects of that program relative to other programs. Table 4-5 presents a matrix meant to facilitate the comparison of two program alternatives. The horizontal dimension of the matrix, Program Cost, denotes the relative cost of each group program alternative. The vertical dimension of the matrix, Program Effectiveness, denotes the goal attainment of each in relation to the others. The nine matrix cells represent the situations that could arise as a result of evaluating the cost-effectiveness of two alternatives. Cells 2, 3, and 6 depict instances where the cost of the target program (Program A)

TABLE 4-5   Matrix for Comparing the Cost-Effectiveness of Two Programs[a]

		PROGRAM COST		
		A MORE COSTLY THAN *B*	*A* & *B* SAME IN COST	*A* LESS COSTLY THAN *B*
PROGRAM EFFECTIVENESS	*A* more effective than *B*	Seek additional information 1	Select *A* 2	Select *A* 3
	A as effective as *B*	Select *B* 4	Seek additional information 5	Select *A* 6
	A less effective than *B*	Select *B* 7	Select *B* 8	Seek additional information 9

Program *A*: Target Program
Program *B*: Comparison Program

[a]Adapted from <u>Development and test of a cost-effectiveness methodology for CMHCs</u> (Vol. 1). Washington, D.C.: National Institute of Mental Health, 1975.

is either the same as or less than the program to which it is being compared (Program B) and where the target program has been found more effective than or as effective as the alternative. In these situations, the target program is the more cost-effective and, all other things being equal, should be selected for continuation or expansion over the alternative. Conversely, cells 4, 7, and 8 represent situations where the alternative program appears more cost-effective and, in this respect, the administratively defensible choice.

Program-selection decisions, of course, should be based on information in addition to cost-effectiveness. This additional information may include (1) consumer reactions, (2) positive or negative related program effects, and (3) relevant context data, such as external sources of funding or political support for a particular program. For example, a microcomputer-based supplemental reading program may prove to be more cost-effective than an alternative utilizing paraprofessional aides. However, the microcomputer program may not be viable because parents perceive it as dehumanizing, jobs will be eliminated, and the federal support commanded by the alternative will be lost. Consumer reaction, related effects, and context information will also be important in making program-selection decisions in those cases where the cost-effectiveness of one program over competing alternatives cannot be readily established (cells 1, 5, and 9). In these cases, this information will normally provide the only rational basis upon which to decide to select a group program alternative.

Communicating Evaluation Results

The evaluation results of group programs are often communicated informally, through verbal exchange or brief summary reports. Informal communication is most appropriate when planning and evaluation activities focus upon developing and improving group programs. In this formative context, those directly involved in program operation—coordinators, supervisors, evaluators, and teachers—work together on a continuous basis to plan, implement, evaluate, and enhance the program. Numerous opportunities exist for these professionals to exchange and act upon evaluation information. Although some documentation of evaluation results is always advised, detailed written reports for communicating information are usually unnecessary.

Occasions do exist, however, when formal procedures are needed for communicating evaluation results. For example, thorough documentation is necessary when those not directly involved with a program—board members, state agency officials—need information about overall program effectiveness to make decisions about expansion or termination. Because incorrect decisions are both difficult to reverse and serious in terms of potential consequences, the procedures and results of evaluation must be clearly documented, so that they can be thoroughly reviewed and critiqued by all interested parties.

Although decisions of this nature are made about a wide variety of special programs, the attention of decision makers is most frequently directed toward group programs. This focus is not surprising, as such programs constitute the bulk of special education activity in most school districts. Group programs incur the greatest cost (Hartman, 1981) and involve the largest number of staff members and pupils of all special education services.

Evaluation results are typically communicated to program decision makers through a brief written report. Because decision makers have many matters competing for their time, an evaluation report must be compelling if it is to succeed in capturing the decision makers' attention. Evaluation reports should be loaded with attractive graphics designed to communicate critical points, short (less than 10 pages), easy to read, and lack technical jargon (Maher & Illback, 1982; Patton, 1978).

Evaluation reports can begin with a one-page abstract naming the program and stating the evaluation questions, major results, and recommendations for program change. The body of the report should commence with a short section on identifying information followed by a section delineating the outcome-evaluation questions and the information gathered in response to each question. Next, a short discussion of results should be presented. Finally, the body should be concluded with recommendations for program change. Implementation-evaluation results as well as methods and procedures used in conducting the evaluation can be included in a report appendix. Box 4-8 provides a format for structuring the formal program evaluation report. Because decision makers may have questions about or

BOX 4-8 *FORMAT FOR COMMUNICATING EVALUATION RESULTS ABOUT GROUP PROGRAMS*

Abstract

    A. Program name
    B. Evaluation questions
    C. Major results
    D. Recommendations for program change

I. Identifying Information

    A. Title of program (e.g., Resource-Room Math Program, Home Instruction Program)
    B. Purpose and goals of program (e.g., program purpose statement taken from the written program design)
    C. Duration of program (e.g., September 1984-June 1985)
    D. Organizational context (e.g., grade-level structure, student population, size of school staff)

II. Outcome-Evaluation Questions and Results

    A. Goal attainment (e.g., "Were goals of the Speech Therapy Program attained?")
    B. Related effects (e.g., "Did the Regular Class Reading Program impact on the pupils in any negative ways?")
    C. Consumer reaction (e.g., "Were pupils who received individual instruction satisfied with it?")
    D. Cause-effect relations (e.g., "To what extent was the Special Class Social Skills Program responsible for improvement in pupils' social functioning?")
    E. Cost-effectiveness (e.g., "Is the Resource Room Math Program more cost-effective than the Cross-Age Tutoring Program?)

III. Discussion of Results

    A. Opinions about the results (e.g., educational significance of degree of goal attainment)
    B. Observations about the program provided (e.g., "It was not implemented as planned.")
    C. Conclusions about program effectiveness (e.g., "Program seemed to be cause of program outcomes.")

IV. Recommendations for Changing the Program

    A. Changes in staffing patterns
    B. Changes in activities and methods
    C. Changes in program evaluation criteria
    D. Changes in funding sources
    E. Changes in physical facilities or site locations
    F. Changes in purpose, goals, and objectives

Appendices

I. Implementation Information

    A. Target population (information about pupil or pupils who have received the program—e.g., data on instructional needs an instructional program was designed to address)
    B. Number of sites and location of each program (e.g., 3 Special Class Language Arts Programs in Smith Elementary School)
    C. Implementation evaluation (e.g., data describing the frequency of program sessions held)
    D. Costs (information about developmental and operational costs of the program)

II. Outcome-Evaluation Methods and Procedures

    A. Goal attainment (e.g., pre-post program assessment approach)
    B. Related effects (e.g., comparison-group approach)
    C. Consumer reaction (e.g., post-program assessment)
    D. Cause-effect relations (e.g., time-series approach)
    E. Cost-effectiveness (e.g., comparison-group approach)

misinterpret information in the evaluation report, it is generally a good idea to schedule a meeting soon after the report is delivered to summarize and discuss results. More detailed information on reporting results can be found in Posavac and Carey (1980), Patton (1978), and in the *Standards for Evaluations of Educational Programs, Projects, and Materials* (Joint Committee, 1981).

SUMMARY

Group programs enhance the efficiency of the special services system. The delivery of group programs, however, is complex. Such programs are built on instructional recommendations contained in the IPs of exceptional pupils. Clarifying the extent to which a group service delivery problem exists includes identifying pupils recommended for group programs, delineating the types of group programs to be provided, and organizing the pupils into meaningful instructional target groups.

In designing group programs, it is important that group goals and objectives reflect the individualized goals and objectives of target-group pupils. Delineating group program goals and objectives helps suggest the emphases for instructional activities and the focuses for outcome evaluation.

Evaluating cause-effect relations and evaluating cost-effectiveness of group programs are both important, yet relatively undeveloped, areas of special education program evaluation. In evaluating cause-effect relations, it is essential that attention be directed at ruling out nonprogram factors that may have been responsible for observed outcomes. The comparison-group, time-series, and regression approaches are outcome-assessment strategies that can be employed in helping to determine whether various group programs produced outcome results.

In evaluating cost-effectiveness, it is essential that propriety be considered. We have suggested that cost-effectiveness evaluation is feasible only if the programs being compared have been in existence for similar amounts of time, have initially equivalent groups, have similar goals and objectives, and have had their costs appropriately analyzed. Finally, it must be clear that the programs being compared differ along important resource dimensions, such as the nature of the staff or instructional methods employed.

The results of group program evaluation are frequently communicated through informal means to allow program staff members to promptly utilize that information for program-improvement purposes. For some situations—such as exchanging information with board members—more formal communication mechanisms are required. In these instances, brief, visually attractive, written reports capable of competing with the numerous events vying for the decision makers' attention are recommended.

5

PLANNING AND EVALUATING
RELATED SERVICES

Related services are provided those exceptional pupils needing supplemental help in order to benefit from special education. Examples of related service programs typically offered through the special services system include counseling, speech therapy, physical therapy, and transportation. These programs are delivered to individual pupils as well as to small groups by specialists such as school psychologists, speech therapists, physical therapists, and bus drivers. Community-agency professionals, such as social workers and public health nurses, also provide related services to exceptional pupils and their families.

Providing related services requires coordination with programs delivered by both the district and community agencies. Related services need to be coordinated with the variety of instructional programs given pupils by the school district as well as with the range of mental health, medical, and family services offered outside of it. In this chapter, we discuss methods and procedures for planning and evaluating related service programs that can enable exceptional pupils to benefit more fully from special education.

OVERVIEW OF RELATED SERVICES

Need for Related Services
in Special Education

Many handicapped children have basic functional disorders—such as in communication, movement, socialization—that impede full participation in special education programs. Children with hearing disorders, for example, typically need to be fitted with hearing aids before they can fully partake of classroom activities. Those with behavior disorders may be the target of counseling designed to help develop the self-control necessary for classroom functioning.

The need to offer interventions to help handicapped children benefit from special education is recognized in both education law and professional practice. PL 94-142, and the state regulations derived from it, require the delivery of support services for this purpose (U.S. Office of Education, 1977b). Concern commonly expressed among professionals for ministering to the needs of the "total child" (Sarason & Doris, 1979) exemplifies the professional support given the related service concept.

Nature and Scope of Related Services

Related services are typically provided only to those pupils whose IPs specify the need for additional support. Designed to supplement special instruction, these services are generally provided on a one-to-one or small-group basis. Yet, regardless of how they are offered, related service programs constitute *group* service delivery efforts. In addition to achieving the related service goals contained in any particular child's IP, each related service program attempts to attain general goals of its own for the entire group of pupils it serves.

Though controversy exists over exactly which services should be classified as related, the following types of programs can be included under this rubric:

Audiology: offered by an audiologist to evaluate and ameliorate hearing impairments

Counseling: delivered by a school counselor, psychologist, social worker, or nurse to assist pupils in social and emotional development

Speech and language therapy: delivered by a speech pathologist to help pupils improve speech and/or language functioning

Physical therapy: provided by a physical therapist to help students develop gross-motor skills

Occupational therapy: delivered by an occupational therapist to enhance fine-motor development

Behavior management: provided by a counselor or psychologist in cooperation with a classroom teacher to improve student behavior

Transportation: designed to carry pupils to, between, and from educational programs

In addition to these programs, others—such as medical diagnosis, health screening, and parent counseling—are sometimes considered related services.

Difficulties in Providing
Related Services

By far, the most frequent difficulties cited by service delivery and policy-making personnel have to do with intra- and interagency coordination (Magrab & Schmidt, 1981). *Intra*agency coordination centers upon assuring that related service programs mesh with other programs in the school district. *Inter*agency coordination involves orchestration of related services delivered by the school with those offered by outside agencies, such as community mental-health centers, rehabilitation facilities, and hospitals.

In the area of intraagency coordination, one common difficulty is that of clarifying the role of related services within the special education system. If teachers and administrators do not understand the purposes, nature, scope, and anticipated outcomes of related service programs, it is unlikely that their actions will be consistent with the functioning of those programs.

A second problem area for intraagency coordination—particularly at the secondary-school level—is resistance among teachers and pupils to related service programs. Many teachers are understandably reluctant to release pupils from class when the related service program conflicts with the coverage of important instructional content. Pupils are likewise hesitant to miss critical material as well as being concerned about the stigma that some related service programs may carry.

In addition to intraagency problems, pitfalls in orchestrating the delivery of related services between and among community agencies have often been encountered. These include delivering redundant services, disagreeing over whose responsibility it is to provide or pay for specific services, and offering services to pupils in a haphazard, ill-planned manner.

CLARIFYING RELATED SERVICE
DELIVERY PROBLEMS

Our approach to planning and evaluating related service programs emphasizes aspects of the goal-based, systems-analysis, and transactional models (see Table 1-1). The goal-based model helps focus attention on the fact that related service programs exist to attain particular outcomes. Elements borrowed from the systems-analysis model highlight the importance of recognizing the relationships between related service programs and the special services, regular education, and community services delivery systems. Finally, the transactional model emphasizes the necessity of learning how consumers experience and react to related service programs.

Assessing Service Delivery Needs

Assessing related service delivery needs can be undertaken at the level of both the individual pupil and the school, or organization. The related service delivery needs of an individual pupil should be determined as part of individualized program problem clarification. Areas of weakness that prevent the student from deriving benefit from education should be identified for planning purposes in conjunction with the process described in Chapter 3.

At the organizational level, needs assessment of related services involves obtaining information about which exceptional pupils require related services and the types of programs recommended for them. This information can be obtained through a procedure similar to that discussed in Chapter 4 for assessing group service delivery needs. For related services, this procedure requires review of the individualized programs of exceptional pupils in the school district to determine the following:

Administrative classification of the pupil (e.g., orthopedically handicapped)

Goal areas where related service programs have been recommended (e.g., manual dexterity)

Specific types of objectives for each goal area (e.g., ability to use scissors in cutting construction paper)

Types of related service programs recommended (e.g., individual occupational therapy)

Frequency, duration, and location of the recommended programs (e.g., twice a week, for entire school year, in Jones Elementary School)

Related service providers (e.g., district occupational therapist)

Table 5-1 illustrates a matrix that can be used for summarizing information about the need for related services. The vertical dimension of the matrix delineates

TABLE 5-1   Related Service Summary Matrix

	GOAL AREAS[a]		
RELATED SERVICE	PHYSICAL	AFFECTIVE	SOCIAL
Counseling	—	15	18
Speech and language therapy	2	3	9
Physical therapy	10	—	4
Occupational therapy	6	1	3
Audiology	9	—	—
Behavior management	—	18	20
Transportation	42	—	—

[a]Pupils may be counted in more than one cell, depending upon recommendations for the kinds of related services needed by the pupil.

types of related services, while the horizontal axis lists the goal areas for the various programs. The intersection of these two matrix dimensions consists of 21 cells, into which data about the numbers of pupils requiring related service programming can be placed. As Table 5-1 shows, 42 pupils in the school district require transportation, 33 need counseling, and 38 are to be the recipients of some form of a behavior-management program. This kind of matrix provides data for clarifying the extent of the related service problem to be addressed by subsequent planning and evaluation tasks.

Assessing the Service Delivery Context

Assessing the organizational context in which related service needs exist entails gathering information about school and community readiness to offer such support programs. Two A VICTORY factors particularly important to related service programs are ability and idea.

Ability. Assessing the ability of the special services system to commit resources to related service delivery can suggest those areas that will need to be addressed if programs are to be successfully designed and implemented. Likewise, evaluating the ability of external agencies (e.g., a community mental-health center) to address district related service needs can indicate areas requiring interagency coordination.

The following questions can be used to guide assessment of this factor:

What kinds of related service programs are currently being provided exceptional pupils by the special services system (e.g., counseling, physical therapy)?

What types of pupils are receiving the programs (e.g., secondary-school pupils classified as emotionally disturbed, elementary-school orthopedically handicapped students)?

How many pupils are receiving the programs?

What professionals are providing the programs (e.g., school psychologist, physical therapist)?

What kinds of related service programs are being provided exceptional pupils by other community agencies (e.g., family counseling, occupational therapy)?

What pupils are receiving those programs (e.g., pupils with emotional handicaps)?

Who is providing those programs, and where are they being delivered (e.g., social workers, at the community mental-health center)?

For the upcoming school year, what new school and community resources may be available for related service provision (e.g., occupational therapy offered through the community mental-health center)?

Information to answer the foregoing questions can be readily obtained by reviewing available related service program design documents and by interviewing school administrators, board of education officials, and officials of community agencies.

Idea. The concern underlying assessment of this factor is to learn if the school staff and parents have an accurate perception of the nature of related service programs—that is, "Do they have the right idea?" Results from this assessment may signal a need to communicate accurate information about related services through meetings or by actually involving the staff in related service program design, implementation, and outcome assessment.

Obtaining contextual information about the idea can be directed by such questions as:

What programs do staff members consider related services to include?
What does the staff consider the goals and objectives of these programs to be?

Answers to these questions can be obtained by contacting representative parents and school staff members using interviews or questionnaires.

Describing the Related Service Delivery Problem

The related service problem description should integrate both needs-assessment and context-assessment information. We have found it useful to describe the related service problem in terms of the following types of information:

Number of pupils needing related services
Specific types and number of related service programs to be provided
Availability of school personnel to deliver needed programs
Types of community-based services available to pupils
Number of pupils receiving related services from external agencies
Discrepancies between number of pupils who need related services and the ability of the special services system to provide them
History of the system in providing related services (e.g., problems encountered, services not provided)
Ideas staff members hold about related services

This information can be described in a problem-clarification summary statement such as those discussed in previous chapters.

DESIGNING RELATED SERVICE PROGRAMS

Describing Related Service Program Purpose, Goals, and Objectives

The design of a related service program, like that of any other special education effort, should be based on a brief general statement of purpose. This statement describes the rationale, scope, and expected results of the program. A statement of purpose for a program in speech and language therapy might be:

The elementary-level speech and language program is meant to help pupils with communication disorders and speech impairments acquire the communications skills necessary to adequately benefit from special education. The program will be staffed by school-district and local hospital therapists holding certificates of clinical competence. The program will offer interventions in both one-to-one and small-group modes.

Following development of the statement of purpose, goals for the related service program should be specified. These goals should be derived from the IPs of pupils designated to receive related services and should reflect those goals most frequently found in pupil IPs. Box 5-1 lists a set of program goals for secondary-school counseling and elementary-school speech therapy.

BOX 5-1 *GOALS FOR PROGRAMS IN COUNSELING AND SPEECH AND LANGUAGE THERAPY*

Counseling

1.   To develop knowledge of acceptable norms for guiding school behavior
2.   To develop skill in interacting positively with peers and teachers
3.   To develop behavioral self-control

Speech and Language Therapy

1.   To develop speech fluency
2.   To develop the ability to use proper sentence structure
3.   To develop an understanding of word and sentence meaning
4.   To develop the ability to use language for communication purposes

Once related service program goals have been described, program objectives are identified. Such objectives can either describe an average number of pupil-individualized objectives to be attained or performance in an area common to all students. For example, a speech-fluency objective might be written to state: "By the end of the school year, pupils enrolled in the program will achieve an average of 80 percent or more of their individualized speech-fluency objectives." As an alternative, the objective might specify that pupils achieve some average level on a speech-fluency task. The choice of which type of objectives format to use should be based on the extent to which pupils share the same individualized objectives and are working under similar conditions to achieve similar proficiencies.

Objectives explicating related service program goals should describe observable, measurable behaviors; be logically related to the goals; and be reasonable expectations of achievement. Moreover, the general caveats stated in Chapter 3 regarding standard setting for individualized goals apply here also: one should have a defensible basis upon which to set criteria for achieving objectives.

Evaluating Related Service
Program Alternatives

The evaluation of related service program alternatives is primarily a task of organizing program resources into configurations representing different program options. The fit of each option with the existing organizational context and the likelihood that each one will result in goal attainment can then be assessed and the most appropriate alternative chosen. The procedures used for evaluating group program alternatives, discussed in Chapter 4, can be employed as a guide to carrying out the task.

Because most school districts do not have the resources necessary to support the full range of related service programs required by handicapped students, it will often be beneficial to explore resource-sharing arrangements with community agencies as possible program options. Resources can be shared among the school district and such agencies as hospitals and mental-health centers in a number of ways. Box 5-2 presents six alternative shared-resource configurations that can be considered in developing related service program options.

BOX 5-2 *SIX ALTERNATIVE WAYS OF SHARING INTERAGENCY RESOURCES*

1. First dollar agreements: When a handicapped child or family is eligible for certain services from the public school and one or more agencies, a promise is made regarding which organization pays first. For example, when a Medicaid-eligible, handicapped child needs physical therapy, Medicaid agrees to pay. Education only pays for physical therapy when a child is not eligible for Medicaid.

2. Complementary dollar agreements: When a handicapped child or family is eligible for certain services from the public school and one or more other agencies, a commitment is made for each organization to pay for certain services. For example, when a Medicaid-eligible, handicapped child needs speech therapy and reconstructive dental surgery, the public school pays for the speech therapy and Medicaid pays for the surgery.

3. Complementary personnel/dollar agreements: When a handicapped child or family is eligible for certain services from the public school and one or more agencies, one organization commits personnel to directly serve the child while the other reserves sufficient funds to pay for other services. For example, when a Medicaid-eligible, handicapped child needs speech therapy and reconstructive dental surgery, the public school directly provides (through a school employee) the speech therapy and Medicaid pays for the surgery.

4. Shared-personnel agreements: When children are screened before entering public school, a commitment is made that allows public health nurses and school nurses to work together in administering parts of the screening program. For example, family health histories are taken by both public health and school nurses during a preschool screening program.

5. Shared facility agreements: When children are screened before entering public school, a commitment is made to use a community hospital facility for carrying out all or part of the program. For example, when preschool screening is conducted for a certain neighborhood, the local hospital is used as the testing site.

Table 5-2 outlines three alternatives for a middle-school counseling program. The program's purpose is to improve the social and emotional adjustment of middle school pupils whose individualized programs recommend counseling. From Table 5-2, it can be seen that the three counseling alternatives differ on a number of resource dimensions. For example, one alternative employs school counselors; the second, twelfth-grade students as cross-age counselors; and the last, staff from the local community mental health center (CMHC).

An analysis of these different resource configurations should attempt to discern which fits best with the organizational context as well as which is most likely to achieve program goals. For example, the extent to which the district has the ability to staff the program with counselors or share the costs of using CMHC staff should be asked of the first and third options, respectively (see Table 5-2). Also questioned should be the fit of parent and staff values as these relate to using students to deliver counseling services to others. Though deliberation of this sort will not always point out the single option that clearly stands above the rest, considering resource requirements, context, and program potential provides a rational basis for selecting the related service program.

Developing the Related Service Program Design

Developing the related service program design involves activities similar to those discussed in Chapter 4. However, because one of the main problems encountered in related service delivery has been coordination, particular care should be taken to assure that the program, as developed, fits with other programs within the district and community. To facilitate coordination, particular attention should be paid to the following:

Scheduling pupils for the related service program so as to avoid removing them from instructional programs for either excessive amounts of time or periods when critical content is covered

Scheduling rooms and other facilities to avoid conflicts with other programs

Arranging transportation of pupils to the related service program site

Delineating clear and concise intra- and/or interagency policies and procedures

Obtaining approval for the program from key intra- and interagency administrators

TABLE 5-2 Three Alternative Ways of Designing a Group-Counseling Program for Exceptional Middle-School Pupils

RESOURCE DIMENSION	TITLE OF PROGRAM		
	PROFESSIONAL SCHOOL COUNSELING	CROSS-AGE COUNSELING	MENTAL-HEALTH CENTER COUNSELING
Human resources	4 certified school counselors employed by the school district	10 twelfth-grade students trained as cross-age group counselors (Maher & Barbrack, 1982)	3 social workers from an outreach unit of the local community mental-health center
Technological resources	Weekly group counseling that emphasizes social problem-solving techniques Pupil goal-attainment scaling follow-up guides Counselor activity logs	Weekly group counseling that employs a 5-step problem-solving approach Pupil contracts for behavior change Supervisor evaluation of program implementation	Weekly individual counseling that utilizes cognitive-behavioral procedures Pupil diaries
Informational resources	No new policies or procedures need to be developed	Procedures for selecting cross-age tutors Policy for providing released time to cross-age counselors	Policies and procedures for sharing inter-agency resources need to be developed
Physical resources	2 small classrooms are needed for 4 class periods, 3 times per week, in middle school	4 classrooms are needed for 2 periods, 2 times per week, in middle school	No rooms in middle school are needed. Counseling sessions to be held in the office of each social worker
Financial resources	$8000 for time of 4 counselors on the project	$400 for training of counselors; $2000 for supervisor cost	$600 for administrative time spent on developing interagency agreements; $6000 reimbursement for mental-health staff costs

The related service design should be placed in written form once all elements of the program have been decided upon. The written design should include a statement of program purpose as well as implementation and outcome sections generally consistent with the generic structure presented in Box 1-2.

Evaluating the Related Service
Program Design

The task of evaluating the related service design is similar to that of evaluating any special education program design. Evaluation includes review of the design document for clarity, comprehensiveness, internal consistency, compatibility, and theoretical soundness. Because so much difficulty has been reported in coordinating services among agencies, we suggest particular attention be given to considerations of clarity, comprehensiveness, and compatibility. Those aspects of the design describing interagency resource arrangements should, in particular, be clearly and fully spelled out; the staff, facilities, equipment, and financial responsibilities of all parties should be defined; and the time period or number of cases over which the agreement will be in effect specified. The compatibility of services offered by each agency should also be carefully checked to assure that efforts fit with district related service needs. Any shortcomings discovered should be corrected before the program begins to operate.

IMPLEMENTING RELATED
SERVICE PROGRAMS

Facilitating Related Service
Program Implementation

Carrying out related service programs in the schools usually involves special education, regular education, and related service staff. We have found several elements of the DURABLE approach of particular importance in facilitating related service program implementation. These elements are discussing, understanding, rewarding, and adapting.

Discussing. Classroom teachers whose pupils are expected to receive related services should be presented with an overview of the nature, scope, and anticipated outcomes of the program, to make sure they understand why pupils are being taken out of class and how they can work to complement the efforts of the related service program. Secondary-school pupils can also be given an orientation to the services they will receive, as can their parents. The value of such orientations has been supported by research that suggests a link between satisfaction with the program and orientation to it (Maher, in press-b).

Understanding. In concert with discussion, understanding should center upon elucidating the concerns of the program staff and consumers with respect to the related service program. Many teachers, for example, are justifiably concerned about students being scheduled for related services during times when important material is being covered in class. High-school students frequently express a hesitancy to attend some related service programs (e.g., speech therapy) because they fear derision from their peers. In such instances, it is important to acknowledge these concerns and to work with students and staff—by rewarding and adapting—to ensure that the program proceeds smoothly.

Rewarding. For a related service program to succeed, it is imperative that the cooperation of the classroom teaching staff be maintained. Thus, encouraging teachers to follow through on their assigned responsibilities—such as releasing pupils from class to attend speech therapy sessions—facilitates program implementation. Teachers can be reinforced for carrying out their responsibilities through verbal praise, notes to them, or letters to their supervisors. More detailed information about the use of positive reinforcement to facilitate implementation can be found in Miller (1978) and Gilbert (1982).

Adapting. The primary means of responding to implementation problems discovered through other aspects of the DURABLE approach is to adapt the program as required. Adapting either the operation of the related service program or the design on which it is based can help alleviate apprehensions held by students and staff. Such actions as rescheduling pupils at times when they can attend without missing important classwork and discussing the nature of the program with students exemplify adaptations made in response to common related service problems.

Evaluating Related Service Program Implementation

Evaluating the implementation of a related service program can document the extent to which the program has been carried out as well as signal those aspects of the program that may need to be revised. Three questions can be used to guide the implementation evaluation of a related service program:

Who received the related service program?
What activities, methods, and staff comprised the program?
What difficulties were encountered?

Determining who received the program. Pupils actually receiving a related service program can be readily identified through a review of program-attendance records kept by those responsible for its delivery. These records should be summarized to indicate the following:

Number of exceptional pupils, by administrative classification (e.g., emotionally disturbed), who received particular related service programs from the special services system

Number of exceptional pupils, by administrative classification, who received related service programs from particular community agencies (e.g., drug-abuse counseling from local substance-abuse preventive clinic)

Average pupil attendance for each related service program delivered

Number and percent of exceptional pupils scheduled to be provided particular related service programs who did not receive them

Low attendance rates for a program or disparities between the number of pupils scheduled to receive it and the number served should be investigated further. The clarity of placement criteria, the care with which criteria are applied, and the opinions of pupils and staff can be analyzed to determine possible causes for failing to reach target group members.

Determining activities, methods, and staffing. This element of implementation evaluation is meant to identify activities and methods actually utilized in the program and the staff delivering them. This information can be compared with the activities, methods, and staff listed in the program design, and discrepancies between actual and intended operation noted for additional investigation.

To facilitate this kind of review, related service staff should be encouraged to maintain a program-implementation log for each of their programs. In this log, the following kinds of information can be recorded:

Dates on which each program session was held and duration of each session

Numbers of students attending each session

Activities and methods used during each session

Comments pertinent to each session (e.g., pupil reaction to a particular counseling method)

Determining program-implementation difficulties. Of concern here is discovering difficulties in carrying out the related service program, why those problems occurred, and how they can be prevented from happening in the future. These data can be gathered by interviewing related service providers, administrators, instructional staff, parents, and pupils connected with the program. Box 5-3 presents a

BOX 5-3 *SAMPLE INTERVIEW QUESTIONS FOR DETECTING DIFFICULTIES IN RELATED SERVICE PROGRAM IMPLEMENTATION*

Questions for Classroom Teachers

1. Were you aware of pupils in your class who were receiving the related service program?
2. If you were aware of these pupils, did you understand why they were being provided the program?
3. If you did not understand, what specific difficulties did this lack of understanding create for you?
4. In what ways was classroom instruction hindered by pupil participation in the related service program?
5. How might such difficulties be prevented in the future?

Questions for Administrators/Supervisors

1.   What kinds of problems were encountered in scheduling pupils for the related service program?
2.   What problems were encountered in coordinating the related service program with pupils' instructional programs?
3.   What problems were apparent in interagency coordination for this program?
4.   How might the problems you have identified be prevented from occurring in the future?

Questions for Related Service Providers

1.   What difficulties did you encounter in carrying out program activities?
2.   What difficulties did you encounter in employing program methods?
3.   What difficulties did you encounter in using program materials?
4.   How might these difficulties be prevented from occurring in the future?

---

set of sample questions upon which interviews about related service implementation problems can be based. These interviews should be undertaken at regular points during program operation, so that serious problems can be immediately located and addressed.

ASSESSING THE OUTCOMES OF RELATED SERVICE PROGRAMS

Outcome evaluation of related service programs can be guided by a range of questions. We will focus upon questions dealing with goal attainment, consumer reaction, and cause-effect relations:

To what extent have the goals of the related service program been attained?
What are the reactions of individuals to the related service program?
Were the outcomes observed produced by the program?

Evaluating Goal Attainment

As has been discussed, related service programs are intended to support those students needing additional help to benefit from special education. Such programs are understandably provided in areas essential to successful functioning in school and society: communication, movement, and socialization, among others. Because of their basic nature, the goals toward which related service programs are directed tend to imply phenomena more easily observed than those typically targeted by academically-oriented instructional programs. It is, for example, possible to literally see improvement associated with a behavioral-management program designed to reduce the frequency of hostile outbreaks; the cognitive effects of interventions to improve such skills as problem-solving are, however, far harder to detect.

Because evidence of progress toward related service goals is often noticeable, observational methods are typically used to measure goal attainment. Here we differentiate two types of observation: behavior recording and behavior rating. The difference between the two is primarily in the degree of subjective judgment used, and to a lesser extent, the interval between the actual observation and recording of behavior.

Behavior *recording* entails observing and documenting well-defined, relatively molecular actions (e.g., making eye contact, emitting an utterance in response to one's name, using obscene language in class). Because the behaviors to be observed are generally easily recognized physical actions recorded as they happen, behavior recording typically requires little judgment on the part of the observer.

Behavior recording can be used to document goal attainment in a variety of naturalistic settings, such as the classroom, playground, home, or counseling group. Two types of recording that can be employed are event recording and duration recording.

Event recording is used when related service program goals and objectives focus on increasing or decreasing the occurrence of specific behaviors. Examples of such behaviors are (1) getting out of one's seat without permission and (2) raising one's hand to ask a question of the teacher.

Event recording involves observing and recording behavior using hand counters or recording charts. Box 5-4 presents an example event-recording form for a counseling program that focused upon achieving the following goal and objective:

To increase the incidence of positive behavior in reading class.
By the semester's end, the pupil will show an increase in the incidence of coming to class on time by 25 percent over baseline estimates.

Other positive behaviors targeted by program objectives are presented on the vertical axis of the recording form.

Some behaviors, such as walking and running, may be valued for their duration, in addition to, or instead of, their incidence. Outcomes of this sort can be measured through duration recording. Behavior duration is measured with a timing device or an instrument to measure distance (e.g., a pedometer). An example of a goal and objective for a physical therapy program amenable to duration recording is:

To increase the length of time spent walking each day.
By the end of the semester, pupils will show an increase in the amount of time walking each school day by an average of 30 percent over baseline (presemester) levels

For more information about behavior-recording techniques, the interested reader should consult Evans and Nelson (1977), Gordon and Kopel (1979), or Kratochwill (1982).

Behavior *rating* is carried out using a rating scale or skill checklist. The types of behaviors assessed are typically more global and less well defined (e.g., self-concept) than those measured through behavior recording. In addition, rating is

BOX 5-4 *EVENT-RECORDING RECORD*

Directions: Enter the incidence with which each behavior described in the left-hand column occurred in your class on each day this week. The incidence is the number of positive behaviors in a category (e.g., the number of times the student raised a hand before asking a question) divided by the sum of positive and negative behaviors in that category. For example, two of three completed classwork assignments for a class period would result in an incidence of 2/3 = .66.

Name of Student: _____

Week of Semester: _____

Positive Classroom Behavior	Mon. Read	Mon. Math	Mon. LA[a]	Tues. Read	Tues. Math	Tues. LA	Wed. Read	Wed. Math	Wed. LA	Thurs. Read	Thurs. Math	Thurs. LA	Fri. Read	Fri. Math	Fri. LA
Enters Class before Period Begins	1.00	1.00	.00												
Asks Permission before Leaving Seat	.50	.80	.60												
Raises Hand to Ask Questions	.50	.60	.33												
Raises Hand to Answer Question	.00	.00	.33												
Completes Assigned Classwork	.66	1.00	1.00												

[a]LA = Language Arts

frequently carried out sometime after the actual behavior is exhibited—at the end of the day, week, or other programming period.

Behavior-rating scales generally present a list of behaviors or other descriptive statements. Each statement is assigned a numeric value, depending upon the respondent's judgment of the extent to which the statement describes pupil behavior. A scale might, for example, ask if a pupil's behavior was hostile (1) frequently, (2) sometimes, or (3) rarely. Responses to questions on a rating scale are frequently summed to arrive at a total score.

Checklists also list behaviors or descriptive statements. They differ from rating scales in that the behavior of interest is generally rated as present or absent and responses are not summed to form a composite score.

Behavior-rating scales and checklists can be used to evaluate related service goal attainment, provided that the instruments employed reflect behaviors that are consistent with program goals. For example, use of this method would be appropriate for the following counseling-program goal and objective:

> To improve pupils' positive school adjustment.
>
> Pupils participating in the counseling program will show an increase in positive end-of-term ratings by classroom teachers over baseline levels, as indicated by the Behavior Rating Profile.

There are many rating scales and checklists that can be considered for evaluating goal attainment of different types of related service programs. Examples of commercially developed instruments include the Behavior Problem Checklist (Quay, 1979a; 1979b; Quay & Peterson, 1967), the Devereux Elementary School Behavior Rating Scale (Spivack & Swift, 1967), the Walker Problem Behavior Checklist (Walker, 1970), and the Behavior Rating Profile (Brown & Hammill, 1978). A listing of behavioral rating scales and checklists can be located in the Buros's *Mental Measurements Yearbooks,* in Walker, Werner, and Bacon (1976), or through the Test Collection at Educational Testing Service in Princeton, New Jersey.

The goal-attainment scaling (preprogram–postprogram assessment) approach. Observational methods can be employed to assess related service program goals through a variety of design approaches. One approach recently applied to related service programs and identified as a practical outcome-evaluation strategy by the American Educational Research Association Task Force on Special Education Program Evaluation (Kennedy, 1982) is goal-attainment scaling. Originally developed for evaluating CMHC psychotherapy programs, this approach is especially recommended when involving pupils, teachers, and parents in related service program planning and evaluation is desired (Maher, 1981; Maher & Barbrack, in press).

The goal-attainment scaling approach is selected during development of the related service program design. As part of the design's outcome evaluation plan, a goal-attainment follow-up guide is constructed. As illustrated in Table 5-3, the goal-attainment follow-up guide is a matrix consisting of from two to five program-goal areas and three to five levels of goal attainment.

TABLE 5-3 Goal-Attainment Follow-Up Guide for a Counseling Program (All goals are equal in weight)

GOAL-ATTAINMENT LEVELS	PROGRAM GOALS		
	Improved School Attendance (based on school-attendance records)	Improved Classroom Productivity (based on teachers' record books)	Improved School Behaviors (based on office records)
Best anticipated success (+2)	100% daily attendance	90–100% completion of academic classroom assignments in all academic classes	0–1 disciplinary referrals to vice-principal
More than anticipated success (+1)	90–99% daily attendance[a]	80–89% completion of academic classroom assignments	2–3 disciplinary referrals to vice-principal[a]
Expected level of success (0)	80–89% daily attendance	70–79% completion of academic classroom assignments[a]	4–5 disciplinary referrals to vice-principal
Less than expected success (–1)	70–79% daily attendance[b]	60–69% completion of academic classroom assignments	6–7 disciplinary referrals to vice-principal
Most unfavorable outcome thought likely (–2)	Less than 70% daily attendance	Less than 60% completion of academic classroom assignments[b]	More than 7 disciplinary referrals to vice-principal[b]

Date of program implementation: January 15, 1979
Date of outcome evaluation: March 15, 1979

Goal-Attainment Score at Jan. 15 = 30.8
Goal-Attainment Score at Mar. 15 = 61.2
Goal-Attainment Change Score   = 30.4

[a] = average level of pupil goal attainment at IEP outcome evaluation
[b] = average level of pupil goal attainment at IEP implementation (baseline)

Source: Maher, C. A. Goal attainment scaling: A method for evaluating educational services. Exceptional Children, in press. Copyright 1983 by Council for Exceptional Children. Reprinted by permission of the publisher and author.

Following construction of the follow-up guide, the content of the related service program is described and a time period for goal attainment set. Program goals are scaled by identifying behavioral indicators representative of various levels of goal attainment. Indicators are specified for the least desirable outcome, through the expected outcome or program objective, to the most desirable program result. Baseline or preprogram assessment data then are recorded on the scale (see Table 5-3). Finally, after a prespecified period, a postprogram assessment is conducted. Assessment results for each goal area are averaged across students and these averages used to calculate the program's overall goal-attainment score. The formula for this score, described by Kiresuk and Sherman (1968), is

$$\text{Goal Attainment Score} = 50 + \frac{10 \ \Sigma \ (w_i x_i)}{[.7 \ \Sigma w_i^2 + .3 \ (\Sigma w_i^2)]^{\frac{1}{2}}}$$

where w_i is the weight assigned to the ith goal scale, x_i is the attainment score (-2 to $+2$) on the ith goal scale, and the summations are across all of the goal scales designated on the goal attainment follow-up guide.

Goal-attainment scores of 50 indicate that, overall, program objectives have been achieved. Scores of 40 and 60 denote achievement below and above expectation, and 30 and 70, attainment far less and far greater than expected, respectively. More information about using goal-attainment scaling can be found in Carr (1979), Maher (in press-a), Maher and Barbrack (in press) and Kiresuk and Lund (1978).

Evaluating Consumer Reaction

Evaluating consumer reactions to related service programs helps elucidate pupil, parent, and staff satisfaction with the program—an important outcome in itself—and sheds light on the practical and educational significance of the outcomes evidenced by pupils. Consumer-reaction evaluation is conducted at the conclusion of the related service program (e.g., the end of the school year) or at some other predetermined time. Methods and procedures for conducting a consumer-reaction evaluation are delineated in the program design as part of the outcome-assessment plan.

Populations considered for consumer-reaction evaluation should include those groups expected to benefit directly or indirectly from the program. Three populations meeting this criterion are (1) pupils participating in the related service program, (2) the parents of those pupils, and (3) teachers in whose classrooms such programs are designed to improve pupil functioning.

Consumer-reaction information can be obtained through questionnaire or structured interview procedures. Box 5-5 is a sample consumer-reaction questionnaire for secondary-school populations enrolled in a counseling program. Box 5-6 presents a set of possible interview questions for obtaining reactions of teachers to a classroom behavior-management program. General areas that might be touched on with parents and classroom teachers include their perception of changes in pupil behavior, the educational significance of those changes, and the value of continued participation of the student in the related service program.

BOX 5-5 *COUNSELING PROGRAM: PUPIL-REACTION QUESTIONNAIRE*

Instructions: Please help us improve our counseling program by answering some questions about the counseling you received. We want to know your honest opinion, whether it is positive or negative. For each question, circle the number that corresponds to your answer.

1. How would you rate the quality of the counseling you received?

3	2	1
Excellent	Average	Poor

2. Did you get the kind of help you wanted?

1	2	3
Definitely not	To a degree	Absolutely

3. If a friend were in need of similar help, would you recommend this counseling program to him or her?

1	2	3
Definitely not	Maybe	Absolutely

4. How satisfied are you with the amount of help you received?

1	2	3
Not very satisfied	Somewhat satisfied	Very satisfied

5. Has the counseling you received helped you to deal more effectively with your problems?

3	2	1
Absolutely	Somewhat	Definitely not

6. If you needed help again, would you come back to the program?

1	2	3
Definitely not	Maybe	Absolutely

7. The things I liked best about the program were:

8. If I were to change one thing about the program, it would be:

BOX 5-6 *TEACHER CONSUMER-REACTION INTERVIEW QUESTIONS*

1. In general, how satisfied were you with meeting locations for behavioral consultation?
2. How well did the service you received meet your needs?
3. How knowledgeable was the person providing you assistance?
4. How satisfied were you with the amount of help you received?
5. Has the assistance you received helped you to deal more effectively with other classroom behavior problems?
6. Did you receive assistance as promptly as you felt necessary?

Evaluating Cause-Effect Relations

Determining whether a related service program was responsible for program outcomes is the focus of evaluating cause-effect relations. Examples of outcome-evaluation questions relevant to this activity are:

> Were observed increases in pupil attendance caused by the individual counseling program?
>
> Did pupils increase their time on-task because of the behavior-management program?
>
> Was improvement in the conversational skills of pupils due to the speech therapy program?

In this section, we consider two ways of evaluating cause-effect relations in related service programs: the time-series and multiple baseline approaches.

Time-series approach. The time-series approach, introduced in Chapter 3, involves collecting data on related service program outcomes prior to, during, and following the program. In using this approach, marked changes in outcome data from baseline to time periods following program implementation offer evidence to support the related service program's role in causing observed outcomes.

The time-series approach is valuable for assessing cause-effect relations because it does a better job ruling out competing explanations for observed outcomes than either preprogram or preprogram-postprogram assessment designs. For example, increases in goal attainment due to other programs, normal pupil growth, or repeated testing should normally evidence themselves over both baseline and intervention periods. As such, the effects of some common competing explanations will "wash out," because only differences between baseline and intervention periods above and beyond those effects will be considered evidence of the program's causative power.

To help illustrate how the time-series approach is employed to evaluate cause-effect relations in related service programs, four possible sets of outcome results are shown (see Figure 5-1). Each sample in the figure is associated with a group-counseling program delivered during the second half of the school year. The program was targeted to socially maladjusted high-school pupils mainstreamed into regular classrooms for academic instruction. The counseling program was designed to improve pupil social functioning so that pupils could participate in the mainstream setting.

Figure 5-1a represents a situation where outcome data were collected at two points, prior to the counseling program and at its conclusion, at the end of January. This outcome-evaluation approach is the preprogram-postprogram-assessment approach. These two data points reveal very little about the effects of program change. Even if a statistical test of preprogram-postprogram change were to reveal a significant difference, it is entirely possible that other factors may have been responsible for the differences between pre- and postprogram outcomes. A case for the program

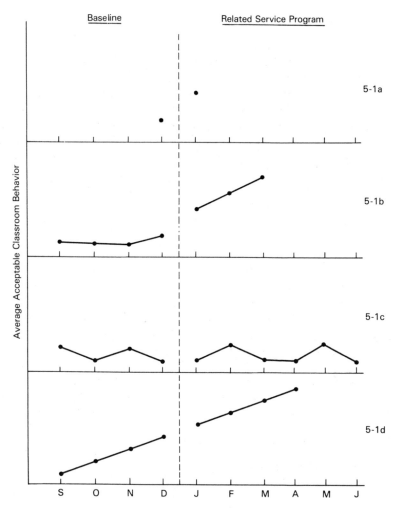

FIGURE 5-1   *FOUR POSSIBLE DATA SETS FROM THE CAUSE-EFFECT EVALUATION OF A COUNSELING PROGRAM*

as cause of the change observed here would need to be based on a thorough investigation and discussion of why competing explanations were *not* tenable causes of the observed results.

Figure 5-1b illustrates the hypothetical addition of data points to those collected through the pre–post approach. This time-series example strengthens the inference that the program caused the observed effect. First, the additional baseline data do *not* show the same increasing trend as that apparent during the intervention phase. This suggests that the observed effect is *not* the result of such external factors as increasing familiarity with testing or normal pupil growth. If these factors had caused the intervention-phase effect, it is likely that they also would have manifested themselves during the baseline condition through a similar increasing trend. Second, the addition of intervention data points suggests that the upward trend in the pre–post study (Figure 5-1a) is a real one and not simply an artifact due to a single erroneous postprogram measurement.

Figure 5-1c illustrates a situation where the time-series data do *not* suggest the group-counseling program to be the cause of any perceptible goal-related effect. This conclusion is based on the absence of any dependable difference between pre-intervention measurements and data following introduction of the program.

In Figure 5-1d, a steady upward trend is evidenced, without interruption, from early baseline through intervention. This pattern suggests that factors other than the counseling program are working to cause pupils' goal attainment. Though

FIGURE 5-2 *BEHAVIOR-MANAGEMENT PROGRAM OUTCOME DATA GATHERED THROUGH AN ACROSS-BEHAVIORS MULTIPLE BASELINE APPROACH*

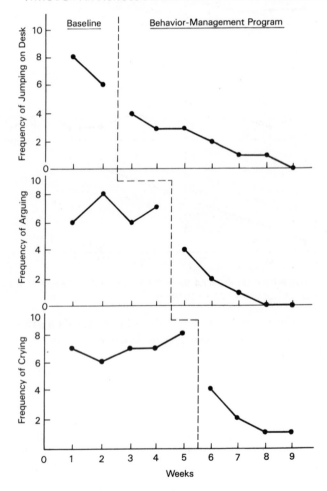

pupils are obviously improving in desired areas, the data do not justify a decision, for example, to expand the program to other schools in the district. From the evaluation data, it appears pupils would improve as dramatically without any counseling intervention at all.

In addition to graphical analysis, time-series data can be analyzed using inferential statistical procedures. Appropriate statistical tests for use with time-series data are discussed in Kazdin (1976), McCain and McLeary (1979), and Kratochwill (1978). The Kazdin and Kratochwill references also provide thorough discussion of the strengths and limitations of graphical and statistical analysis of time-series data.

The multiple baseline approach.   The multiple baseline approach is an extension of the time-series approach. It is used when related service program goals and objectives focus upon changing more than one behavior or upon changing one behavior across situations or settings.

In using the multiple baseline design with two or more behaviors, a baseline is first established for each behavior. When this has been accomplished, the related service intervention meant to modify the first behavior is begun while baseline data continue to be collected for the second behavior. After a prespecified period, intervention focused upon modifying the second behavior is begun. If the frequency of occurrence of each behavior appears to change only *after* introduction of the program designed to affect it, then support for the program's cause-effect power is evident (see Figure 5-2).

The multiple baseline design can also be employed to evaluate the occurrence of a particular behavior across different situations and settings. For example, the effect of a behavioral-management program on lateness to class could be evaluated across different classes. Again, the program is supported as cause of the changed behavior only if lateness is reduced following staggered introduction of the program in different classes.

SUMMARY

Related services are intended to help pupils benefit from special instruction. Related service programs are provided by schools and other community agencies. The major difficulty encountered in providing related services appears to be coordinating these services both within the school district and between the school district and other agencies.

The extent to which a related service problem exists is determined through review of recommendations for related services contained in the individualized programs of exceptional pupils. When combined with relevant contextual information, such an approach to related service needs assessment helps indicate what new programs and what interagency agreements need to be developed.

Related service program implementation can be facilitated through discussing the program with classroom teachers, target pupils, and parents. Attempts should be made to schedule pupils so that important classwork is not missed because of their participation in the related service program. Efforts to evaluate related service program implementation should concentrate on determining who received the program; what activities, methods, and staff were used; and what difficulties in program delivery were encountered.

Outcome assessment of related services programs primarily is based upon data derived from behavior recording and behavior rating. These methods most directly measure the outcomes sought from related service programs—improved pupil performance in communication, movement, and socialization. Among the approaches recommended for assessing related service goal attainment is goal-attainment scaling. For purposes of determining whether a related service program caused observed effects, the time-series and multiple baseline designs are suggested.

PLANNING AND EVALUATING PERSONNEL DEVELOPMENT SERVICES

Educating exceptional pupils requires the involvement of many individuals, including teachers, administrators, specialists, and parents. In order to effectively perform their educational service delivery functions, these personnel must possess specific job-related competencies. Personnel development is the component of the special services system responsible for assuring that these critical proficiencies are developed and maintained. In a very real sense, the success and failure of the system depends upon the extent to which effective personnel development is delivered to those involved in educating exceptional pupils.

In this chapter, we discuss planning and evaluation methods and procedures that can help in providing meaningful personnel development programs.

OVERVIEW OF PERSONNEL DEVELOPMENT SERVICES

Need for Personnel Development Services in Special Education

Personnel development is a necessary part of the special education services delivery system for a variety of reasons. In our view, the most important reasons relate to (1) the dynamic nature of special education and its related fields; (2) employee stress and burnout; and (3) professional and legal requirements.

That special education is a dynamic and rapidly changing field is obvious to anyone who has been involved in it. Notions of cognitive and language development, learning disability, student assessment, and parent involvement, among many others, have evolved dramatically. In the 1970s, for example, mildly handicapped children were popularly conceived to process information differently, depending upon both the modality through which it was presented and their own particular cognitive strengths (Salvia & Ysseldyke, 1981). Special educators typically attempted to assess the extent to which individual children were "visual" or "auditory" learners, and adjusted their teaching methods accordingly. This notion of cognitive processing has been replaced by more theoretically sound and empirically researched views (e.g., see Sternberg, 1981) that have very different implications for both assessment and instruction.

The foregoing illustration is only one in a long list of new developments in special education and its related fields. That this developmental trend is continuing is illustrated by such things as the many new applications to special education of microcomputer and video-disc technology (Bennett, 1982d) and the growing application of neuropsychological techniques to assessment and instruction (Hartlage, 1982). Clearly, some organized mechanism for updating educators' competencies seems necessary if the services they provide are to keep up with the latest advances in the field.

In addition to necessitating routine in-service education for special educators, the changing nature of special education has had one other dramatic effect of direct consequence for personnel development. Federal and state legislation, in particular PL 94-142, has partially shifted the responsibility for educating the handicapped from the shoulders of special educators to those of populations relatively unfamiliar with exceptional education. Regular education teachers, school principals, parents, and paraprofessionals, among others, all now share in this educational enterprise. These populations also need to be trained if they are to effectively carry out new roles and responsibilities.

The relief of stress and prevention of "burnout" provides a second underlying rationale for ongoing personnel development. Heavy caseloads, increased paper work, repeated adversarial encounters between school personnel and parents, and violence in the schools have all served to create an atmosphere of stress that has caused many educators to leave their positions in search of other employment. Sarason (1971) and Trachtman (1981), in discussing the relative isolation in which teachers and specialists work in public schools, and the lack of incentive and reward systems for improved on-the-job performance, have argued that job satisfaction of school employees will continue to decrease unless systematic efforts to develop and improve professionals' knowledge, attitudes, and skills are undertaken. Providing effective programs of personnel development may assist in making the special education delivery context a more productive and satisfying work environment (e.g., Dunette, 1976; Forman, 1982; Maher & Illback, in press).

One final reason exists for providing organized personnel development services in special education: such services are mandated by federal and state law and encouraged by many professional organizations. We discuss this reason last because we strongly feel that schools should provide, and staff should engage in, personnel development programs because these activities represent good professional practice and not solely because they are legally mandated.

The most prominent legal requirement for in-service education is the Comprehensive System of Personnel Development (CSPD) provision of PL 94-142 (U.S. Office of Education, 1977b). This provision requires local districts to assess annually the training needs of all personnel involved in educating handicapped students and provide programs designed to meet documented needs. Design of a CSPD at the district level is intended to be a broad-based participatory effort, involving the school staff, parents, and the community. Local-level programs are monitored by the state education agency, which in turn reports to the federal government on the status of statewide CSPD efforts.

Many professional associations, at the national, state, and local levels, also either require in-service experiences for continued licensure and certification or strongly encourage those experiences for membership. For example, the National Association of School Psychologists (NASP) provides certificates of continuing professional development based upon members' documentation of their involvement in a variety of personnel improvement efforts (National Association, 1979).

Nature and Scope of Personnel Development Services

Personnel development is delivered in the form of programs targeted to various staff populations responsible for educating exceptional pupils. Table 6-1 provides a listing of various targets of personnel development and the programmatic responsibilities of these groups that might be enhanced through in-service education.

Personnel development programs can focus on one or more personnel needs. We choose to organize these needs into three domains: knowledge, affect, and skill. Personnel development programs that focus on the knowledge domain typically involve increasing the program participant's awareness of, or knowledge about, some aspect of special education. These programs usually take the form of didactic courses and seminars, lectures, and reading in professional books and journals. For example, regular classroom teachers might be provided with a seminar series designed to increase their awareness of state rules and regulations for educating mainstreamed handicapped children.

Programs having to do with the affective domain usually involve improving the participant's feelings about, appreciation of, or attitudes toward, others or oneself. Often, personnel development programs that focus on affective development utilize small-group discussions, role playing, media presentations, and peer consulting relationships. School principals, for instance, might become involved in a series of discussion groups with parents of handicapped children to develop greater empathy for the problems encountered by such parents.

TABLE 6-1   Special-Education Service Personnel and Typical Programmatic Responsibilities

SERVICE	PERSONNEL	PROGRAMMATIC RESPONSIBILITIES
Assessment	Educational diagnostician	Academic evaluation
	Psychologist	Psychological evaluation
	Social worker	Social assessment
	Nurse	Assessment of physical health
Instruction	Special education teacher	Academic instruction in self-contained and resource rooms
	Speech therapist	Pupil speech/language development
	Regular education teacher	Academic instruction of mainstreamed handicapped children
Related Services	Counselor	Individual and group counseling
	Bus driver	Pupil transportation
Administration	Principal	Supervision of mainstream programs
	Director of special education	Development of special education curriculum/supervision of special education staff
	School superintendent	Policy development
Personnel Development	Staff development specialist	In-service program design, implementation, and evaluation

Skill development programs focus on one or more performance competencies. These programs often employ role playing, simulation exercises, case studies, performance feedback, and clinical supervision. For example, a "master" school psychologist may work with less-experienced peers to develop their skill in formulating instructionally relevant recommendations from assessment.

Difficulties in Providing Personnel Development Services

A number of difficulties are encountered in delivering personnel development programs. One is identifying the specific area and staff that should be the targets of training efforts. Many different staff populations come into contact with exceptional children. The areas in which each of these populations could conceivably be trained are numerous. The problem for personnel development is assessing the needs of various populations and ordering documented training needs so that the most critical ones are addressed first.

A second difficulty in delivering personnel development programs relates to the prevalent view that in-service training is a one- or two-hour lecture provided on the district's annual or semiannual in-service training day. Such a view results in programs that because of their brevity meet few, if any, staff needs. This, in turn, creates among the staff a perception of personnel development as a waste of valuable time.

Finally, one of the most serious deficiencies that we have observed with special education in-service training efforts is the lack of direction that appears to characterize most staff development programs. All too often, those receiving a program as well as those responsible for its development, implementation, and evaluation seem to lack a clear idea of what the activity is meant to achieve. Because such aimlessness is a threat to the utility and the reputation of personnel development efforts, we place substantial emphasis on defining precisely what an in-service program is meant to accomplish.

CLARIFYING PERSONNEL DEVELOPMENT SERVICE DELIVERY PROBLEMS

Our approach to planning and evaluating personnel development programs reflects aspects of the goal-based, goal-free, and transactional models (see Table 1-1). The goal-based model centers attention on the importance of designing personnel development programs from priority needs of the staff. The goal-free model emphasizes the related effects that may result from personnel development programs, while the transactional model focuses on the reactions of participants to the program they have received.

Assessing Service Delivery Needs

Assessing personnel development needs is the process of identifying those staff competencies requiring further development. This process can be best carried out through a multidisciplinary Personnel Development Team (PDT). The PDT can be organized at a school or district level. It is used to assure that the interests of all personnel involved in educating exceptional pupils are represented in the staff development planning and evaluation process. Our experience indicates that a PDT consisting of seven to nine members is a practical working group. Team members should be selected to represent regular and special education teachers, related specialists (e.g., psychologist, nurse), principals, and parents of exceptional pupils (see Maher, 1982a, for more information on the PDT concept).

The personnel development needs-assessment process conducted by the PDT consists of two elements: (1) identifying personnel problems related to educating exceptional students and (2) determining the specific needs that most likely underlie those problems.

Identifying personnel development problems.   The first element of the needs-assessment process is directed at identifying a limited set of problems upon which to focus subsequent efforts to determine needs. The types of problems sought are ones that are both critical in terms of special education services delivery and amenable to staff development efforts.

Implicit in this approach to needs assessment is our belief that the needs of every staff population cannot be assessed comprehensively; the resources for such an undertaking simply do not exist in most school districts. Rather, choices must be made about how limited resources for needs assessment can be spent. Our approach is to use resources to clarify those problems most central to adequate service delivery and most amenable to staff development. This approach can be supplemented by using less formal and comprehensive strategies to meet legal or political mandates for dealing with a broader range of staff populations or problems.

The first activity we suggest in identifying problems for comprehensive needs assessment is to delineate all *major* anticipated and existing difficulties in the delivery of district services to exceptional children. For instance, these difficulties might include decreasing resources, teacher burnout, time spent in due-process meetings, growing paper work, and minority disproportions in EMR classes. Problems can be identified through group discussions and listed on a blackboard or flip chart as soon as they are raised. The nature of each problem is briefly described, so that all PDT members are aware of what problem is being referred to. No discussion of possible causes of the problem is undertaken at this point.

Once the PDT is confident that it has identified most major existing or anticipated service delivery problems, an attempt is made to order those problems in terms of priority for action. While a number of methods exist for determining priorities, we recommend asking each PDT member to distribute independently a total of 100 points over the problem set, assigning points in proportion to each problem's gravity. The point values for each problem are next averaged across team members and the problems ranked according to the results. The ranking and average point values for a sample problem set are:

Decreasing resources	50 points
Disproportionate placement	20
Time spent in due-process hearings	15
Teacher burnout	11
Increasing paper work	4
	100 points

The extent to which each problem is the result of staff deficiencies in knowledge, attitude, or skill, or would be alleviated by improvements in those areas, should next be considered by the PDT. Consideration of each problem is facilitated by asking the following question: "What programmatic functions, if any, do staff members perform that might in some way contribute to this service delivery problem?" This question should be asked separately for assessment, instructional, related service, and administrative staff populations. The extent to which the problem is viewed as a staff development problem is then expressed by each individual as a proportion from .00 to 1.00 and then averaged across all team members. For example, decreasing resources is a problem that is typically neither caused by the staff nor likely to be substantially improved through increasing staff skills, knowledge, or attitudes. Thus, the extent to which that problem is related to staff development might be expressed as .00.

A second problem, disproportionate placement, might be perceived differently. Assessment personnel staffing the preplacement evaluation program might lack knowledge or skill, or hold attitudes that contribute to this problem. Regular classroom teachers might also be contributors, because of their responsibility for referral. Finally, administrative personnel could be involved as causal agents, because of their involvement in monitoring the referral, evaluation, and placement process. Disproportionate placement might, therefore, be viewed as related to staff development and this perception expressed as a proportion of, say, .75.

The extent to which other problems are viewed as related to staff development in a district might be as follows:

Time spent in due-process hearings	.70
Teacher burnout	.30
Increasing paper work	.20

When the PDT has completed offering its perceptions of the priority given district problems and the extent to which each problem might be addressed through staff development, problems are assigned priorities for comprehensive needs assessment. Needs-assessment priorities are calculated by multiplying the point value assigned each problem for importance by the decimal value representing the extent to which the problem is one of staff development. Applying this procedure might produce the following set of priorities for needs assessment:

Disproportionate placement	$20 \times .75 = 15.0$
Time spent in due-process hearings	$15 \times .70 = 10.5$
Teacher burnout	$11 \times .30 = 3.3$
Increasing paper work	$4 \times .20 = 0.8$
Decreasing resources	$50 \times .00 = 0.0$

In looking over this example, we can see that the needs-assessment priority of 15 given disproportionate placement is one and one-half times the priority given increased due-process hearings and four times the priority of teacher burnout. These weights suggest the importance of determining specific staff needs with respect to each problem area and can be used as a rough basis for apportioning available resources for needs assessment.

The problem-identification process concludes with a brief description of those problems receiving high priority for needs assessment and the hypothesized relationship of each problem to staff development. A sample problem description for disproportionate placement might read as follows:

At present the ethnic-racial makeup of regular school-age children in our district is 60 percent white, 30 percent black, and 10 percent Hispanic. The ethnic-racial makeup for the educable mentally retarded program, however, is 50 percent black, 20 percent Hispanic, and 30 percent white. The disproportionate placement of minority children in the EMR program suggests the *possibility* that some minority students who are not handicapped or who have other handicaps, such as learning disability, may be inappropriately classified as educable mentally retarded. Such inappropriate classification may be due to a number of factors, including inappropriate assessment tools and deficiencies in staff attitudes, knowledge, or skill. Possible deficiencies in staff competency could involve regular education teachers' attitudes toward these children and their skill in addressing their educational needs within the context of the regular education program; child-study-team members' knowledge and skill in assessing adaptive behavior, a central criterion for the diagnosis of educable mental retardation, or their skill in differentiating legitimate languages such as black English from language disorder; and placement-team members' attitudes toward the most appropriate educational placement for minority children.

Determining personnel development needs.   This element of the personnel development needs-assessment process is directed at identifying specific training needs associated with the high-priority service delivery problems selected by the PDT. The first step in determining specific needs is noting the staff populations that are to be targets of comprehensive needs assessment. These populations should be taken directly from the problem description previously developed. For example, regular education teachers and members of the child-study and placement teams would be designated for needs assessment in the problem description of disproportionate placement cited previously.

For each staff population, the special education services and programs that will constitute the focus of needs assessment should next be specified. For example, with respect to the problem of disproportionate placement, the programs and services of concern might include, for regular education teachers, the *referral program* (assessment service); for child-study-team members, the *preplacement evaluation program* (assessment service); and for placement-team members, the *individualized program* (instructional service), the document upon which placement decisions are based.

Through logical analysis, those competencies (knowledge, skills, attitudes) that staff must possess in order to successfully implement the programs of concern are specified (Bennett, 1980a). Competencies can be identified by reviewing the literature relevant to a particular job, observing individuals deliver the program and talking with them about its requirements, and brainstorming with those familiar with the program. This step should result in a listing for each staff population of the competencies needed to adequately implement the programs of concern to the PDT.

For example, after consultation with regular education teachers, review of the relevant literature, and brainstorming, it might be hypothesized that regular education teachers must possess the following competencies in order to adequately implement a referral program:

Knowledge of the behaviors and symptoms associated with various handicapping conditions

Knowledge of the basic characteristics, languages, and cultures of minority children

Knowledge of alternative curricular and behavior management strategies

Skill in applying alternative strategies

Skill in differentiating between behaviors indicative of potential handicap and behaviors associated with cultural differences

Respect for cultural differences

Methods for determining the extent to which staff members possess the competencies needed to carry out their programmatic functions are next selected. Perceived-need methods, such as the questionnaire and interview, are far and away the most widely used means of gathering data on personnel needs. The data that these methods provide, reflect a staff population's perception of its own training needs (or those of another population). For example, to learn more about how regular education teachers view their own training needs relative to referral, a questionnaire such as that depicted in Box 6-1 might be distributed to a sample of teachers.

BOX 6-1 *NEEDS-ASSESSMENT QUESTIONNAIRE*

Directions: This questionnaire is being distributed to a sample of regular education teachers so that our district Personnel Development Team can get feedback about which topics teachers feel should be emphasized in this year's staff development program. Please give us your feedback by entering the number that best describes your feelings in the blank space next to each item. Do not write your name anywhere on this form.

I feel that in-service training on the following competencies would enhance my ability to deliver services to handicapped children. . .

| 1—Not at all | 3—Quite a bit |
| 2—Only somewhat | 4—To a great extent |

_____   1.   Knowledge of the behaviors associated with various handicapping conditions.
_____   2.   Knowledge of the basic characteristics of minority children.
_____   3.   Knowledge of the language characteristic of minority children.
_____   4.   Knowledge of the cultures of minority children.
_____   5.   Knowledge of alternative curricular strategies.
_____   6.   Knowledge of alternative behavior management strategies.
_____   7.   Skill in differentiating between behaviors indicative of potential handicap and behaviors associated with cultural difference.
_____   8.   Appreciation of cultural differences.

Please describe any other areas in which you desire training:

Sampling staff perceptions is an important part of any comprehensive needs-determination effort. As any experienced administrator or in-service-program designer will testify, staff development programs can succeed or fail depending on the degree to which the staff feels such programs are responsive to its needs.

Perceived needs, however, are not the whole story. Staff members may perceive needs that cannot be verified by objective means; or, alternatively, may fail to perceive needs that can be otherwise documented. For example, one administrator we know received feedback from child-study-team members expressing a desire to learn more about writing IP goals and objectives. After examining a sample of IPs produced by team members and having that sample evaluated by local consultants and neighboring directors of special education, the administrator concluded that her team members possessed the necessary competencies to write more-than-adequate goals and objectives. When reported to team members, this feedback bolstered their confidence in their work and saved the time and expense of an unnecessary training experience.

We have likewise noted cases where needs were independently documented but *not* perceived as such by staff. For example, we were able to document a training need in basic test-interpretation concepts for members of child-study teams in one state and one major metropolitan school district (Bennett, 1980b; Bennett & Shepherd, 1982). The method we used to assess training needs was a test of knowledge and ability to apply job-related concepts of test interpretation. In our informal conversations with child-study-team members, we were surprised to find, not simply a failure to perceive the training need, but a failure to grasp that such basic concepts as reliability and validity were relevant to test interpretation at all!

The methods typically used to document "real" need include observation, product review (e.g., of IPs), attitudinally-oriented interviews and questionnaires, and, on occasion, performance or paper-and-pencil tests. While testing professionals can be a touchy business, it can be accomplished if it is made clear that (1) the test is for training-needs determination and not staff evaluation, (2) the anonymity of participants is guaranteed, (3) the study will be carried out by the PDT member representing that staff group, and (4) the test will be relatively short.

Our advice on selecting methods is, to the extent possible, to use both perceived- and real-need methods, because both types provide valuable information for in-service program planning. Box 6-2 presents strengths and limitations of commonly used methods of needs assessment.

Following the selection of methods, instruments must be constructed, a sample chosen (in cases where the entire staff population will not be assessed), and data

BOX 6-2 *STRENGTHS AND LIMITATIONS OF COMMONLY USED PERSONNEL DEVELOPMENT NEEDS ASSESSMENT METHODS*

I. Interview

  A. Strengths
    1. Unrestricted in terms of topics covered
    2. Can reveal perceived needs, problems, causes, and possible solutions
  B. Limitations
    1. Time-consuming
    2. May not reveal actual knowledge or skill-training needs
    3. Effectiveness depends on skills of interviewer
    4. Results often difficult to organize and interpret
    5. Obtrusive; no anonymity

II. Questionnaire

    A.   Strengths
        1. Efficient—can reach large number of people
        2. Can reveal perceived needs and affective needs
        3. Relatively easy to organize and interpret data when structured format used
        4. Anonymity of individuals guaranteed
    B.   Limitations
        1. Range of topics and responses limited
        2. May not reveal actual knowledge or skill-training needs
        3. Response rates typically low

III. Observation

    A.   Strengths
        1. Can reveal actual training needs
        2. Results relatively easy to organize and interpret when structured format used
        3. Useful when activity being observed is important in and of itself
    B.   Limitations
        1. Time-consuming
        2. May not reveal perceived need
        3. Adequate schedules require skill to construct
        4. Obtrusive

IV. Product review

    A.   Strengths
        1. Can reveal actual training needs
        2. Results relatively easy to organize and interpret if structured format used
        3. Useful when results of an activity are deemed important
        4. Unobtrusive
    B.   Limitations
        1. Time-consuming
        2. May not reveal perceived needs
        3. Adequacy of the activity must be inferred from the product
        4. Adequate review guides require skill to construct

V. Test

    A.   Strengths
        1. Can reveal actual knowledge and skill needs
        2. Results easy to organize and interpret
    B.   Limitations
        1. Will not reveal perceived needs
        2. Will not reveal affective needs
        3. Threatening to some staff members
        4. Adequate tests difficult to construct

gathered. Questionnaire and interview, test, product review, and observational schedule construction have been treated in detail in a number of sources, and will not be discussed here (e.g., see Cronbach, 1970; Thorndike & Hagen, 1977). Suffice it to say that these activities require considerable skill that may warrant the input of an evaluation consultant if in-house resources are not adequate.

    In collecting data, there is generally little reason to assess all members of a staff or document population (e.g., a population of IPs) when that population is large. Sampling often proves to be the more practical strategy, because it requires the participation of fewer professionals as survey respondents and less time for data collection and analysis on the part of PDT members.

The analysis of needs-assessment data should identify those competencies frequently cited as needs by members of a staff population as well as those that are most frequently implicated through other evaluation methods. Furthermore, areas of agreement and disagreement between competencies identified through perceived- and real-need methods should be sought. The most powerful candidates for in-service program development will, in our view, generally be those needs identified through *both* method types. Also, attempts should be made to determine if any of the same needs exist across populations. This information will be useful in determining if the same program can be used for training a number of populations.

Because most school districts do not have the resources required to address every documented training need, we recommend ranking needs in order of priority for program design as the concluding component of the needs-determination process. As for problem description, a need should be given priority to the extent that it is likely to be (1) related to a serious service delivery problem and (2) responsive to in-service efforts.

Assessing the Service Delivery Context

The personnel development needs that have been identified must be seen within an organizational context if effective personnel development services are to be provided. Knowledge of important contextual factors helps suggest whether current organizational conditions will support in-service training efforts as well as the specific conditions that must be changed to increase the chances of success. In gathering context information, those responsible for personnel development can be guided by questions such as those presented in Box 6-3. We will briefly discuss two of the eight areas listed in Box 6-3: obligation and resistance.

BOX 6-3 *PERSONNEL DEVELOPMENT READINESS QUESTIONS*

Ability

1. Have the persons responsible for planning, implementing, and evaluating CSPD been clearly specified?
2. Have financial resources been allotted for CSPD activities?

Values

1. What values are implicit in the district's staff-development efforts?
2. Do the values of the staff, administrators, and community appear consistent with those of personnel development?

Idea

1. In general, do staff members understand the purpose, nature, and scope of personnel development?
2. What misperceptions about in-service training do staff members hold?

Circumstances

1. Is the district administration generally supportive of a formal system of personnel development?
2. Are key administration supporters of CSPD likely to continue to hold their jobs for the foreseeable future?
3. Are present district policies and procedures relevant to CSPD likely to continue for the foreseeable future?

Timing

1. Will new or additional persons, materials, or finances be available to support CSPD efforts during the coming year?
2. Has a new mandate been enacted by the district during the past year supporting increased CSPD activities?

Obligation

1. Have key administrators in the agency perceived or articulated a need for systematic approaches to personnel development in the district?
2. Have regular and special services staff members perceived or articulated a need for further training with respect to education of the handicapped?

Resistance

1. Are any key administrators not supportive of systematic approaches to personnel development?
2. Are any regular or special services staff members not supportive of continued training in education of the handicapped?

Yield

1. Do key administrators perceive direct benefits from their own involvement in staff development programs?
2. Do regular and special education staff perceive direct benefits from their own involvement in personnel development programs?

Obligation. Obligation is characterized by the extent to which staff members believe that they should become actively involved in personnel development efforts. Inferences about staff obligation can be based on data gathered in several ways. First, staff behavior toward personnel development programs, such as participation in needs-assessment activities and attendance at program sessions, can be observed. Informal interviews with representative members of the staff can also be conducted, to obtain views on the importance of in-service program participation. A third method of assessing staff obligation—as well as other A VICTORY factors—is through administration of a questionnaire.

Resistance. Resistance refers to the extent to which staff members oppose becoming involved in personnel development. Resistance can be assessed by means of observation, interview, or permanent product review. Observation, for example, might focus on determining the extent to which staff members have participated actively in small-group training activities delivered during in-service workshops in the past and if staff members returned to the workshop sessions following lunch and coffee breaks. Interviews may be used to explore why staff members have seemingly refused to participate in personnel development programs. For example, interviews may reveal that particular staff members resisted a program because they felt it focused on irrelevant skills.

Resistance can also be inferred from review of permanent products. Written workshop exercises, for example, can be reviewed to suggest the extent to which the staff invested the effort expected of individuals interested in the program.

Describing the Personnel Development
Service Delivery Problem

A personnel development problem-clarification statement should include the following information:

The target population(s) requiring training

The specific needs of each identified population in terms of competencies and the commonality of need with other groups

The priority for program design assigned each need

Relevant contextual information about the readiness of the district for personnel development efforts

This information should be presented in a narrative that can serve as the basis for program-design activities.

DESIGNING PERSONNEL
DEVELOPMENT PROGRAMS

Describing Personnel Development Program
Purpose, Goals, and Objectives

The purpose of a personnel development program is based upon a need for improving the job-related competencies of one or more staff populations as reflected in the problem-clarification statement. The purpose should clearly indicate the rationale, scope, and major outcomes of the program to be designed. An example of a statement of purpose for a personnel development program is as follows:

The purpose of the program is to help regular classroom teachers in the Washington Elementary School better educate minority children. The program will be under the direction of the school social worker and will be delivered over the course of the school year. As a result of participating in the program, teachers will increase their knowledge of and respect for minority cultures and their skill in differentiating cultural differences from potential handicapping conditions.

Personnel development program goals are derived from the statement of purpose and the needs reflected in the problem-clarification statement. As such, goals reflect desired outcomes having to do with knowledge, affect, or skill. Four program goals that can be derived from the statement of purpose just described are:

To improve regular education teachers' *knowledge* of minority cultures

To improve regular education teachers' *knowledge* of nonstandard English dialects

To increase regular education teachers' *respect* (affect) for cultural diversity

To improve regular education teachers' *skill* in differentiating between language differences and language disorders

The objectives of a personnel development program are written statements delineating observable, measurable behaviors that will be used to indicate goal attainment. Program objectives must reflect program goals. For example, objectives for cognitive goals should specifically describe the knowledge to be gained; affective objectives should denote observable indicators of improved feelings or attitudes; skill objectives should delineate specific, job-related competencies. Program objectives should be realistic expectations of what staff members might accomplish given the resources available for program development.

Evaluating Personnel Development Program Alternatives

Once program purpose, goals, and objectives have been described, program alternatives can be evaluated. In doing this, we recommend categorizing goals according to type (that is, knowledge, affective, skill). This categorization is helpful because different goal types lend themselves more or less well to particular delivery options. For example, knowledge goals frequently lend themselves to didactic presentations delivered through workshops or university courses; skill goals lend themselves to formats such as supervision and peer consultation.

Following the categorization of goals, a variety of delivery options should be examined in relation to the goals. This task is often overlooked in personnel development program design, since in-service training is almost universally associated with the one-day district-wide seminar or lecture presentation. Failure to see in-service training in terms of the breadth of methods that can be employed can turn staff development into a tedious routine despised by participants and presenters. Box 6-4 delineates a variety of personnel development alternatives for use in program design.

BOX 6-4 *PERSONNEL DEVELOPMENT PROGRAM ALTERNATIVES*

WORKSHOPS
    Lecture Presentations
    Media Presentations
    Case Study Seminars
    Simulations and Role Playing
    Brainstorming Sessions
    Staff Share-a-thon

GRADUATE COURSES

PROFESSIONAL CONFERENCES

CONSULTING RELATIONSHIPS
   Peer Consultation/Assistance
   External Advisor

SUPERVISION

PROFESSIONAL READING
   Journals
   Resource Books

In evaluating various program alternatives, we have found the following questions helpful:

> If the program being considered is an on-site workshop, what financial resources and released-time arrangements are necessary? Can they be made readily available?
>
> If the program being considered is a consulting relationship, to what extent and when are both parties willing to work together?
>
> If the program being considered requires directed reading, how will the outcomes of this activity be documented and monitored? By whom?

These questions are illustrative, not exhaustive; they denote some of the inquiries that can be made in assessing alternatives. Answers to them should be supplemented with a discussion of overall advantages of each option, including knowledge of the service delivery context obtained during the problem-clarification phase. The alternative that presents the greatest likelihood of achieving desired goals within the conditions imposed by the existing context should be the option selected.

Developing the Personnel Development
Program Design

The task of developing the personnel development program design is primarily one of arranging the conditions needed for the program to operate (e.g., budget, rooms, activities, staffing) and deciding upon the roles and responsibilities of various staff members. With respect to operational conditions, one element deserving particular attention is that of incentives. Many personnel development programs fail because personnel are generally given few inducements to participate. Incentives should be built into the program at the design stage. Such inducements might include released time for participation, points applied to salary-guide increments, and reimbursement for graduate tuition or professional books purchased.

Care should also be given to ensure that interesting experiences are built into programs. To the extent possible, workshops should be designed to include a variety of activities. These activities should be interspersed to keep any one activity from becoming routine. So, for example, a workshop for regular education teachers on the language characteristics of minority children might begin with a lecture presentation followed by a video tape giving examples of children with language disorders and differences. It might conclude with a small-group exercise in which each group is required to watch tapes depicting a series of children, decide whether to refer each child for language assessment, and discuss the reason for each decision.

To stimulate interest, workshop activities should also, to the maximum degree consistent with goals and objectives, emphasize the active participation of staff. Role playing, simulation, small-group discussion, and other "hands-on" exercises should be used frequently. Overreliance on passive delivery modes, such as lecture and media presentation, can be both deadly boring and grossly ineffective in achieving desired in-service program outcomes.

On the topic of staff roles and responsibilities, particular attention should be paid to arrangements with outside training consultants. Consultants should be fully briefed on the purpose, goals, and objectives of the program and the role they are expected to fulfill. District in-service staff coordinators should, in turn, be sure that they understand the honorarium, travel, and equipment requirements of the consultant. All design arrangements can then be finalized in a written plan generally consistent with that presented in Table 1-1.

Evaluating the Personnel Development Program Design

Since personnel development programs require sanction and support of administrators and staff alike, we suggest that these professionals be actively involved in the design-evaluation process. Representatives of both the school administration and staff targeted to receive the program can be given a copy of the design and asked to read it and respond to various design-evaluation questions. These include:

> Do you understand the nature and scope of the in-service program? Do you understand what staff competencies the program is meant to impact and how it will accomplish this? Are the populations to which the program is directed clearly stated? (Clarity)
>
> Does the program design seem to cover all considerations relevant to carrying out the in-service program? (Comprehensiveness)
>
> Are all parts or aspects of the program logically related? If not, which appear inconsistent? (Internal consistency)
>
> Does the staff development program seem compatible with current conditions in the district? Does it fit in well with other existing district in-service programs? Does it duplicate the efforts of other programs? Does the program seem responsive to the staff need it was designed to address? (Compatibility)
>
> Are the training methods and content described educationally meaningful, given current notions of good practice and educational theory? (Theoretical soundness)

Information obtained from these questions should be used to modify or refine the program design as needed, prior to implementation.

IMPLEMENTING PERSONNEL
DEVELOPMENT PROGRAMS

Facilitating Personnel Development
Program Implementation

Throughout this chapter, we have alluded to the importance of involving staff in in-service program-design efforts. Making staff members feel that their concerns continue to be important is essential to successful implementation. Three elements of the DURABLE approach are particularly helpful in facilitating the implementation of and staff involvement in a personnel development program. These elements are discussing, understanding, and building.

Discussing. The nature and scope of the personnel development program should always be discussed with program participants. Discussion can occur either at a faculty meeting or at the beginning of the in-service program. Based on this discussion, participants should be better informed about (1) the rationale and need for the personnel development program; (2) the major outcomes or goals expected to result from staff participation; (3) expected professional benefits accruing from involvement; (4) the kinds of activities in which they will be engaged; and (5) the time period and dates over which the program will occur. If a Personnel Development Team (PDT) has been involved in designing the program, a member of that team should lead the discussion with program participants.

Understanding. In conjunction with discussing, an understanding of participants' concerns about the program should be sought. For example, in order to appropriately implement a personnel development program, it may be necessary to understand the extent to which participants (1) perceive the program as threatening, (2) consider the program credible, (3) believe the program is addressing their needs, and (4) predict the program can be implemented successfully. This information can be useful in adapting the program prior to or during its implementation.

Building. Building can be employed at any time during program implementation but is especially important just prior to and during the initial stages of the program. Essentially, the program designers and trainers attempt to communicate to participants a sense of enthusiasm about the value of the program. It is our experience that unless those responsible for the personnel development program show enthusiasm for it, the interest of participants in attending the program will be significantly reduced.

Evaluating Personnel Development
Program Implementation

Assessing the extent to which a personnel development program has been implemented is important for a variety of reasons. First, in order to conduct a meaningful assessment of program outcome, it is necessary to know what was actually delivered. Second, evaluation of personnel development program implementation provides information on the feasibility of conducting the program at other sites. Finally, this type of evaluation can suggest operational problems or other aspects of the program to be improved.

Evaluating the implementation of a personnel development program can be guided by five questions. These will be considered next.

Was the personnel development program carried out as planned? This question focuses on obtaining information about how discrepant the implemented program was from the intended one. In answering this question, the most common implementation variables to assess are:

Extent to which scheduled activities occurred

Amount of human and financial resources utilized, given those originally allocated to the program

Types of instructional and experiential methods used

Materials used, such as handouts, worksheets, audiovisual (AV) materials and equipment

Extent to which those who conducted the program followed the prescribed instructional or supervisory procedures

Percent attendance and professional role of those participating in the program

Information of this type can be gathered through interviews with trainers and in-service program participants.

Were instructional methods adequate? This question can be answered through participant questionnaire and interview, direct observation, and reviews of permanent products. Information should be gathered about the adequacy of such variables as the (1) audibility and visibility of AV materials and other media, (2) legibility and clarity of handouts and worksheets, and (3) utility of various exercises and related experiential activities.

Were instructors appropriate for conducting the program? Information to answer this question usually is best obtained by means of direct observation or through participant questionnaire or interview. Judgments can be made on the (1) extent to which the instructors appeared to hold the attention of the participants, (2) responsiveness of the instructors to participants' questions and concerns, and (3) extent to which the instructors seemed to have a grasp of the subject matter.

Did staff members participate in the program? This question focuses on the nature and extent of participant involvement in the program. Important variables include the extent to which targeted staff members (1) attended the program, (2) enthusiastically took part in program activities, and (3) cooperated in terms of completing program assignments. Information can be gathered by checking attendance rosters to determine who attended, and by observing activities to infer the degree of involvement in them.

Were facilities adequate? This question centers upon (1) the size and arrangement of the room, (2) room temperature and ventilation, and (3) seating, lighting, and acoustics. It can best be answered through informal discussion with participants.

The information derived from these questions documents what was delivered, suggests the advisability of running the program again at other sites, and identifies areas for which the program needs to be improved.

ASSESSING THE OUTCOMES OF PERSONNEL DEVELOPMENT PROGRAMS

Assessing personnel development program outcomes has been a relatively neglected planning and evaluation activity. Several explanations can account for lack of attention to it. First, personnel development programs often have been planned and carried out as isolated events, each single-day workshop standing apart from other workshops and ongoing in-service activities. Rarely has it been the case that an in-service program has been planned and executed as a sequence of interrelated activities (e.g., workshops, supervision, reading) carried out across a significant period of time. The view of in-service programs as isolated events understandably reduces the profitability of outcome evaluation. Why spend a week constructing instruments and analyzing data to draw conclusions about a one-day workshop?

Second, the ultimate purpose of personnel development is undoubtedly to improve pupils' learning. However, many factors affect how students learn; teasing out increased learning due to staff development from that due to other factors is a hopelessly impossible task. Third, the school staff may be resistant to personnel development outcome assessment. The staff may view this kind of evaluation as *personnel* or *personal* evaluation rather than *program* evaluation. Fourth, evaluation of the outcome of any program requires human resources to carry out the task. When limited evaluation personnel exist, personnel development outcome evaluation usually is at the bottom of the list.

We believe that some personnel development outcomes can be practically evaluated if appropriate questions are asked and workable approaches employed. In the next section, we will focus on questions of goal attainment, related effects, consumer reaction, and cause-effect relations:

> To what extent have the goals of the personnel development program been attained?
> Have any related effects been observed following implementation of the personnel development program that may have resulted from the program?
> How have consumers reacted to the personnel development program?
> Was the personnel development program the cause of the observed outcomes?

Evaluating Goal Attainment

Evaluating the goal attainment of personnel development programs centers on questions of knowledge, attitude, and skill development. Examples of such questions are:

To what degree have school principals become more knowledgeable about the major provisions of PL 94-142?

To what extent have regular classroom teachers developed improved attitudes toward children with physical handicaps?

To what extent have multidisciplinary team members improved conflict-resolution skills designed to foster cooperation at team meetings?

In evaluating in-service goal attainment, several outcome-evaluation approaches can be employed, including (1) preprogram-postprogram assessment and (2) a time-series evaluation. We will consider the preprogram-postprogram assessment approach here.

Preprogram-postprogram assessment.   In this approach, the level of goal attainment is measured prior to program implementation and again following the program's conclusion. Judgments then can be made about the extent of goal attainment and the amount of change over the baseline, or preprogram, period.

The measures used to assess personnel development goals must be relevant to goal content. The same kinds of measures used in assessing personnel-development needs are appropriate for goal-based evaluation, and will not be detailed here. In general, though, knowledge goals are primarily assessed by means of paper-and-pencil measures, such as tests, while affective and attitudinal goals are assessed by means of questionnaires or structured-interview procedures. Personnel development goals that focus on skill development may be difficult to assess, since their evaluation may demand naturalistic observation not often possible given legal and political constraints (e.g., teacher contracts). When direct classroom observation of the staff is not possible, performance in role-playing situations, either live or on video tape, might be considered. Also, analysis and reviews of permanent products or work samples (e.g., IEPs, teacher-made materials) might be useful in inferring improved skill levels. Table 6-2 provides an outline of various methods that can be employed for measuring goal attainment in personnel development programs.

TABLE 6-2   Methods for Evaluating Personnel Development Goal Attainment

METHOD	GOAL TYPE		
	KNOWLEDGE	AFFECT	SKILL
Questionnaires		X	
Essays	X		
Oral reports	X		
Interviews	X	X	
Situational exercises			X
Work samples			X
Ratings by peers and supervisors	X	X	X
Tests	X		

To illustrate the preprogram-postprogram–assessment approach to evaluating the goal attainment of a personnel development program, consider a goal and objective taken from an in-service training-program design for multidisciplinary teams (Maher, 1981):

> To improve team ability to write complete individualized programs (IEPs). Following training, there will be an increase of 40 percent over baseline in the number of complete IEPs written by the team, as defined by a checklist for a complete program.

In employing the preprogram-postprogram–assessment approach with this goal and objective, all or a representative sample of IPs written by team members prior to training would be reviewed, using the checklist to detect missing or incomplete IP elements (e.g., no date for program review, lack of measurable objectives). An IP would be considered complete only if all elements were fully specified.

The number of complete IPs relative to all IPs would then be determined and expressed as a percent. This percent value would serve as a baseline measure of goal attainment. Following the training program, which might occur via weekly workshops over a month's time (see Maher, 1980), a postprogram assessment of the goal and objective would be conducted, using the same permanent product-review method.

Figure 6-1 presents data on goal attainment of the training-program goal and objective before and following training-program implementation. As the bar

FIGURE 6-1   *PERCENT OF COMPLETE INDIVIDUALIZED PROGRAMS BEFORE AND AFTER TEAM IN-SERVICE TRAINING*

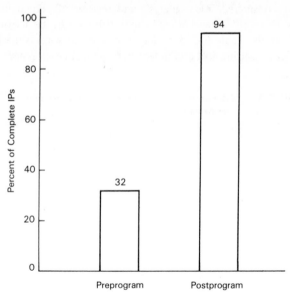

graph reveals, a large increase is apparent in percent of IP completeness at time of postprogram assessment. The three-fold increase in completeness of 62 percentage points over baseline conditions indicated that this goal was attained.

The preprogram-postprogram–assessment approach can be readily employed for evaluating the goal attainment of a personnel development program, provided goals and objectives are clearly and specifically described. However, the approach is weak in determining whether the program was the cause of goal attainment and if factors not part of the program were causes of the observed effects.

Evaluating Related Effects

Evaluating the related effects of a personnel development program consists of identifying positive and negative outcomes not reflected in personnel development goals and objectives. For example, following an in-service program meant to increase regular classroom teachers' understanding of cultural differences, participating teachers might be observed making attempts to involve more minority children in after-school academic activities. Such behavior might be hypothesized as a positive related effect of the personnel development program.

Preprogram-postprogram assessment is one useful means for evaluating related effects. Using this approach involves four activities:

Describing preprogram conditions
Determining extent of implementation of the personnel development program
Describing postprogram conditions
Determining related effects

Describing preprogram conditions.   This activity involves gathering information about the behavior of teachers and the learning of exceptional pupils prior to the implementation of a personnel development program. The information obtained serves as a basis for evaluating possible related effects on teachers and pupils following the in-service program. Toward this end, information can be collected about the following kinds of variables:

Level of pupils' skill development
Nature of interactions between exceptional pupils and their exceptional and normal peers
Nature of interactions between teachers and pupils
Expectations of teachers, parents, and pupils for learning of exceptional students

Information about pupils' skill development can be obtained from pupil IPs. This information forms the basis for looking at effects not reflected in goals and objectives of the personnel development program.

Information about interaction between and among exceptional pupils and their normal or exceptional peers can be collected by behavioral-observation procedures. For example, the number of times that regular education pupils initiate discussion with special education pupils during a group project might be counted as might the number of times regular students help special pupils with classwork. Interactional patterns might be described in terms of the number of times teachers provide social reinforcement to exceptional pupils, the frequency with which exceptional pupils initiate discussion with teachers, or the extent to which pupils do not comply with teacher requests.

The expectations of others for the learning of exceptional pupils might also be sampled. Structured interviews with teachers, parents, and pupils could, for example, focus upon identifying expectations for the degree of goal attainment to be realized by the pupils. Detailed discussions of methods for classroom observation, interviewing, and summarizing the results of pupil-teacher interactions can be found in Brophy and Good (1969), Kratochwill (1982), Cartwright and Cartwright (1974), and Guba and Lincoln (1981).

Determining extent of program implementation. This activity is intended to determine if the personnel development program was delivered as planned. If investigation reveals that the program was not delivered, it is obviously inappropriate to conclude that any effects observed in teachers and pupils upon postprogram assessment are related to the program.

Describing postprogram conditions. To give related effects an opportunity to manifest themselves, a period of time—perhaps a few weeks or months—should be allowed to elapse before postprogram assessment is conducted. When undertaken, outcome assessment should focus upon the same pupil and staff variables targeted during preprogram assessment.

Determining related effects. Analysis of data obtained from the preprogram-postprogram assessment centers upon determining the nature of any observed pupil or staff changes and ruling out competing explanations for those effects. Changes observed might be positive or negative, such as (1) increased positive interactions between minority pupils and teachers after a cultural-awareness program, (2) use of adaptive behavior scales to the total exclusion of other measures after an inservice program on assessing minority children, and (3) increased expectations for EMR student learning after a cognitive-skills in-service program.

Before concluding that a related effect has been detected, all reasonable competing explanations for that effect should be explored. Reasonable explanations include normal pupil growth, regression, other programs, and instrumentation, as well as other factors discussed previously.

Evaluating Consumer Reaction

Consumer-reaction evaluation is without doubt the most frequently employed type of personnel development outcome assessment. While goal-based evaluation focuses on obtaining direct evidence of improvement, consumer-reaction evaluation concerns itself with the *perceptions* of those involved directly and indirectly with the program.

Postprogram approach. Consumer-reaction evaluation can be carried out using the postprogram-assessment approach. In this way, the reactions of consumers are obtained following the program only. This approach focuses primarily on persons who have participated directly in the program, such as a group of teachers provided classroom behavior-management training. In addition, it can include persons who did not directly participate in the program but who have some vested interest in it, such as school principals.

A number of variables can be assessed in a consumer-reaction evaluation. The two variables most frequently assessed are:

Satisfaction, either with the program as a whole, or with certain aspects of the program (e.g., quality of instruction, utility of activities)
Perceptions of the extent to which program goals, or individual participant goals, were attained

As a matter of practice, a consumer-reaction evaluation should be conducted for all personnel development programs. This type of evaluation communicates an interest in the opinions of program participants and can be used to identify improvements as well as suggest the advisability of expanding the program to the other sites. Methods used to evaluate consumer reactions include the questionnaire and interview surveys.

Evaluating Cause-Effect Relations

An evaluation of the cause-effect relations of a personnel development program seeks to determine whether the program was responsible for the observed outcome results. In this type of evaluation, it is necessary to rule out factors other than the personnel development program that may have been responsible for detected outcomes. Unless such factors as those discussed earlier can be ruled out, it is not appropriate to conclude that the personnel development program was the probable cause of observed effects.

Three outcome-evaluation approaches are directly applicable to evaluating cause-effect relations in personnel development programs. The first, the preprogram-postprogram–assessment approach, has already been discussed in chapters 4 and 5. The second approach, the multiple baseline design, will be briefly detailed, as will the comparison-group approach, the third method of evaluating cause-effect relations in personnel development programs.

Multiple baseline approach. The multiple baseline design, an extension of the time-series approach, is particularly useful in evaluating cause-effect relations in instructional-training programs and programs in which supervision is the primary training method. This design can be employed when it is possible to both deliver the program to various participants at different points in time and collect data prior to and during each delivery. Figure 6-2 illustrates the use of the multiple baseline design to evaluate whether clinical supervision was effective in increasing school psychologists' involvement in counseling and IEP planning and evaluation activities. As seen in Figure 6-2, increases in both outcome levels were observed only following the implementation of the in-service program with each school

FIGURE 6-2 *USING THE MULTIPLE BASELINE DESIGN TO ASSESS PERSONNEL DEVELOPMENT CAUSE-EFFECT RELATIONS[a]*

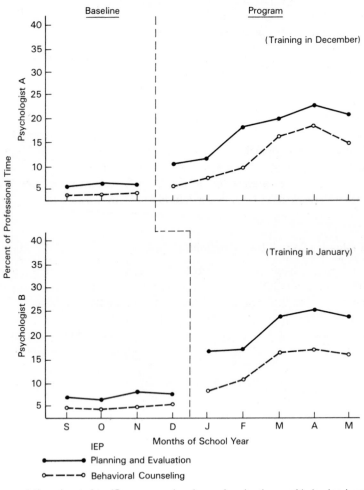

[a]Percentage of time devoted to IP program planning and evaluation, and behavioral counseling activities for Psychologist A (top graph) and Psychologist B (lower graph)

Source: Maher, C. A. Time management training for school psychologists. Professional Psychology, 1981, 12, 613–620. Copyright 1981 by American Psychological Association. Reprinted by permission of the publisher and author.

psychologist. Hence, the results suggest that the program was responsible for the observed outcomes.

Comparison-group approach. This approach involves comparing a group of staff members who received a particular personnel development program with a group of staff members who either did not receive any program or received some alternative training experience. With the comparison-group approach, the personnel development program is considered to have had an effect over and above the alternative condition if staff members who received the program achieve greater outcome levels than the comparison group. Once a personnel development program is judged as having an effect relative to another program such as a no-program condition, consideration then can be given to whether the program produced that result.

Two versions of the comparison-group approach can be employed as a basis for evaluating cause-effect relations in a staff development program. These are the (1) randomized and (2) nonrandomized comparison-group approaches. In the randomized comparison-group approach, staff members are randomly assigned to either the personnel development program or to the comparison condition. When random assignment is employed, chances are that both groups will share relevant background characteristics (e.g., number of years' teaching experience, level of professional education, level of competency in the area targeted by the program, extent of exposure to nonprogram influences, such as experiential learning). Random assignment, therefore, helps rule out competing explanations for program effects, by providing two groups that are theoretically affected by plausible alternative factors to the same degree. For example, the effects of normal growth, regression, instrumentation, and so on should be the same in both groups; therefore, any differences in outcome levels that are observed are most likely owed to differences in the in-service program received. As detailed in Campbell and Stanley (1966), Cook and Campbell (1979), and many other sources, random assignment is the most powerful means available for ruling out nonprogram factors as causes of observed effects.

Two kinds of evaluation situations, if found to prevail, suggest use of the randomized comparison-group approach. The first situation is one in which a large number of staff members are viewed as possible targets for a program yet only some staff can be provided with the program, owing to limited resources. In this situation, it may be possible to randomly assign staff to program and no-program conditions, thereby giving all staff members an equal chance of being selected for the program. A second situation is one in which two alternative programs are available. In this case, members of the staff can be randomly assigned to either condition.

In the *non*randomized comparison-group approach, intact groups of staff members are assigned to the personnel development program and the comparison condition. An example of such a situation is one in which all elementary-school teachers in School X received instructional training from a master teacher based there, while teachers in School Y did not. In using the nonrandomized comparison-group approach, the evaluation results are more defensible when various validity threats are ruled out, especially when it can be documented that the two groups (e.g., teachers in schools X and Y) were similar on relevant background variables (e.g., preprogram instructional-skill levels, years' teaching experience), and that the schools were similar on organizationally relevant variables, such as teacher-student ratio and curricula.

A particular situation where the nonrandomized comparison group would be *inappropriate* is when staff participate in in-service efforts on a voluntary basis. In such an event, it would not be sound practice to compare a volunteer group with teachers who did not register for the program. This is so because outcome differences between the two groups could be due to nonprogram factors, such as lower initial skill levels among volunteers than nonvolunteers. For evaluating cause-effect relations when personnel development programs are provided to volunteer groups, preprogram-postprogram assessment is recommended.

SUMMARY

Personnel development is essential for developing and maintaining critical job competencies related to providing an appropriate education to exceptional pupils. Personnel development, however, is a complex and often difficult undertaking in school districts. In particular, staff members sometimes do not feel obligated to help plan personnel development activities or participate in training programs. Furthermore, members of the staff are often unclear about the potential benefits of in-service education.

This chapter has considered personnel development services to include a broad array of programs and activities. Among these programs and activities are staff supervision, professional readings and site visits, as well as parental and paraprofessional training.

An important aspect of planning and evaluating personnel development services is the active involvement of staff. A Personnel Development Team has been suggested as a useful means of assuring such involvement. Through a PDT, representatives of teacher, administrator, and parent groups can bring important and diverse perspectives to bear on determining the priority of staff development needs and on designing, implementing, and evaluating in-service programs.

The outcome assessment of personnel development programs has been a relatively neglected planning and evaluation activity. When outcome assessment is conducted, the question most frequently addressed is that of consumer reaction to in-service training. With clearly stated program goals and objectives, other evaluation questions, such as those of goal attainment, related effects, and cause-effect relations, can begin to be addressed.

7

PLANNING AND EVALUATING
ADMINISTRATIVE SERVICES

Administrative services coordinate all aspects of the special education services delivery system. As such, they are the management or "executive" function that makes the system work. Administrative services take the form of programs targeted to managing particular demands and constraints placed on the services delivery system. Included among these programs are student case management, program-compliance monitoring and reporting, program planning and evaluation, cost analysis, and staff supervision. This chapter discusses planning and evaluating these different administrative programs.

OVERVIEW OF ADMINISTRATIVE SERVICES

Need for Administrative Services
in Special Education

Our view of special education administrative services is based largely upon systems-analysis models of planning and evaluation. In addition to emphasizing the relationship of elements within a program, these models highlight the interaction of programs with one another and the effects outside forces have on programs.

In keeping with our systems orientation, we see the need for administrative programs as emanating from a variety of complex organizational demands and constraints placed upon schools. Organizational demands are requirements imposed by forces both external to and within the school district. External organizational demands are the legislative, litigative, and professional mandates governing special education. Examples of external demands are the requirements of PL 94-142, the precedent-setting decisions issued through such legal actions as *Armstrong* vs. *Kline* and the *Standards for Educational and Psychological Tests.* Internal organizational demands are pressures brought to bear by constituencies within the school district. These include the stipulations of teacher contracts as well as the requests of parent and community groups.

Organizational demands influence the special services system in different ways. Some demands have the most profound effects. For example, the very existence of special education is due to societal demands—embodied in PL 94-142 and in case law—for educating handicapped children. Organizational demands also affect the special services system in subtler ways. External mandates help mold the day-to-day operation of the system, by specifying procedures for such things as determining service eligibility, monitoring and reporting, cost accounting, and planning and evaluating educational programs.

Organizational constraints are the quantity and quality of resources available for delivering special education services. Into this category fall (1) human resources, such as teachers and specialists; (2) technological resources, including methods and materials; (3) financial support; (4) physical resources; and (5) informational resources, such as locally developed policies and procedures.

Organizational demands and constraints interact in a number of ways. To be satisfied, some demands—such as those for services—require the expenditure of resources. The level of resources actually available, of course, helps determine the extent to which these demands will be met. Satisfying other demands generates resources. For example, state and federal education agencies typically require a certified report of the number of children served, before disbursing entitlement monies. Still other demands may impose additional resource constraints, as when community forces press for increasing computer-literacy programs at the expense of programs for the handicapped.

Managing the various organizational demands and constraints imposed upon the special services system is the job of administration. Such management is critical to the continued functioning of the services delivery system. Without it, the system would have no means for allocating resources to the requirements placed upon it.

Nature and Scope
of Administrative Services

Organizational demands and constraints are managed through a series of targeted programs. Each of these targeted programs is responsible for managing a different set of demands and constraints. For example, the most basic demand placed on the services delivery system is providing a free appropriate public education to handicapped children. Satisfying this demand encompasses a variety of administrative responsibilities, including overseeing development of the individualized program, ensuring that the student is provided due-process guarantees mandated by law, and systematically coordinating the different services that may need to be delivered. The administrative program commonly assigned these responsibilities is student case management.

In addition to providing a free appropriate public education, external demands are also placed on the services delivery system for monitoring and reporting overall compliance with legal requirements. Compliance monitoring and reporting programs are composed of organized procedures for gathering basic statistical data on the handicapping conditions of children served, the types of services provided, and the degree of success achieved in meeting mandated evaluation time lines, among other things. This information is regularly transmitted to superintendents, boards of education, and state agencies responsible for overseeing demand compliance.

A third critical demand placed on a special education administration is developing and assessing programs. Among other things, this responsibility is meant to satisfy legal regulations for tailoring services to pupil needs and parent concern for improving programs. The administrative program targeted to this demand is planning and evaluation—the focus of this book.

To respond successfully to demands placed on the system, an administration must also manage resources. Cost-analysis procedures—or programs—must exist for projecting financial needs, arriving at the most cost-effective allocation of available resources, and monitoring expenditures to ensure that they remain within budget constraints.

Because personnel resources are almost universally limited, programs must also be targeted toward staff supervision. Administrators must assign personnel to those activities that will return the maximum benefit to the children served by the system. In addition, they must evaluate the staff for purposes of professional development, promotion, and dismissal, and be responsive to their need for advice and direction.

Difficulties in Providing
Administrative Services

One of the foremost difficulties in the delivery of administrative services relates to time. Most administrators spend the bulk of their time reacting to problems: due-process actions brought by parents, complaints from the state department on the completeness of pupil records, pressure from the superintendent regarding the need to limit expenditures to budgeted amounts. This crisis mode of operation is problematic for a number of reasons. First, it leaves the staff with the distressing—but accurate—perception that their lives are being controlled by external events; priorities change from one crisis to the next, and stability never seems to arrive. Second, it leaves little time for other important administrative responsibilities, such as improving existing programs. Finally, it creates a vicious cycle; the more time spent reacting to crises, the less time for taking preventive measures.

We believe that the special education services delivery system can be proactively administered by developing targeted programs to oversee the various demands and constraints imposed upon it. Administration through targeted programs should help the services delivery system operate in a more orderly and purposeful manner.

CLARIFYING ADMINISTRATIVE SERVICE DELIVERY PROBLEMS

The administrative problem-clarification process consists of three elements: assessing service delivery needs, determining their context, and describing the administrative problem.

Assessing Service Delivery Needs

Administrative service needs can be assessed through a process that involves (1) identifying demands and constraints placed on the services delivery system, (2) specifying needed management functions, (3) determining the extent to which existing programs successfully perform those functions, (4) assigning priorities to improving specific programs, and (5) estimating resources required for needed improvements.

Identifying demands and constraints. Identifying organizational demands requires a thorough review of the responsibilities mandated by education law and regulations, responsibilities assigned the administrator by the school district, concerns expressed by parents and the community, and principles of good administrative practice. Examples of organizational demands include providing a free appropriate public education, monitoring the system's compliance with education regulations, and developing and assessing programs.

Because responsibilities, concerns, and, to a lesser extent, principles, change, the organizational demands placed on the services delivery system should be reviewed frequently. Education law and regulations in particular need to be closely monitored, as they are often modified by interpretive statements, court decisions, and new laws and regulations. These changes can be followed through such periodicals as *Education of the Handicapped* (Capitol Publications) and *Liaison Bulletin* (National Association of State Directors of Special Education).

The organizational constraints imposed upon services delivery systems typically fall into the categories previously cited: human, financial, informational, technological, and physical.

Specifying management functions. The administrative functions needed to manage different demands and constraints are derived from an analysis of those organizational factors. For example, providing a free appropriate public education implies a number of specific functions collectively referred to as case management. Among these might be:

coordinating services provided the child

ensuring that promised services are provided

ensuring that due-process guarantees are afforded

monitoring the child's progress

updating and maintaining the child's record file

involving the parent in the educational decision-making process and responding to parent concerns

directing the child and parent to needed services outside the school

Other critical demands, such as program-compliance monitoring and reporting, can also be broken down into their basic management requirements. Program-compliance monitoring and reporting can be thought to require such functions as gathering and reporting the following types of information:

the names and number of students receiving special services

the numbers of children receiving particular related services

the names and number of students referred but not evaluated within mandated time limits

the names of students in out-of-district placements

the names of children received for services from other districts

A final example of the analysis of administrative functions relates to managing financial constraints. Managing cost constraints might be thought to require such functions as

projecting, or budgeting, future support needs

allocating available funds (i.e., revising budgets to bring them into line with appropriations)

tracking expenditures as they occur

comparing the costs and benefits of various program alternatives

billing purchasers of services (e.g., other school districts sending children for special education)

paying service providers (e.g., professionals providing contracted services)

Determining the adequacy of existing procedures. Once the administrative functions needed to manage specific demands and constraints have been identified, the extent to which those functions adequately address demands and constraints should be assessed. Needs can be said to exist in those areas in which program functions do not adequately address organizational demands and constraints. In terms of the case-management procedures already discussed, the inquiry would focus on determining the (1) accuracy, timeliness, and accessibility of student-record data, (2) coordination of services delivered by different professionals, and (3) provision of due-process guarantees. Box 7-1 provides a sample rating scale to help assess the

BOX 7-1 *RATING SCALE FOR CASE-MANAGEMENT NEEDS ASSESSMENT*

```
DIRECTIONS: This form lists some of the important functions that a
special education case-management program must perform.  Read each
statement and indicate the frequency with which your current case-
management program performs each function.


  Always        Often          Sometimes         Rarely          Never
    5             4                 3               2               1


_____1. Assigns a case-manager for each handicapped child.

_____2. Requires at least monthly contact between the case manager and
        other professionals providing services to the child.

_____3. Requires at least monthly contact among professionals
        providing services to the same child in related areas.

_____4. Provides same-day responses to requests for student record
        information.

_____5. Provides insertion of new information in student records
        within a week of receiving that information.

_____6. Requires at least bimonthly contact between the case manager
        and the child's parents.

_____7. Provides immediate access to listings of community services
        for the handicapped (e.g., dental, medical, adaptive living,
        transportation, advocacy).
```

degree to which demands are adequately addressed by existing case-management functions.

The Rating Scale for Case-Management Needs Assessment (see Box 7-1) can be given to a small sample of individuals familiar with the district's current case-management procedures (e.g., principals, team members, special teachers). The proportion of individuals indicating a particular response for each question can then be calculated to gain a rough indication of the specific functions the existing program is not performing adequately. Table 7-1 presents sample data from a hypothetical school district.

Analysis of the data in Table 7-1 suggests possible problems in case-management functions relating to access and maintenance of student records (questions 4 and 5). Because this information only indicates that a problem *may* exist, the administrator should follow up by meeting with the staff to discover if there is a problem and what the specific difficulties are. These meetings might, for example, reveal that student record files are scattered across different offices in the district, are poorly organized, or are rarely signed out. In addition, investigation might uncover long delays in entering new information into pupils' record files.

Assigning priorities to program improvements. In cases where the demands and constraints related to particular administrative functions are not adequately addressed, the importance of improving the function should be evaluated. Impor-

TABLE 7-1 Summary of Case-Management Needs Assessment Results

QUESTION #	RESPONSE CATEGORY[a]				
	ALWAYS	OFTEN	SOMETIMES	RARELY	NEVER
1. Assigned manager	1.00	.00	.00	.00	.00
2. Manager/professional contact	.35	.45	.15	.05	.00
3. Professional/professional contact	.30	.50	.15	.05	.00
4. Record requests	.00	.05	.10	<u>.50</u>	<u>.35</u>
5. Record updates	.00	.00	.00	<u>.35</u>	<u>.65</u>
6. Manager/parent contact	.45	.35	.15	.05	.00
7. Resource access	.50	.35	.10	.05	.00

[a]Numbers indicate proportions of respondents selecting each option.

tance can be expressed in relation to other district needs through a simple ranking procedure. Needs can be ranked according to the seriousness of consequences resulting from ignoring each one. The administrator's ranking of needs can be cross-validated by getting input from representatives of key constituencies. This input will aid in choosing the most important needs for action and in gaining support among the staff and parents for the decision that is made. Table 7-2 presents an example of a ranked list of administrative needs.

For example, a district might find that a major administrative need exists in the case-management function responsible for maintaining pupil records. Addressing this need might take precedence over other program-improvement needs: con-

TABLE 7-2 Ranking of Needs According to Seriousness

RANK	NEED	CONSEQUENCE OF IGNORING NEED
1	Student-record improvement	Continue using current program with risk of inaccurate school-aid application, loss in funding, loss of individual student records.
2	In-service training for resource-room teachers in Orton-Gillingham reading method	Teachers continue using current repertoire of reading methods; some students not taught effectively.
3	Assessment tools for speech pathologist to use in diagnosing speech/language difficulties	Pathologist continues to use informal measures; speech difficulty not documented through formal means—some subtle difficulties missed.

tinued use of a dysfunctional pupil-record system might result in reporting errors—
that could inadvertently reduce the district's school-aid reimbursement—and in lost
student records. Besides depriving the school of important information, lost records
could open the district to legal action by the parents of children affected by the
loss.

Estimating required resources. The resource levels necessary for improving
an administrative program can be conveniently expressed as dollar costs. Dollar
costs are convenient for considering the feasibility of program-improvement efforts
because money represents the primary resource concern of most districts and because other resource requirements can usually be expressed in financial terms.

Cost estimates for improving the administrative program will necessarily be
very gross. Exactly what the program will involve has yet to be decided, and hence,
a good estimate of costs will not be possible. In most cases, however, *rough* figures
can be generated through contact with other administrators who may have installed
similar programs. Estimates should take account of the approximate cost of additional staff, equipment, and supplies that may be required to develop and operate
the program.

Assessing the Service Delivery Context

We will discuss three of the eight A VICTORY factors employed in assessing
the administrative service delivery context: values, circumstances, and yield.

Values. The values factor refers to the extent to which the principles of the
administrative program are consistent with those held by the staff and community.
Values are particularly important to assess in programs that are to employ innovative technologies. For instance, many parents are concerned with the use of computers to store pupils' records because they feel that using computers conflicts
with their personal privacy. School administrators have likewise expressed reserva-
tions about automating student-record systems, especially when these systems are
electronically linked to intermediate-unit or state-agency data banks. These administrative systems are at odds with district values for local control.

Circumstances. The circumstances dimension of the A VICTORY model
relates to the extent to which prevailing factors facilitate or impede the program's
integration into the district. For instance, the superintendent and school board
may support efforts to automate record procedures for special education pupils
as long as the resulting system is consistent with long-term district plans to automate the records of general education pupils.

Yield. The extent to which members of the administrative staff perceive
benefits for themselves and students resulting from the program is encompassed
by yield. The administrator may justifiably feel that a computerized cost-analysis
program will make financial management easier. The secretary, who has to operate

the machine, may view the situation quite differently. With no computer experience, and fearful of learning this new skill, the secretary may perceive little yield for participating in the cost-analysis program.

Describing the Administrative Service Delivery Problem

The description of the administrative service delivery problem should summarize the results of problem clarification. It should include the demands and constraints not being adequately addressed by current programs, recommended program and functional enhancements, the priority given improving particular administrative functions, and the ball-park cost of developing improved programs. In addition, contextual factors relevant to developing and operating enhanced administrative programs should be described. A sample description of an administrative service delivery problem is given in Box 7-2.

BOX 7-2 *DESCRIPTION OF ADMINISTRATIVE SERVICE DELIVERY PROBLEM*

Demands or Constraints Not Met

Federal and state demands for keeping accurate pupil records are not fully satisfied by the current special services record-management system. Because pupil records also form the basis for state-aid reimbursements, the current record system is also impacting upon the management of the district's financial resources.

Recommended Program and Functional Improvements

Pupil records maintained through the district's case-management program are distributed across a number of school-district offices. In addition, multiple files are kept for many children, making needed information difficult to access. It is recommended that a computer-based record-keeping system be designed that would locate all critical pupil information in a central file accessible to case managers and other district administrators.

Priority Assigned Improvements

Improvements in the student record-keeping function of the case-management program should be given high priority because of the legal and financial importance associated with pupil records. Loss of records could result in liability on the part of the district. In addition, poorly organized pupil records can result in providing erroneous reports of the number of children receiving special services.

Estimated Cost of Improvements

The cost of developing an automated pupil-record system is roughly estimated to be $15,000 to $25,000. This estimate is based upon contacts with three other districts in the county currently using computerized systems.

Relevant Contextual Factors

Ability: Approximately $30,000 is available for new program development in the current fiscal year. In addition, two child-study team members have worked in districts using computerized record systems and have agreed to help plan the new system.

Values: A number of special education teachers have voiced opposition to the system, because they feel the system would invade students' privacy.

Circumstances: The superintendent is planning to expand the district's computing capabilities over the course of the next five years. Superintendent and administrative support for the special education record-keeping system is contingent on compatibility with the planned expansion.

The problem description serves as the basis for deciding to proceed with the administrative program design. This decision will typically hinge on the program's fit with contextual factors—especially whether estimated costs can be covered by available funds. The decision to proceed will necessarily apply only to designing the program. A final decision to install the program will need to wait until the program is designed and firmer estimates of development and operating costs have been produced.

DESIGNING ADMINISTRATIVE PROGRAMS

Describing Administrative Program Purpose, Goals, and Objectives

The design of any program typically begins with a statement of the program's purpose, and administrative programs are no exception. The program's purpose, which should be clearly related to the need for the program, serves both to organize design efforts and as information for those involved or interested in the program. The purpose should present the general rationale for the program, its scope (that is, major activities, client population, staff), and major outcomes. A statement of purpose for a case-management program might be the following:

> The district's case-management program is meant to coordinate the provision of a free appropriate public education for the individual handicapped child. The program involves maintaining student records, regularly meeting with those individuals involved in providing services to the child, ensuring that due-process requirements are adhered to, and maintaining contact with the student's parents. The primary staff for the program is the case manager, who is usually a designated member of the child-study team.

The statement of the administrative program's purpose should be followed by a listing of one or more goals and objectives that the program is intended to accomplish. Such goals and objectives allow those responsible for sanctioning the program to understand more clearly what it is they are being asked to approve; they also serve as explicit benchmarks for an administrative program's outcome assessment. Goals and objectives should reflect the functions the administrative program is being designed to perform. Examples of statements of goals and objectives for a case-management program are given in Box 7–3.

BOX 7–3 *GOALS AND OBJECTIVES OF A CASE-MANAGEMENT PROGRAM*

Goal # 1: The program should result in coordinated service delivery.

Objective #1: A case manager should be assigned to each handicapped child.

Objective #2: Each professional providing service to a particular child should be aware of the other services the child is receiving.

Goal #2: The program should result in efficient maintenance of pupil records.

Objective #1: The whereabouts of individual students' records should be known at all times.

Objective #2: New information should be inserted in students' records within a week of receipt by the case manager.

Evaluating Administrative
Program Alternatives

When the purpose, goals, and objectives of an administrative program have been clearly specified, the task of delineating and evaluating various alternative approaches to achieving those requirements should begin. In the case of administrative programs, a great deal can be learned about alternative administrative approaches by contacting other special education directors or by meeting with the administrators of other programs in the district. The district business administrator, for example, will often be able to suggest different approaches to the management and analysis of costs; the guidance director, approaches to the management of student records and cases; and the research and evaluation director, methods and procedures for planning and evaluation. Finally, a review of the special education literature to find descriptions and analyses of different administrative methodologies can be undertaken.

For example, two common alternatives for performing the case-management student record-keeping function are manual and automated systems. In the manual record-keeping system, student information is housed in file folders stored in metal cabinets. Such files take up a great deal of room, are frequently misplaced, and sometimes exist in duplicate or triplicate for the same student. In addition, the information they contain is often inaccurate, missing, or out-of-date. As a supplement to these record files, index cards duplicating a subset of the information housed in student folders are often kept. These "tickler" files are used to trigger critical events such as reevaluation and individualized program review for individual students. Both tickler and main files serve as the basis for program reporting and compliance monitoring; the number of children provided different types of services is calculated by tabbing through the files and making a manual count on which state- and federal-education aid is based.

Automated, or computerized, student record-keeping systems exist in a number of different forms. Automated systems have been provided to districts through data-processing-service bureaus where the district accesses the service bureau's computer through a leased display terminal and telephone line. Systems have also been built to run on the "main-frame" computers that many districts employ for payroll and other business purposes. Finally, systems are available for use on small, relatively inexpensive micro-computers (Bennett, 1982d).

The evaluation of administrative program alternatives should take into account a number of critical factors. These include the (1) developmental and operating costs of each alternative, (2) amount of time involved in developing each, (3) degree of community, staff, superintendent, child, and board acceptance, and (4) benefits likely to be derived. Box 7-4 contains a chart that displays the differences among three automated student-record management alternatives for a hypothetical district. Alternative A represents a contractual arrangement with a data-processing service bureau; Alternative B, developing a system to run on the district's business computer; and Alternative C, purchase of a micro-computer and student-information management software. The chart is illustrative and is not meant to endorse any particular approach to automating case management.

Analysis of the data presented in Box 7-4 suggests a number of interesting differences among the three alternative student-record management programs.

BOX 7-4 *COMPARISON OF PROGRAM ALTERNATIVES*

Part I

DIRECTIONS: This chart is meant to assist the administrator in assessing different program alternatives. For developmental and operating costs, enter the estimated costs of putting the program into a state of readiness to operate (developmental costs) and the estimated annual costs of running the program (operating costs) once it has been developed. For developmental time, enter the amount of elapsed time in days required to put the program into a state of readiness.

	Program Alternative		
	A	B	C
	Data Processing	On-site	Micro-
Program Dimension	Service	Computer	Computer
DEVELOPMENT COST			
Staff Time	$ 1,000	$15,000	$ 1,000
Materials	0	100	1,400
Equipment	0	8,000	3,000
Travel	500	1,000	500
Consultants	0	1,000	1,000
Telephone	100	100	100
Mail	10	10	10
Printing	0	100	0
Miscellaneous	50	50	50
Total	1,660	25,360	7,060
OPERATING COST			
Staff Time	$7,000	$10,000	$7,000
Materials	400	400	500
Equipment	3,000	0	0
Travel	0	0	0
Consultants	0	0	0
Telephone	1,400	10	10
Mail	10	10	10
Printing	100	100	100
Miscellaneous	7,100	200	300
Total	$19,010	$10,720	$ 7,920
FIVE-YEAR COST	$96,710	$78,960	$46,660
DEVELOPMENT TIME	5 days	180 days	5 days

```
                            Part II


DIRECTIONS:  For each program alternative, rate the following program
dimensions. Use a + to indicate a good rating, a - to denote a poor
rating, a ! to indicate an average judgment, and n/a for not
applicable. , Place the symbol corresponding to your  rating on the
line belonging to the appropriate dimension and column headed by the
proper alternative.

                         Program Alternative


                           A              B              C
                     Data Processing   On-site        Micro-
Program Dimension        Service       Computer       Computer


ACCEPTANCE
  Staff                     !              !              !
  Parents                   !              !              +
  Board                     -              +              +
  Superintendent            -              +              +
  Students                 n/a            n/a            n/a


PROGRAM BENEFITS
  Efficiency                +              +              +
  Effectiveness             +              +              +
  District Image            +              +              +
  Staff Morale              !              !              !


OTHER
  Control                   -              !              +
```

With respect to Program A (contracted data-processing services), the comparison of program alternatives makes it clear that the developmental costs for installing the program are relatively slight. These costs primarily involve the time needed by the staff to research the various data-processing companies and select the most favorable outfit. The annual operating costs of the program under Alternative A are, however, substantial. These costs include basic service charges (miscellaneous), terminal and printer leasing fees (equipment), and telephone bills from the constant contact that must be maintained between the terminal and service bureau in order for the district to use the computer.

Reading down the table, we also note that Alternative A has a relatively short development time, essentially the time involved in finding a service bureau that has a program capable of meeting the district's record-management needs. Acceptance of Alternative A is rated poor to average, given the fact that the work will be contracted out instead of being done in-house; program benefits are considered average to good. Finally, the fact that student data will be stored off-site and that the district will *not* have decision-making power about when and how processing is done is denoted by a poor control rating.

With respect to Alternative B (developing an in-house system using current main-frame computing capabilities), we are immediately struck by the heavy development costs. These costs are primarily for purchasing an additional terminal and printer to use with the district's existing business-computer facilities, time spent by district data-processing and special education staff in creating the computer programs necessary to manipulate student records, consultants to assist in the development process, and travel to districts with automated systems to get ideas and advice.

The annual operating costs for Alternative B are smaller than those for A because equipment is purchased and costs are therefore categorized as developmental. In addition, charges for constant telephone communication are not incurred—the terminal is directly connected to the on-site district computer—and no fee is paid for the services of a data-processing company. Operating costs above Alternative A are found in time spent by district data-processing staff in maintaining the system—that is, correcting problems discovered in the computer programs and making modifications to suit changes in district record-keeping requirements.

Alternative B obviously demands more time to install and, because it utilizes existing district resources, is rated average to good in terms of acceptance. The alternative is rated highly—as are the others—in ability to increase the effectiveness of the case-management program. It is rated average on the dimension of control because, though control of the system remains within the district, it lies outside the special services division. In this arrangement, priority is typically given to those business functions that are the first responsibility of the district's computer facilities (e.g., payroll, accounting). The processing requests of others will normally wait until those functions have been performed.

The third possibility, Alternative C (micro-computer system), promises developmental costs in between those of alternatives A and B. The cost of purchasing equipment for this alternative is far less than for B. Staff-time costs are limited to that needed to locate and assess the various software products and micro-computers available for the job. Finally, some additional costs not found in A or B are incurred—for materials and supplies, such as diskettes, needed for program start-up.

In terms of operating costs, Alternative C requires the smallest recurring expense of any option. It incurs the $7,000 cost of a half-time secretary—as do the other systems—as well as some modest additional cost for maintenance and repairs (miscellaneous). Alternative C requires little time for development—primarily that needed to examine available systems. It receives good acceptance ratings from parents and school boards, who typically want to see more micro-computers in the schools, and should improve program efficiency and effectiveness—as should the others. Finally, Alternative C keeps control of the student-record system within the special services department.

The Five-Year Cost is also helpful in comparing program alternatives. The Five-Year Cost includes the development cost plus five times the annual operating cost of the program. Using this measure, Alternative C might be viewed as demanding the smallest commitment of resources over a five-year period for our district.

Developing the Administrative
Program Design

It is our philosophy that written designs be developed for all programs involving the participation of significant numbers of people or requiring procedures of great complexity or importance. In many small districts with limited special education services, these criteria will seldom be met. For such cases, a detailed, written program design will be unnecessary; a page or two of documentation supplemented by informal understandings may suffice. However, in larger districts, the effectiveness and the efficiency of the administrative service program will depend on the extent to which staff members understand exactly what it is they are expected to do and achieve. A program responsible for managing the cases of a few hundred handicapped students, for example, will require explicit procedures for recording critical due-process events and deciding when to destroy student records, among other things.

When a written program design is deemed necessary, that document should state the purpose of the program as described earlier in this chapter, as well as the implementation and outcome requirements of the program (see Box 1-2). Implementation requirements, as previously stated, cover the conditions needed for operation (i.e., human, information, technological, financial, and physical resources); methods and activities; roles, responsibilities, and relationships; sequence and timing of activities; and the amount of variation permissible across program sites. Outcome requirements recapitulate the statements of goals and objectives developed earlier in program design and also attempt to relate general program activities to goals and objectives.

For an administrative case-management program, selected portions of the implementation section of a sample design are presented as Box 7-5. This box illustrates a number of important points about the design process. First, while it is often useful to be as specific as possible in describing the various aspects of a program (e.g., each staff member, each activity, all materials), it is rarely practical to do so. Second, working through the design process will usually identify problems and issues not evident in earlier thinking about the program. These problems and issues will often be minor, resulting in fine-tuning the budget or modifying the original program conceptualization. Occasionally, major difficulties will be discovered that suggest reevaluating other program alternatives. Though this may seem like a step backwards, reconsidering now may save a lot of pain later, when the administrative program begins to fail and substantial human and financial resources have already been expended.

BOX 7-5 *PLAN FOR AN ADMINISTRATIVE CASE-MANAGEMENT PROGRAM*

II. Implementation

   A.   Preconditions for operation
      1.   Human resources
         a.   Five licensed school psychologists or social workers to fill three full-time equivalent case-manager positions. One manager to be employed on a full-time basis by the program. Four managers to devote half-time to the program. One half-time secretary to maintain and update student records.
         b.   Support required from all members of child study staff, instructional staff, etc., in reporting critical events to the case manager and in working together to deliver services in a coordinated manner.
      2.   Information resources
         a.   Policies and procedures
            (1) All students referred for or currently receiving special education services will come under the purview of the program.
            (2) For each such student, a full record of all referral, evaluation, classification, placement, and basic identifying information will be maintained. Such record will be opened upon initial referral for services and kept in perpetuity.
            (3) A log file of all accesses to the student record will be kept, indicating the date and name of the person viewing the record.
         b.   Evaluation plan
            (1) The program will be evaluated in terms of (1) the extent to which program implementation is in compliance with the program design, (2) the extent to which program goals and objectives have been achieved, and (3) the extent of parental satisfaction with the case-management process.
            (2) Evaluation of program implementation will occur in November and February of each school year and will be conducted for formative program improvement purposes. Such evaluation will involve (1) review of number, type, and qualifications of staff; (2) interviews with case managers and other staff members to determine levels of staff support for the program; (3) checking the existence of program policies and procedures and evaluation plans; (4) review of case-management computer equipment; (5) a budget audit; (6) analysis of the level of use of assigned physical resources; (7) observation of case-coordination meetings and meetings with parents.
            (3) Evaluation of goal attainment will occur in June of each school year and will be conducted to facilitate improvement of the program for the following school year and to draw summative conclusions about the program's efficacy. Evaluation will include review of a sample of student records to check their availability, timeliness, and accuracy; review of the access log file; interviews with case-management staff to identify problems in achieving goals; interviews with service delivery staff to assess the extent of cooperation in the planning and delivery of intervention services.
            (4) Evaluation of consumer satisfaction will occur in June of each school year and will be conducted for the same purposes as evaluation of goal attainment. Consumer-satisfaction evaluation will involve interviews and questionnaire surveys of a sample of parents whose children were served by the case-management program during the school year.
      3.   Technological resources
         a.   Materials
            (1) Computer paper, diskettes, file cabinets, manila folders, log books, case-information update forms, etc.
         b.   Equipment
            (1) TRS-80 micro-computer, dot matrix printer.

4. Financial resources

a. Developmental budget		b. Operational budget	
Staff time	$2,000	Staff time	$85,000
Materials	2,400	Materials	1,500
Equipment	6,000	Equipment	500
Travel	500	Travel	0
Consultants	1,000	Consultants	200
Telephone	100	Telephone	200
Mail	10	Mail	200
Printing	0	Printing	100
Miscellaneous	50	Miscellaneous	300
Total	$12,060	Total	$88,000

5. Physical resources
   a. Use of office space for a case manager one day per week in each of 10 schools. Use of office space five days per week for a case manager at the high school.

B. Methods and activities
   1. Meetings between case manager and staff delivering services to each child.
   2. Meetings among those delivering closely related services to the same child.
   3. Regular contact with parents through telephone and school visitation.
   4. Maintenance and update of pupil records.
   5. Routine monitoring of pupil progress through the special services system.

C. Roles and responsibilities
   1. Case manager
      a. Coordinate delivery of services to child, maintain contact with parents, ensure provision of due-process guarantees, supervise maintenance of student records.
   2. Child-study staff
      a. Inform case manager of all critical evaluation, classification, placement, and annual review information.
   3. Special education teachers
      a. Inform case manager of any problems relating to education of the child.
      b. Coordinate delivery of services with other district staff providing services to child.
   4. Related service staff
      a. Inform case manager of any problems relating to education of the child.
      b. Coordinate delivery of services with special education teacher and others providing service to the child.
   5. Secretarial staff
      a. Enter student data into automated record system.
      b. Initiate production of automated case-management status reports at request of case manager.
      c. Type correspondence, file, and answer telephones.

D. Sequence and timing of activities
   1. Upon initial referral of the pupil for special education evaluation, a case manager is assigned.
   2. Case manager creates pupil record.
   3. Pupil-record information is entered into automated record system by secretary.
   4. Secretary prints weekly listing of children referred but not evaluated within 60 days and gives listing to case managers.
   5. Case managers follow up on delinquent evaluations and report results of follow-up to the director of special services.

Evaluating the Administrative
Program Design

The design of most administrative programs can be evaluated by requesting feedback from one or two colleagues. For administrative programs that require the participation of significant numbers of staff members, however, more substantial efforts should be attempted. For a case-management program requiring the participation of 10 to 20 professionals, feedback on the design should be sought from those expected to staff the program. Feedback should be directed at identifying practical problems with the program as designed, clarifying ambiguous elements, assessing the program's soundness, and evaluating the program's fit with existing programs and procedures. Design-review feedback should be incorporated to the extent possible before program-implementation begins.

IMPLEMENTING ADMINISTRATIVE
SERVICE PROGRAMS

Facilitating Program Implementation

The effort needed to facilitate smooth program implementation will frequently be a function of the number of individuals involved in the administrative program. Clearly, programs such as case management, which require the cooperation and coordination of many different staff members, possess the potential for more frequent and complex implementation pitfalls than cost analysis, which typically requires the involvement of only the administrator, business manager, and secretary. In programs where staff cooperation and coordination is important, we have found three DURABLE factors to be particularly relevant: rewarding, building, and evaluating.

Rewarding. With large-scale programs, such as case management, implementation can be greatly facilitated through the use of intrinsic reinforcement. To work effectively, case-management programs require those on pupil-evaluation teams, special education classroom teachers, and other members of the staff to constantly forward updated information to the case coordinator. For example, the case manager must be informed whenever a reevaluation is completed, a modification in the child's schedule made, or an address or telephone number changed. Getting the staff to routinely provide this information can be difficult unless it somehow makes the staff member's job easier.

In our experience with automated record-keeping systems, staff members were encouraged to forward pupil information regularly because their jobs were made easier as a result. For team members, lists of children due for reevaluation and rapid readjustments of case load to permit a more equitable distribution of work were offered. For teachers, alphabetized class lists and student addresses were returned to make classroom record keeping easier.

Building. We have typically used "building" to refer to communicating positive expectations about a program to the staff. For some programs—particularly those involving computers or other innovations—building should emphasize communicating *realistic* expectations. Many administrators and case managers hold the misapprehension that a computer will magically solve all their problems of case management, compliance monitoring and reporting, and cost analysis. They believe that the computer will organize their pupil records, give them compliance information at the press of a button, and immediately save them time and money.

Those school systems that have automated their administrative functions know that computers are not the panacea some make them out to be. Computers will not make a disorganized pupil record system run right. If paper records are improperly filed and frequently lost, the same fate would probably befall the computer diskettes on which pupil information is kept. Computers will not provide information at the touch of a button. Before anything comes out, operating procedures will need to be learned, and pupil, program, or cost data entered. Finally, computers will not immediately save time or money. In the beginning, the staff will need to perform double duty, maintaining both manual and automated systems, to verify that the computer is performing accurately. In addition, expenses above those paid for the manual system will accrue from equipment repairs, diskettes, paper, and printer ribbons.

Building, then, should make the staff aware of both the benefits and problems likely to result from implementing a new administrative program. Enthusiasm should be communicated, but balanced against a realistic presentation of difficulties expected to occur.

Evaluating Administrative
Program Implementation

Formally evaluating administrative program implementation is most important for those programs incorporating significant numbers of staff members or complex operational procedures. For these programs, plans for implementation—as well as outcome—evaluation should be built into the program design. Implementation evaluation should focus on determining the degree to which promised resources were made available, available resources used, planned activities conducted, and roles and responsibilities carried out. Such evaluation should utilize interviews with staff; reviews of program documents (e.g., cost reports and budgets), equipment, and facilities; and, to the extent possible, observation of activities.

For case-management programs, implementation evaluation might entail observing case meetings to determine the extent to which they were facilitating the pupil's education. Box 7-6 presents a list of questions for use in observing such meetings. Other implementation-evaluation methods include interviews with the service delivery staff to explore the coordination of services to the child, spot checks of student records to see how up-to-date and accurate they appear to be, and discussions with child-study and secretarial staff to probe for problems in the recording and maintenance of student-record information.

BOX 7-6   *QUESTIONS FOR GUIDING OBSERVATION OF CASE-MANAGEMENT MEETINGS*

Discussion Regarding Meeting Procedures

1. Is the purpose of the meeting clearly stated (either verbally or in a written agenda)?
2. Are the roles of the team members clearly defined (beyond name and title)?
3. Is a statement made about the desirability of participation by all team members?
4. Are the problems to be discussed during the meeting clearly stated?
5. Does a member keep some written record of the meeting (includes filling out forms at the end of the meeting)?

Student Progress

6. Are the student's strengths as well as weaknesses discussed?
7. Are multiple sources of data cited (e.g., classroom observation and standardized tests)?

Team Process

8. Are team members attentive listeners (i.e., do they look at speaker, nod, etc.)?
9. Do team members clarify others' remarks by questioning, paraphrasing, or elaborating?
10. Do team members seek information and opinions from others?
11. Does the team stay on task?

Making Recommendations

12. Do team members verbalize their opinions regarding the problem?
13. Do members attempt to make, through discussion, recommendations that all are willing to support (i.e., reach a consensus decision)?
14. Are recommendations made?
15. Are recommendations clearly stated?

Implementing Recommendations

16. Is a method specified for monitoring the results of recommendations?
17. Is a timetable for monitoring stated?
18. Are staff roles for implementing the recommendations fully described?
19. Does the team evaluate its meeting as having attained/not attained its goals for the meeting?

Meetings with Parents Present

20. At the beginning of the meeting, are parents asked about their expectations for the meeting (e.g., what they hope to learn from it)?
21. Are the parents' due-process rights explained?
22. Are parents included in the meeting through the use of direct questions, comments, and explanations directed to them, and by asking if they have any questions for the team?
23. Is the parents' input requested during the meeting?
24. Is the parents' input responded to by paraphrasing, comparing to other sources of information, etc.?
25. Is language at a level that the parent can understand? When technical terms are used, are they accurately defined in a way that parents can comprehend?

Source: Adapted from Christenson, S., Graden, J., Potter, M., Taylor, J., Yanowitz, B., & Ysseldyke, J. Current research on psychoeducational assessment and decision making: Implications for training and practice (Monograph #16). Minneapolis: Institute for Research on Learning Disabilities, University of Minnesota, 1981. Used by permission.

ASSESSING THE OUTCOMES
OF ADMINISTRATIVE SERVICE PROGRAMS

Administrative services typically require the least resource support of any service in the special education system. They involve few staff members, little equipment, minimal space, and small budgets. Because it makes little sense to expend large amounts on evaluating programs that themselves demand minimal support, we recommend formally assessing the outcomes of administrative programs in only select cases. These include cases where significant resource commitments are involved or numerous clients are served. Program monitoring and compliance reporting, for instance, will meet this criterion in larger districts because state-aid reimbursement depends upon the child counts resulting from this program. This program's outcomes mean substantial sums of money to the school district. Its outcomes (e.g., the accuracy of child-count figures) should be carefully evaluated.

A range of questions—from goal attainment to program change—can be asked about those administrative programs for which outcome evaluation is deemed appropriate. While each of these questions may be important in different instances, we focus our discussion on questions of consumer reaction and cost-effectiveness.

Evaluating Consumer Reaction

Administrative programs are meant to help administrators manage the demands and constraints placed upon the special services system. The extent to which these programs appear to help staff members manage is therefore an important consideration.

For outcome-evaluation purposes, consumer reactions should be elicited from the staff only after the administrative program has been operating for a reasonable period of time. This postprogram-assessment approach gives the staff the opportunity to work thoroughly with the program and formulate solid impressions of it. One direct method of obtaining consumer reactions through this approach is to talk with those involved with the program. Consumers can be asked about the relevance of the administrative program to special services management, its effectiveness in assisting management, and its practicality. For case management, managers and members of child-study teams might be asked if the individual student records produced by the program are relevant to the performance of their jobs, helpful in managing student cases, and easy to access and maintain.

An indirect means of evaluating consumer reaction is through the frequency and breadth of use of the administrative service program. For example, some computerized record-management systems automatically keep records of the number and type of requests made. If members of the staff frequently use the system for a variety of purposes—such as looking at student records and generating lists of students needing reevaluation—then the utility of the system would be supported.

Evaluating Cost-Effectiveness

Chapter 4 discusses the conditions required for dependable cost-effectiveness evaluations. The degree of goal attainment of the program must be known, a suitable comparison program targeted at achieving the same goals through a different method should be available, and both programs should be at comparable stages in their development. Finally, both programs should, in fact, have been implemented in different ways.

For many school programs, these conditions are difficult to satisfy. For administration in particular, there is little opportunity to target different programs to the same task. Therefore, we recommend that judgments of cost-effectiveness be very tentative. In situations where more dependable information is needed, we highly recommend obtaining the assistance of a business administrator and profesfesional evaluator familiar with the peculiarities of cost-effectiveness evaluation.

For administrative programs, we suggest (1) determining costs, (2) evaluating resource expenditures in light of outcomes produced, and (3) assessing flexibility— that is, the cost of adapting the program to achieve different outcomes, such as those resulting from modified state-education regulations, board of education directives, or other environmental conditions.

The evaluation of costs entails looking back at the program over the course of the year to determine exactly what expenditures were incurred and why. Reviewing incurred expenses is important for at least two reasons. First, expenses are sometimes erroneously charged. Expenses may appear for charges never incurred, and some incurred costs may emerge late or not at all. It is obviously critical to correct these errors before judging cost-effectiveness. There is little point in comparing the erroneous costs of one program with the actual costs of another.

Costs should also be reviewed for the benefit of future program planning. Particular line-item expenditures should be compared with budgets, to determine where projections and expenses differ significantly. Discrepancies should be investigated to assess whether they are due to errors in budgeting or unusual environmental conditions beyond the control of the budgeting process. Overly optimistic or pessimistic line-item projections should be noted, so that these errors are not repeated in future budgets.

Discrepancies between budget projections and actual costs will be particularly frequent in new administrative programs, especially those utilizing innovations such as computer and telecommunications technology. Experience with a particular innovation is, by definition, limited, and errors are bound to occur. It is not uncommon to underbudget the costs of micro-computer applications by a factor of two or three. We have found that many districts omitted budget items for software needed to make the computer work, staff training, equipment repairs, and supplies such as floppy diskettes and paper. In these instances, it is advisable to suspend evaluation of cost-effectiveness until enough experience has been gathered to know the typical operating costs of the program.

In taking a retrospective look at the resource costs of an administrative program, it is also often valuable to break out the amount and type of staff time required to carry out the program. Staff-time expenditures should be analyzed to determine whose time is being devoted to what aspects of the program. Actual and original time projections should also be compared.

When the cost and staff-time requirements of the administrative program are known, attempts can be made to evaluate the program's costs in light of the outcomes produced. As stated in Chapter 4, this evaluation requires comparing the program's expenses and outcomes to alternative methods for achieving the same goals. Because appropriate comparison programs will often be unavailable, surrogate comparisons might be considered. For example, the current automated compliance monitoring and reporting system might be compared with data or impressions of the old manual reporting system; the micro-computer–based student record-keeping system might be contrasted with the main-frame approach used in a neighboring district with similar characteristics. These "impressionistic" comparisons must be made with *great* care. Efforts should be made to rule out as many competing causes for observed results as possible. Conclusions should emphasize the shortcomings of the data.

The actual evaluation of costs in light of effects can be accomplished in a variety of ways. One means of conducting this evaluation is to compare the resource amounts required by different alternatives to produce the same product unit. How much time does it take the program of compliance monitoring and reporting to produce the annual child-count report compared to the old method? How long does it take the case-management program to complete a record for a newly referred student?

In considering the resources needed to produce a product unit, it is good practice to take account of both actual staff time and elapsed time. One may, for example, find the staff time required to produce management reports (e.g., lists of children due for reevaluation) by a micro-computer–based compliance-monitoring system comparable to the neighboring district's main-frame system. However, the elapsed-time requirements of the two systems may be far different. Because the main-frame system serves many purposes and clients throughout the school district, the elapsed time needed to respond to a request for a management report may be days. The micro-based system, because it is dedicated solely to serving special education management requirements, might produce the report within hours of the request.

A second means of weighing the costs and outcomes of an administrative program is in terms of dollar costs and the degree to which goals have been achieved. How much does the automated program of compliance monitoring and reporting cost, and what level of goal attainment has it achieved? How does this compare to the old program? What is the total dollar cost of the micro-computer–based record-keeping system, and how successfully has it met its goals? How does this compare to the neighboring district's main-frame system? A framework for making such comparisons is presented in Chapter 4.

A final consideration in evaluating administrative program cost-effectiveness is flexibility. Flexibility refers to the probable cost of changing a program to produce modified outcomes resulting from superintendent's, board's, or state's policy shifts. Examples of modified outcomes include the frequent changes in forms that characterize many state-level programs of compliance monitoring and reporting. Computerized systems developed by districts to produce these reports will inevitably need to accommodate format modifications. While some systems may be able to adjust to format changes at the flick of a switch, others will require substantial

revision. The cost of adapting to changes in outcome requirements should, therefore, be a fundamental part of cost-effectiveness evaluation whenever frequent
program modifications are anticipated.

SUMMARY

The approach to planning and evaluating administrative programs taken in this
chapter was based upon systems-analysis models, which emphasize the interrelationships within and among programs. In keeping with this perspective, administration
was defined as the executive function responsible for managing the various demands
and constraints placed upon the special education service delivery system. Administration manages these demands and constraints through targeted programs such as
case management, cost analysis, and planning and evaluation.

The chapter suggested clarifying administrative service delivery problems
through a needs-assessment process based on analyzing the demands and constraints
placed on the special services system. The process involved identifying demands and
constraints, specifying the administrative functions needed to manage those demands and constraints, determining the extent to which existing programs successfully perform those functions, assigning priorities to improving specific programs,
and estimating the resources required for needed improvements. In conjunction
with context information, the results of the needs assessment describe the administrative service delivery problem and form the basis for a decision to proceed with
program design.

With respect to administrative program design, particular attention was paid
to evaluating program alternatives. Four elements were suggested for consideration.
For each alternative, these were developmental and operating costs, development
time, district and community support, and expected benefits.

In the section on implementation, it was noted that administrative programs
requiring the cooperation and coordination of the staff can encourage needed participation through intrinsic reinforcement. Emphasis was also placed upon building
realistic expectations so that staff members would be prepared for the problems
that are inevitably encountered in implementing all innovative programs. Finally,
formal evaluation of program operation was recommended primarily for programs
incorporating significant numbers of staff or complex operational procedures.

Assessing the outcomes of administrative programs was discussed in terms of
evaluating consumer reaction and cost-effectiveness. For sampling consumer reaction, direct and indirect methods were noted. Among these methods were discussing the relevance, effectiveness, and practicality of the administrative program with
consumers, and inferring reaction through the frequency and type of use to which
the program is put. Cost-effectiveness evaluation was discussed in terms of estimating costs, judging expenses in light of realized outcomes, and determining program
flexibility. Finally, we stressed the need to recognize the shortcomings of cost-
effectiveness results when appropriate comparison programs are unavailable.

REFERENCES

AD HOC WORKING GROUP. Learning disabilities, dyslexia, and vision: Restatement of policy by ophthalmologists' associations. *New York Orton Society Newsletter*, 1982, *5*(4), 4.

ANGOFF, W. Scales, norms, and equivalent scores. In R. Thorndike (Ed.), *Educational measurement*. Washington, D.C.: American Council on Education, 1971.

ANGOFF, W. Personal communication, December 16, 1982.

APGA policy statement: Responsibilities of users of standardized tests. Falls Church, VA: Association for Measurement and Evaluation in Guidance, American Personnel and Guidance Association, 1980.

Armstrong v. Kline. 629F. 2d (3d Cir. 1980), cert. denied subnom.

BENNETT, R. Methods for evaluating the performance of school psychologists. *School Psychology Monograph*, 1980, *4*(1), 45–59. (a)

BENNETT, R. *The special education teacher diagnostician: Professional training needs.* Paper presented at the International Conference of the Association for Children with Learning Disabilities, Milwaukee, February 1980. (b)

BENNETT, R. Assessment of exceptional children: Guidelines for practice. *Diagnostique*, 1981, *7*, 5–13. (a)

BENNETT, R. Evaluating individualized education programs. *Diagnostique*, 1981, *7*, 91–100. (b)

BENNETT, R. Professional competence and the assessment of exceptional children. *Journal of Special Education*, 1981, *15*, 438–446. (c)

BENNETT, R. Cautions for the use of informal measures in the educational assessment of exceptional children. *Journal of Learning Disabilities*, 1982, *15*, 337–339. (a)

BENNETT, R. Criterion-referenced measurement in the classroom. *New Jersey Journal of School Psychology,* 1982, *1,* 3–13. (b)

BENNETT, R. The use of grade and age equivalent scores in educational assessment. *Diagnostique,* 1982, *7,* 139–146. (c)

BENNETT, R. Applications of microcomputer technology to special education. *Exceptional Children,* 1982, *45,* 106–113. (d)

BENNETT, R. A multi-method approach to assessment in special education. *Diagnostique,* in press.

BENNETT, R., & MAHER, C. Issues in evaluating the impact of special education. In P. Sleeman & L. Messineo (Eds.), *Designing learning programs and environments for students with special learning needs.* Springfield, Il.: Charles C. Thomas, in press.

BENNETT, R., & SHEPHERD, M. Basic measurement proficiency of learning disability specialists. *Learning Disability Quarterly,* 1982, *5,* 177–184.

BERGAN, J. R. Path-referenced assessment in school psychology. In T. R. Kratochwill (Ed.), *Advances in school psychology* (Vol. 1). Hillsdale, N.J.: Lawrence Erlbaum, 1981.

BERK, R. (Ed.). *Criterion-referenced testing: State of the art.* Baltimore: Johns Hopkins University Press, 1980.

BLOOM, B. S., HASTINGS, J. T., & MADAUS, G. F. *Handbook on formative and summative evaluation of student learning.* New York: McGraw-Hill, 1971.

BROPHY, J. E., & GOOD, T. L. *Teacher-child dyadic interaction: A manual for coding classroom behavior.* Austin: Research and Development Center for Teacher Education, University of Texas at Austin, 1969.

BROWN, L. L., & HAMMILL, D. D. *The behavior rating profile: An ecological approach to behavioral assessment.* Austin: Pro-Ed., 1978.

BUROS, O. K. (Ed.). *The eighth mental measurements yearbook.* Highland Park, N.J.: The Gryphon Press, 1978.

CALIFORNIA STATE DEPARTMENT OF EDUCATION. *Program evaluator's guide.* Princeton, N.J.: Educational Testing Service, 1979.

CAMPBELL, D. T., & STANLEY, J. C. *Experimental and quasi-experimental designs for research.* New York: Rand-McNally, 1966.

CARLBERG, C., & KAVALE, K. The efficacy of special versus regular class placement for exceptional children: A meta-analysis. *Journal of Special Education,* 1980, *14,* 295–309.

CARR, R. A. Goal attainment scaling as a useful tool for evaluating progress in special education. *Exceptional Children,* 1979, *46,* 88–95.

CARTWRIGHT, C. A., & CARTWRIGHT, A. P. *Developing observational skills.* New York: McGraw-Hill, 1974.

Code of ethics and competencies for teachers of learning disabled children and youth. Kansas City: Division for Children with Learning Disabilities, Council for Exceptional Children, 1978.

COMPTROLLER GENERAL OF THE UNITED STATES. *Disparities still exist in who gets special education.* Washington, D.C.: U.S. General Accounting Office, 1981.

COOK, T. C., & CAMPBELL, D. T. *Quasi-experimentation: Design and analysis issues for field settings.* New York: Rand-McNally, 1979.

CRONBACH, L. J. *Essentials of psychological testing* (3rd ed.). New York: Harper & Row, 1970.

CRONBACH, L. J. *Designing evaluations of educational and social programs.* San Francisco: Jossey-Bass, 1982.

CRONBACH, L. J., AMBRON, S. R., DORNBUSCH, S. M., HESS, R. D., HORNIK, R. D., PHILLIPS, D. C., WALKER, D. F., & WERNER, S. S. *Toward reform of program evaluation: Aims, methods, and institutional arrangements.* San Francisco: Jossey-Bass, 1980.

CRUICKSHANK, W. Least-restrictive placement: Administrative wishful thinking. *Journal of Learning Disabilities,* 1977, *10,* 193–194. (a)

CRUICKSHANK, W. Myths and realities in learning disabilities. *Journal of Learning Disabilities,* 1977, *10,* 57–64. (b)

CTB/McGRAW-HILL. *California Achievement Tests: Technical bulletin 1.* Monterey, Cal.: Author, 1979.

DAVIS, H. T., & SALASIN, S. E. The utilization of evaluation. In E. L. Struening & M. Guttentag (Eds.), *Handbook of evaluation research* (Vol. 1). Beverly Hills, CA: Sage, 1975.

DELBECQ, A. L., VAN de VEN, A. H., & GUSTAFSON, D. H. *Group techniques for program planning.* Glenview, Il.: Foresman & Company, 1975.

DENO, S., & MIRKIN, P. *Data-based program modification: A manual.* Minneapolis: Leadership Training Institute, University of Minnesota, 1977.

DUNNETTE, M. D. Basic attributes of individuals in relation to behavior in organizations. In M. D. Dunnette (Ed.), *Handbook of industrial/organizational psychology.* Chicago: Rand McNally, 1976.

DUNST, C. J. Program evaluation and the Education for All Handicapped Children Act. *Exceptional Children,* 1979, *46,* 24–31.

EDUCATIONAL TESTING SERVICE. *Sequential Tests of Educational Progress (STEP III): Manual and technical report.* Menlo Park, Cal.: Addison-Wesley, 1980.

EVANS, I., & NELSON, R. O. Assessment of child behavior problems. In A. R. Cimerano, K. S. Calhoun, & H. E. Adams (Eds.), *Handbook of behavioral assessment.* New York: John Wiley & Sons, 1977.

FORMAN, S. G. Stress management learning for teachers: A cognitive-behavioral program. *Journal of School Psychology,* 1982, *3,* 180–187.

GAGNE, R. M., & BRIGGS, L. J. *Principles of instructional design* (2nd ed.). New York: Holt, Rinehart & Winston, 1979.

GILBERT, T. F. Analyzing productive performance. In L. W. Frederiksen (Ed.), *Handbook of organizational behavior management.* New York: John Wiley & Sons, 1982.

GLASER, R. Instructional technology and the measurement of learning outcomes. *American Psychologist,* 1963, *18,* 519–521.

GOODMAN, L., & BENNETT, R. Use of norm-referenced assessment for the mildly handicapped: Some basic issues reconsidered. In T. Miller & E. Davis (Eds.), *The mildly handicapped student.* New York: Grune and Stratton, 1982.

GORDON, S. B., & KOPEL, S. *A practical guide to behavioral assessment.* New York: Springer, 1979.

GOTTMAN, J. M., & GLASS, G. V. Analysis of interrupted time series experiments. In T. R. Kratochwill (Ed.), *Single subject research: Strategies for evaluating change.* New York: Academic Press, 1978.

GROSSMAN, H. (Ed.). *Manual on terminology and classification in mental retardation.* Washington, D.C.: American Association on Mental Deficiency, 1973.

GUBA, E. G., & LINCOLN, Y. S. *Effective evaluation.* San Francisco: Jossey-Bass, 1981.

HAMBLETON, R. K., & EIGNOR, D. R. Guidelines for evaluating criterion-referenced tests and test manuals. *Journal of Educational Measurement*, 1978, *15*, 321–327.

HANSCHE, J. H., GOTTFRIED, N. W., & HANSCHE, W. J. *Special education classification: A multivariate analysis.* Paper presented at the annual meeting of the National Association of School Psychologists, Houston, April 1981.

HARTLAGE, L. Neuropsychological assessment techniques. In C. R. Reynolds & T. B. Gutkin (Eds.), *Handbook of school psychology.* New York: John Wiley & Sons, 1982.

HARTMAN, W. Estimating the costs of educating handicapped children: A resource-cost model approach—summary report. *Educational Evaluation and Policy Analysis*, 1981, *3*, 33–47.

HELLER, K., HOLTZMAN, W., & MESSICK, S. *Placing children in special education: Strategy for equity.* Washington, D.C.: National Academy Press, 1982.

HOWELL, K. W., KAPLAN, J. S., & O'CONNELL, C. T. *Evaluating exceptional children: A task analysis approach.* Columbus, OH: Charles E. Merrill, 1979.

INTERNATIONAL READING ASSOCIATION. Board action. *Reading Today*, June 1980.

JENKINS, J., & PANY, D. Standardized achievement tests: How useful for special education? *Exceptional Children*, 1978, *44*, 448–453.

JOINT COMMITTEE ON STANDARDS FOR EDUCATIONAL EVALUATION. *Standards for evaluations of educational programs, projects, and materials.* New York: McGraw-Hill, 1981.

KAUFMAN, J. M. Historical trends and contemporary issues in special education in the United States. In J. M. Kaufman & D. P. Hallahan (Eds.), *Handbook of special education.* Englewood Cliffs, N.J.: Prentice-Hall, 1981.

KAUFFMAN, R. A. *Educational system planning.* Englewood Cliffs, N.J.: Prentice-Hall, 1972.

KAZDIN, A. E. Statistical analysis for single case experimental designs. In M. Hersen & O. Barlow (Eds.), *Single-case experimental designs: Strategies for behavior change.* New York: Pergamon Press, 1976.

KAZDIN, A. E. Assessing the clinical or applied significance of behavior change through social validation. *Behavior Modification*, 1977, *1*, 427–452.

KENNEDY, M. M. *Recommendations of the Division H task force on special education program evaluation.* Washington, D.C.: American Educational Research Association, 1982.

KENNY, P. A quasi-experimental approach to assessing treatment effects in the non-equivalent control group design. *Psychological Bulletin*, 1975, *82*, 345–362.

KIRESUK, T., & LUND, S. B. Goal attainment scaling. In C. C. Attkisson, W. A. Hargreaves, M. J. Horowitz, & J. E. Sorensen (Eds.), *Evaluation of human service programs.* New York: Academic Press, 1978.

KIRESUK, T. J., & SHERMAN, R. E. Goal attainment scaling: A general method for evaluating comprehensive community mental health programs. *Community Mental Health Journal*, 1968, *4*, 443–453.

KRATOCHWILL, T. R. (Ed.). *Single subject research: Strategies for evaluating change.* New York: Academic Press, 1978.

KRATOCHWILL, T. R. Advances in behavioral assessment. In C. R. Reynolds & T. B. Gutkin (Eds.), *Handbook of school psychology.* New York: John Wiley & Sons, 1982.

LAMBERT, N. (Ed.). *Special education assessment matrix.* Monterey, CA.: CTB/McGraw-Hill, 1981.

Larry P. et al. v. Wilson Riles et al. United States District Court for the Northern District of California, Case No. C-71-2270RFP, 1974, 1979.

LEVIN, H. Cost effectiveness evaluation. In M. Guttentag & E. L. Struening (Eds.), *Handbook of evaluation research* (Vol. 2). Beverly Hills, CA: Sage, 1975.

LEVINE, V. The role of outcomes in cost-benefit evaluation. *New directions in program evaluation,* 1981, *9,* 21–40.

LIEBERMAN, L. Itard: The great problem solver. *Journal of Learning Disabilities,* 1982, *15,* 566–568.

LINN, R. L. The validity of inferences based on the proposed Title I evaluation models. *Educational Evaluation and Policy Analysis,* 1979, *1,* 23–32.

LINN, R. L. Measuring pretest-posttest performance changes. In R. A. Berk (Ed.), *Educational evaluation methodology: The state of the art.* Baltimore: Johns Hopkins University Press, 1981.

LIVINGSTON, S., & ZEIKY, M. *Passing scores: A manual for setting standards of performance on educational and occupational tests.* Princeton, N.J.: Educational Testing Service, 1982.

Lora v. Board of Education of the City of New York. Opinion, United States District Court for the Eastern District of New York, Case No. 75, Civ. 917, July 2, 1979.

MacGINITIE, W. *Gates-MacGinitie Reading Tests: Teachers manual (Level A)* (2nd ed.). Boston: Houghton Mifflin, 1978.

MacMILLAN, D., & MEYERS, C. Larry P.: An educational interpretation. *School Psychology Review,* 1980, *9,* 136–148.

MADAUS, G. F., AIRASIAN, P. W., HAMBLETON, R. K., CONSALVO, R. W., & ORLANDI, L. R. Development and application of criteria for screening commercial, standardized tests. *Educational Evaluation and Policy Analysis,* 1982, *4,* 401–415.

MAGRAB, P. R., SCHMIDT, L. M. Interdisciplinary collaboration: A prelude to coordinated service delivery. In J. O. Elder & P. R. Magrab (Eds.), *Coordinating services to handicapped children: A handbook for interagency coordination.* Baltimore: Paul H. Brookes Publishing, 1981.

MAHER, C. A. Training special service teams to develop individualized education programs (IEPs). *Exceptional Children,* 1980, *47,* 206–211.

MAHER, C. A. Improving the delivery of special education and related services in public schools. *Child Behavior Therapy,* 1981, *3,* 29–44.

MAHER, C. A. A team approach for planning and evaluating personnel development program. *Exceptional Children,* 1982, *49,* 230–236. (a)

MAHER, C. A. Using performance feedback for improving the program planning skills of school psychologists. *Professional Psychology,* 1982, *12,* 630–638. (b)

MAHER, C. A. Goal attainment scaling: A method for evaluating special education services. *Exceptional Children,* in press. (a)

MAHER, C. A. Organizational behavior management. In C. A. Maher & S. G. Forman (Eds.), *Providing effective services in school organizations: A behavioral approach.* Hillsdale, Il.: Erlbaum, in press. (b)

MAHER, C. A., & BARBRACK, C. R. Preventing high school maladjustment: Effectiveness of professional and cross-age behavioral group counseling. *Behavior Therapy,* 1982, *13,* 259–270.

MAHER, C. A., & BARBRACK, C. R. Evaluating individual counseling of conduct problem adolescents: The goal attainment scaling method. *Journal of School Psychology,* in press.

MAHER, C. A., & ILLBACK, R. J.   Planning for the delivery of special services: A multidimensional needs assessment framework. *Evaluation and Program Planning*, 1982, *4*, 249–259.

MAHER, C. A., & ILLBACK, R. J.   Framework for applying organizational psychology in schools. In C. A. Maher, R. J. Illback, & J. E. Zins (Eds.), *Organizational psychology in the schools: A handbook for practitioners*. Springfield, Il.: Charles C. Thomas, in press.

MAHER, C. A., & KRATOCHWILL, T. R.   Evaluation of special service programs: An overview. *School Psychology Monograph*, 1980, *4*, 1–24.

Mattie T. et al. v. C. E. Holladay et al.   United States District Court for the Northern District of Mississippi, Case No. DC-75-31-S, 1979.

McCAIN, L. J., & McCLEARY, R.   The statistical analysis of the simple interrupted time-series quasi-experiment. In T. C. Cook & D. T. Campbell (Eds.), *Quasi-experimentation: Design and analysis issues for field settings*. Chicago: Rand McNally, 1979.

MERCER, J. R.   *Labeling the mentally retarded*. Berkeley: UCLA Press, 1973.

MERCER, J. R., & LEWIS, J.   *Technical manual: SOMPA system of multicultural pluralistic assessment*. New York: Psychological Corporation, 1979.

MILLER, C., & CHANSKY, N.   Psychologists' scoring of WISC protocols. *Psychology in the Schools*, 1972, *9*, 144–152.

MILLER, C., CHANSKY, N., & GREDLER, G.   Rater agreement on WISC protocols. *Psychology in the Schools*, 1970, *7*, 190–193.

MILLER, L. M.   *Behavior management: The new science of managing people at work*. New York: John Wiley & Sons, 1978.

MURPHY, R. J., & BRYAN, A. J.   Multiple-baseline and multiple-probe designs: Practical alternatives for special education assessment and evaluation. *Journal of Special Education*, 1980, *14*, 325–335.

NATIONAL ASSOCIATION OF SCHOOL PSYCHOLOGISTS. *Certificate for continuing professional development*. Washington, D.C.: National Association of School Psychologists, 1979.

NATIONAL INSTITUTE OF MENTAL HEALTH. *Development and test of a cost-effectiveness methodology for CMHCS*. Washington, D.C.: National Institute of Mental Health, 1975.

NATIONAL STUDY OF SCHOOL EVALUATION. *Evaluative criteria for evaluation of secondary schools* (5th ed.). Arlington, Va.: National Study of School Evaluation, 1978.

NEA REPRESENTATIVE ASSEMBLY. Nea resolutions 1981. *NEA Reporter*, 1981, *20*, 9–16.

PARC v. Commonwealth of Pennsylvania.   343 F. Supp. 279, 302 (E.D. Pa. 1972).

Parents in Action on Special Education (PASE) v. Hannon.   Opinion, United States District Court for the Northern District of Illinois, Case No. 74-C-3586, July 11, 1980.

PARLETT, M., & HAMILTON, D.   Evaluation and illumination: A new approach to the study of innovatory programmes. In D. Hamilton & M. Parlett (Eds.), *Beyond the numbers game*. Berkeley: McCutchan, 1978.

PATTON, M. Q.   *Utilization-focused evaluation*. Beverly Hills, CA: Sage, 1978.

PAUL, J. L.   Service delivery models for special education. In J. M. Kauffman & D. P. Hallahan (Eds.), *Handbook of special education*. Englewood Cliffs, N.J.: Prentice-Hall, 1981.

PENNINGTON, L.   Provision of school psychological services. *School Psychology Digest*, 1977, *6*, 50–70.

PLAS, J. If not grade equivalent scores—then what? *Measurement in Education,* 1977, *8*(2), 4–7.

POPHAM, W. J. *Educational evaluation.* Englewood Cliffs, N.J.: Prentice-Hall, 1975.

POSAVAC, E. J., & CAREY, R. G. *Program evaluation: Methods and case studies.* Englewood Cliffs, N.J.: Prentice-Hall, 1980.

PRASSE, D. *The Larry P. decision.* Special issue of *School Psychology Review,* 1980, *9*(2).

PRESCOTT, G., BALOW, I., HOGAN, T., & FARR, R. *Metropolitan Achievement Tests Survey Battery: Teacher's manual for administering and interpreting.* New York: Psychological Corporation, 1978.

PROGER, B., & MANN, L. Criterion-referenced measurement: The world of grey versus black and white. *Journal of Learning Disabilities,* 1973, *6,* 72–84.

PROVUS, M. *Discrepancy evaluation.* Berkeley: McCutchan, 1972.

QUAY, H. C. Classification. In H. C. Quay & J. S. Werry (Eds.), *Psychopathological disorders of childhood.* New York: John Wiley & Sons, 1979. (a)

QUAY, H. C. Patterns of aggression, withdrawal, and immaturity. In H. C. Quay & J. S. Werry (Eds.), *Psychopathological disorders of childhood.* New York: John Wiley & Sons, 1979. (b)

QUAY, H. C., & PETERSON, D. R. *Manual for the behavior problem checklist.* Champaign-Urbana: University of Illinois, 1967.

REICHARDT, C. S. The statistical analysis of data from nonequivalent group designs. In T. R. Cook & D. T. Campbell (Eds.), *Quasi-experimentation: Design and analysis issues for field settings.* Chicago: Rand McNally, 1979.

RESCHLY, D. J. *SOMPA: A symposium.* Special issue of *School Psychology Review,* 1979, *8*(2).

RESCHLY, D. J. Psychological testing in educational classification and placement. *American Psychologist,* 1981, *36,* 1094–1102.

REYNOLDS, C. *Test bias: In God we trust: All others must have data.* Paper presented at the annual meeting of the American Psychological Association, Los Angeles, August 1981.

ROSSI, P. H., & FREEMAN, H. E. *Evaluation: A systematic approach* (2nd ed.). Beverly Hills, CA: Sage, 1982.

SAGE, D. Administration of special education. In J. M. Kauffman & D. P. Hallahan (Eds.), *Handbook of special education.* Englewood Cliffs, N.J.: Prentice-Hall, 1981.

SALVIA, J., & YSSELDYKE, J. E. *Assessment in special and remedial education* (2nd ed.). Boston: Houghton-Mifflin, 1981.

SARASON, S. B. *The culture of the school and the problem of change.* Boston: Addison-Wesley, 1971.

SARASON, S. B., & DORIS, J. *Educational handicap, public policy, and social history: A broadened perspective on mental retardation.* New York: Free Press, 1979.

SCRIVEN, M. Evaluation perspectives and procedures. In W. J. Popham (Ed.), *Evaluation in education: Current applications.* Berkeley: McCutchan, 1974.

SEASHORE, H., & RICKS, J. *Test service bulletin 39.* New York: Psychological Corporation, 1950.

SECHREST, L., & YEATON, W. Assessing the effectiveness of social programs. Methodological and conceptual issues. *New Directions in Program Evaluation,* 1982, *9,* 41–56.

SINGER, J. H. Evaluating program placement in an institution for the mentally retarded: A multivariate approach. *Journal of Special Education,* 1978, *12,* 133–142.

Specialty guidelines for the delivery of services by school psychologists. *American Psychologist,* 1981, *36,* 670–681.

SPIVACK, G., & SHURE, M. B. *Social adjustment of young children: A cognitive behavioral approach to solving real life problems.* San Francisco: Jossey-Bass, 1974.

SPIVACK, G., & SWIFT, M. *The elementary school rating scale.* Devon, Pa.: The Devereaux Foundation, 1967.

STAKE, R. E. (Ed.). *Evaluating the arts in education: A responsive approach.* Columbus, OH: Merrill, 1975.

Standards for educational and psychological tests. Washington, D.C.: American Psychological Association, 1974.

STANLEY, J. Reliability. In R. Thorndike (Ed.), *Educational measurement.* Washington, D.C.: American Council on Education, 1971.

STERNBERG, R. J. Testing and cognitive psychology. *American Psychologist,* 1981, *36,* 181–189.

STEVENS, G. Bias in the attribution of hyperkinetic behavior as a function of ethnic identification and socioeconomic status. *Psychology in the Schools,* 1981, *18,* 99–106.

STRAIN, P. S., & KERR, M. M. *Mainstreaming of children in schools: Research and programmatic issues.* New York: Academic Press, 1981.

STUFFLEBEAM, D. L., FOLEY, L., GEPHART, D., MERRIMAN, M., & PROVUS, M. *Educational evaluation and decision making.* Itaca, Ill: F. E. Peacock, 1971.

THORNDIKE, R. *The concepts of over- and under-achievement.* New York: Teachers College Press, 1963.

THORNDIKE, R. Dilemmas in diagnosis. In W. MacGinitie (Ed.), *Assessment problems in reading.* Newark, DE: International Reading Association, 1973.

THORNDIKE, R. L., & HAGEN, E. P. *Measurement and evaluation in psychology and education* (4th ed.). New York: John Wiley & Sons, 1977.

TOBIAS, S., COLE, C., ZIBRIN, M., & BODLAKOVA, B. *Bias in the referral of children to special services.* Paper presented at the meeting of the American Educational Research Association, Los Angeles, April 1981.

TRACTMAN, G. On such a full sea. *School Psychology Review,* 1981, *10,* 138–181.

U.S. OFFICE OF EDUCATION. Assistance to states for education of the handicapped: Procedures for evaluating specific learning disabilities. *Federal Register,* 1977, *42,* 65082–65085. (a)

U.S. OFFICE OF EDUCATION. Education of handicapped children: Implementation of Part B of the Education of the Handicapped Act. *Federal Register,* 1977, *42,* 42474–42518. (b)

VELDMAN, D. *Fortran programming for the behavioral sciences.* New York: Holt, Rinehart & Winston, 1967.

WALKER, H. M. *Walker problem behavior identification checklist.* Los Angeles: Western Psychological Corporation, 1970.

WALKER, R. T., WERNER, T. J., & BACON, A. *Behavior checklists.* Morgantown, W. Va.: Research and Training Center, West Virginia University, 1976.

WALLACE, G., & LARSEN, S. C. *Educational assessment of learning problems: Testing for teaching.* Boston: Allyn & Bacon, 1978.

WARREN, S. A., & BROWN, W. G. Examiner scoring errors on individualized intelligence tests. *Psychology in the Schools,* 1973, *10,* 118–122.

WINDLE, C., & WOY, J. R.   Implications of the CMHC amendments of 1975 for program evaluation. In W. Neigher, R. J. Hammer, & G. Landsberg (Eds.), *Emerging developments in mental health program evaluation.* New York: Argold, 1977.

WINER, B. J.   *Statistical procedures in experimental design.* New York: McGraw-Hill, 1971.

WORTHEN, B., & OWENS, T.   Adversarial evaluation. *Journal of School Psychology,* 1978, *16,* 39–48.

YSSELDYKE, J.   Issues in psychoeducational assessment. In G. Phye & D. Reschly (Eds.), *School psychology: Perspectives and issues.* New York: Academic Press, 1979.

YSSELDYKE, J.   Implementing the "Protection in Evaluation Procedures" provisions of PL 94-142. In Department of Health, Education, & Welfare (Ed.), *PEP: Developing criteria for the evaluation of protection in evaluation procedures provisions.* Philadelphia: Research for Better Schools, 1980.

ZEIKY, M., & LIVINGSTON, S.   *Manual for setting standards on the basic skills assessment tests.* Princeton, N.J.: Educational Testing Service, 1977.

INDEX